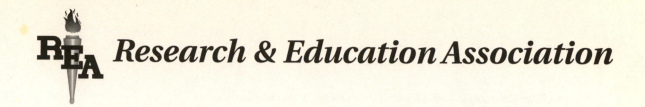

Research & Education Association

The Best Teachers' Test Preparation for the

MTEL™
General Curriculum
(Field 03)

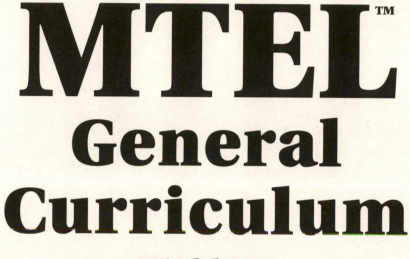

With CD-ROM for Windows®
REA's TESTware® for the MTEL

Staff of
Research & Education Association

Visit our Educator Support Center at:
www.REA.com/teacher

The General Curriculum Test Objectives presented in this book were created and implemented by The Massachusetts Department of Education and NES®. For further information visit the MTEL website at *www.mtel.nesinc.com.*

For all references in this book, Massachusetts Tests for Educator Licensure® and MTEL™ are trademarks of The Massachusetts Department of Education and National Evaluation Systems, Inc.™ NES® is a registered trademark of National Evaluation Systems, Inc.™

Research & Education Association
61 Ethel Road West
Piscataway, New Jersey 08854
E-mail: info@rea.com

The Best Teachers' Test Preparation for the Massachusetts Tests for Educator Licensure® (MTEL™) *General Curriculum* With TEST*ware*® on CD-ROM

Printed in the United States of America

Library of Congress Control Number 2006923801

International Standard Book Number 0-7386-0254-X

Windows® is a registered trademark of Microsoft Corporation.

REA® and TEST*ware*® are registered trademarks of Research & Education Association, Inc.

CONTENTS

About Research & Education Association

Founded in 1959, Research & Education Association is dedicated to publishing the finest and most effective educational materials—including software, study guides, and test preps—for students in middle school, high school, college, graduate school, and beyond.

REA's Test Preparation series includes books and software for all academic levels in almost all disciplines. Research & Education Association publishes test preps for students who have not yet completed high school, as well as for high school students preparing to enter college. Students from countries around the world seeking to attend college in the United States will find the assistance they need in REA's publications. For college students seeking advanced degrees, REA publishes test preps for many major graduate school admission examinations in a wide variety of disciplines, including engineering, law, and medicine. Students at every level, in every field, with every ambition can find what they are looking for among REA's publications.

REA's practice tests are always based upon the most recently administered exams and include every type of question that you can expect on the actual exams.

REA's publications and educational materials are highly regarded and continually receive an unprecedented amount of praise from professionals, instructors, librarians, parents, and students. Our authors are as diverse as the fields represented in the books we publish. They are well-known in their respective disciplines and serve on the faculties of prestigious high schools, colleges, and universities throughout the United States and Canada.

Today, REA's wide-ranging catalog is a leading resource for teachers, students, and professionals.

We invite you to visit us at *www.rea.com* to find out how "REA is making the world smarter."

Acknowledgments

We would like to thank REA's Larry B. Kling, Vice President, Editorial, for supervising development; Pam Weston, Vice President, Publishing, for setting the quality standards for production integrity and managing the publication to completion; John Paul Cording, Vice President, Technology, for coordinating the design, development, and testing of REA's TEST*ware*®; Christine Reilley, Senior Editor, for project management and preflight editorial review; Diane Goldschmidt, Senior Editor, for post-production quality assurance; Michelle Boykins and Heena Patel, software project managers, for their software testing efforts; Christine Saul, Senior Graphic Artist, for cover design; and Jeff LoBalbo, Senior Graphic Artist, for post-production file mapping.

We gratefully acknowledge David M. Myton, Ph.D., Renay M. Scott, Ph.D., Karen Bondarchuck, M.F.A., John A. Lychner, Ph.D., Janet E. Rubin, Ph.D., Ellen R. Van't Hof, M.A., Nelson Maylone, Ph.D., and Ginny Muller, Ph.D., for providing foundational material for this book. We also thank Al Davis, M.A., M.S., for editing this book in accordance with the MTEL General Curriculum test objectives and Joan and Norman Levy for creating Practice Test 2.

We also gratefully acknowledge Caragraphics for page composition.

Teach...
Inspire...
Lead...

INTRODUCTION

With this book in hand, you've taken an important step toward becoming a certified teacher in the State of Massachusetts. REA's Massachusetts Tests for Educator Licensure (MTEL) General Curriculum test preparation book is designed to help candidates pass the General Curriculum (Field 03) subject matter test section for an Elementary license. The MTEL General Curriculum test is composed of the following segments: language arts, mathematics, history and social science, science and technology/engineering, child development, and integration of knowledge and understanding. Each subtest area that appears on the official test is comprehensively reviewed, and two full-length practice tests are provided to hone your knowledge. Following each test, you will find an answer key with detailed explanations designed to help you more completely understand the test material and its difficulty. A diagnostic grid will help you determine where your strengths and weaknesses lie. When you successfully complete this book, you will be well-equipped with the knowledge, practice, and strategies to pass this most important exam.

ABOUT THE TEST

What is the MTEL General Curriculum and what is it used for?

The MTEL must be taken by individuals seeking certification to teach in Massachusetts. Prospective teachers are required to take and pass two tests: a two-part test in communication and literacy skills and an additional test for the subject of the candidate's chosen area of certification. In this case, the subject area is Elementary Education, which requires the taking of the General Curriculum test and the Foundations of Reading test to obtain a license. The General Curriculum test encompasses the following subareas: language arts, mathematics, history and social science, science and technology/engineering, child development, and integration of knowledge and understanding.

If I apply for licensure in Massachusetts after having prepared in another state, do I have to take the test?

Yes. Out-of-state candidates applying for their initial educator license in Massachusetts must pass all applicable Massachusetts licensure tests.

Please note: The Northeast Regional Credential (NRC) is available if you hold an educator's license (a license of eligibility or a letter of eligibility is not sufficient). Issued pursuant to the Interstate Agreement on Qualification of Personnel, an NRC entitles you to be employed for a period not exceeding two years in a Massachusetts school. To find out if the jurisdiction in which you hold your educator's license/license allows you to qualify for an NRC, please contact the Massachusetts Department of Education or check the Web site at *http://www.wested.org/cs/we/view/pj/185/*.

How is the test content determined?

Each test has test objectives for the corresponding field that describe the content eligible to be included in that test. These objectives were derived from the Regulations for the Licensure of Educational Personnel in Massachusetts and the Massachusetts Curriculum Frameworks, where appropriate. A broadly inclusive group of Massachusetts public-school educators and college faculty at institutions of higher education were involved in the development and validation of the tests. The MTEL program is particularly matched to the context within which it is used and the purposes that it serves.

Who administers the test?

The MTEL is administered by the Massachusetts Department of Education. A comprehensive test development process was designed and implemented specifically to ensure that the content and difficulty levels of the exam are appropriate.

When and where is the test given? How long will it take?

The MTEL is administered five times a year at six locations across the state, as detailed in the MTEL Registration Bulletin (a download link is below). Additionally, on two of the five test dates, the MTEL will be offered at seven out-of-state locations, subject to the requirement that there be a minimum number of candidates per area. To receive information on upcoming test dates and locations, you may wish to contact the test administrator as follows:

Massachusetts Tests for Educator Licensure
National Evaluation Systems, Inc.
P.O. Box 660
Amherst, MA 01004-9013
Tele: 413-256-2892
Fax: 413-256-8221
Web site: *http://www.doe.mas.edu/mtel*

Download the MTEL Registration Bulletin here: *http://www.mtel.nesinc.com/MA9_bulletinforms.asp*.

The tests are scheduled to be completed within a maximum of four hours.

Is there a registration fee?

To take the General Curriculum test, you must pay a fee. A complete summary of the registration fees is included in the MTEL Registration Bulletin (see link above). You may register online at: *http://www.mtel.nesinc.com/*.

HOW TO USE THIS BOOK AND TEST*ware*®

What do I study first?

Read over our review material, and then take the first practice test on the included CD-ROM. This will help you pinpoint your areas of weakness. Study those sections in which you had the most difficulty first, and then move on to those areas that presented less of a challenge to you. Our CD-ROM features two full-length practice tests that correlate with book tests 1 and 2. **We strongly recommend that you begin your preparation with TEST*ware*® tests.** The software provides the added benefit of instantaneous, accurate scoring and enforced time conditions.

Wisely scheduling your study time is also a key component to your success on the MTEL. To best utilize your study time, follow our flexible study schedule at the end of this chapter. The schedule is based ideally on a seven-week program, but can be condensed if needed.

FORMAT OF THE MTEL GENERAL CURRICULUM

What is the basic format the MTEL General Curriculum?

The MTEL General Curriculum test is designed to assess the candidate's knowledge, proficiency, and depth of understanding (at a level required for a baccalaureate major) of the elementary subject matter required for a Massachusetts Elementary teaching license. The multiple-choice items on the test cover the subareas as indicated below. The open-response items may relate to topics covered in any of the subareas and will typically require a breadth of understanding of the elementary field and the ability to relate concepts from different aspects of the field. Responses to the open-response items are expected to be appropriate and accurate in the application of the subject knowledge, to provide high-quality and relevant supporting evidence, and to demonstrate a soundness of argument and understanding of the elementary field.

About the Subject Reviews

The subject reviews in this book are designed purposefully to provide you critical insight into the content and format of the MTEL. For smarter study, we break down this part of test preparation into more manageable "chunks." Before you begin reviewing, it is important to note that your own schooling experience has taught you most of what is needed to answer the questions on the actual tests. Our review is written to help you fit and shape information acquired over the years into a context ideally suited for taking the MTEL.

You may also be taking test preparation classes for the MTEL, or have purchased other study guides and textbooks. Reviewing class notes and textbooks along with our subject reviews will provide you with an even better foundation for passing the MTEL.

SCORING THE MTEL GENERAL CURRICULUM

The subareas of Language Arts, Mathematics, History and Social Science, and Science and Technology/Engineering each average 21 multiple-choice questions and account for 17% of the test. Child Development averages 15 multiple-choice questions and accounts for 12% of the test. And the subarea of Integration of Knowledge and Understanding has two Open-Response items and accounts for the final 20% of the test.

The criterion-referenced MTEL is designed to measure a candidate's knowledge and skills in relation to an established standard rather than in relation to the performance of other candidates.

Multiple-Choice Questions

A candidate's performance on subareas with multiple-choice questions is based strictly on the number of test questions answered correctly. Candidates do not lose any points for wrong answers. Each multiple-choice question counts the same toward the total score.

These items are scored electronically and checked to verify accuracy.

Open-Response Questions

Open-response questions are scored holistically by two or more qualified educators. Scorers receive training in scoring procedures and are monitored for accuracy and consistency. Scorers are typically licensed teachers, administrators, arts and sciences faculty, teacher education faculty, and other content specialists.

Scorers judge the overall effectiveness of each response. That is, scorers are trained to provide an overall judgment, not to indicate specific errors.

A score is assigned to each response based on a scale that describes various levels of performance from weak to strong or thorough. If a candidate's response is blank, unrelated to the assignment, illegible, or in a language other than the target language, the candidate will receive no points for that question, and may or may not meet the qualifying score for the test, depending on performance on the other questions.

Score Results

Score results are mailed approximately five weeks following the test administration date. The Score Report Mailing Date for each test administration is listed in the table on the back of the MTEL Registration Bulletin. If, one week after the Score Report Mailing Date, you still have not received your scores, contact the testing company directly at (413) 256-2892.

Test-Taking Strategies

Although you may not be familiar with tests like the MTEL, this book will help acquaint you with this type of exam and help alleviate test-taking anxieties. Here are the key ways you can more easily get into an MTEL state of mind:

Become comfortable with the format of the MTEL. Practice tests are the best way to learn the format of the MTEL. When you take a practice test, try to simulate the environmental conditions of the actual testing facility. Remember, you are in training for the MTEL, and simulated testing conditions will only help you perform better. Stay calm and pace yourself. After simulating a test even once, you boost your chances of doing well, and you will be able to sit down for the actual MTEL with much more confidence.

Read all the possible answers. Examine each answer choice to ensure that you are not making a mistake. Jumping to conclusions without considering all the answers is a common test-taking error.

Use the process of elimination. GUESS if you do not know. If you do not know the answer immediately after reading the answer choices, try to eliminate as many of the answers as possible. Eliminating just one or two answer choices gives you a far better chance of selecting the right answer.

Do not leave an answer blank. There is no penalty for wrong answers, and you might even get it right if you have to guess at the answer.

Familiarize yourself with the test's directions and content. Familiarizing yourself with the directions and content of the MTEL not only saves you valuable time, but can also aid in reducing anxiety before the test. Many mistakes are caused by anxiety. It's simply better to go in knowing what you will face.

Mark it right! Be sure that the answer oval you mark corresponds to the appropriate number in the test booklet. The test is multiple-choice and is graded by machine. Marking just one answer in the wrong place can throw off the rest of the test.

After the Test

When you finish your test, hand in your materials and you will be dismissed. Then, you are free. Go home and relax. Meet with friends. Go out to dinner. Or go shopping. Whatever you do, make it a great day! After all you have done to get this far, you deserve it!

MTEL General Curriculum Study Schedule

The following study schedule allows for thorough preparation to pass the MTEL General Curriculum. This is a suggested seven-week course of study. This schedule can, however, be condensed if you have less time available to study, or expanded if you have more time. Whatever the length of your available study time, be sure to keep a structured schedule by setting aside ample time each day to study. Depending on your schedule, you may find it easier to study throughout the weekend. No matter which schedule works best for you, the more time you devote to studying for the MTEL General Curriculum, the more prepared and confident you will be on the day of the test.

Week	Activity
1	Take the first practice test on CD-ROM as a diagnostic exam. Your score will indicate where your strengths and weaknesses lie. Try to take the test under simulated exam conditions, and review the explanations for the questions you answered incorrectly.
2	Study the MTEL General Curriculum test objectives to get a better idea of the content on which you will be tested. You should make a list of the objectives that you know you will have the most trouble mastering so that you can concentrate your study on those areas.
3	Study *The Best Teachers' Test Preparation for the MTEL General Curriculum*. Take notes on the sections as you work through them, as writing will aid in your retention of information. Keep a list of the subject areas for which you may need additional aid.
4	Identify and review references and sources. Textbooks for college composition, science, social studies, arts, and mathematics courses will help in your preparation. You may also want to consult the Massachusetts curriculum Web site at *www.doe.mass.edu*.
5	Condense your notes and findings. You should develop a structured outline detailing specific facts. You may want to use index cards to aid you in memorizing important facts and concepts.
6	Test yourself using the index cards. You may want to have a friend or colleague quiz you on key facts and items. Then, take the second practice test on CD-ROM. Review the explanations for the questions you answered incorrectly.
7	Study any areas you consider to be your weaknesses by using your study materials, references, and notes. You may want to retake the test on CD-ROM.

General Curriculum

Review

Language Arts

History and Structure of English

0001   **Understand the history and structure of the English language.**

For example: major developments in the history of the English language (e.g., invention of the printing press, standardization of written language, development of dictionaries); major linguistic origins of the English language (e.g., Anglo-Saxon roots, Celtic influences, Greek and Roman elements); derivatives and borrowings; differences between oral and written English (e.g., level of formality, diversity of oral dialects, uniformity of written language); fundamental language structures (i.e., phonology, morphology, syntax, and semantics); parts of speech (e.g., noun, verb, adjective, adverb, conjunction, preposition); sentence types (e.g., simple, compound, complex) and sentence purposes (e.g., declarative, imperative, interrogative); and rules of English grammar and conventions of edited American English.

History of English

Modern English developed from the language of the **Angles**, the **Saxons**, and the **Jutes**, Germanic tribes who invaded the British Isles during the early Middle Ages. These invaders—who forced the native Celts to migrate north and west to Scotland, Ireland, Wales, and Cornwall—spoke a dialect now known as **Anglo-Saxon** or **Old English**, which resembled some dialects now spoken in the Netherlands. English, especially as it is now spoken in Ireland, Scotland, and Wales, retained some words from the original Celtic languages. The best-known example of Old English is the epic poem *Beowulf*. Some differences between written Old English and contemporary English can be gleaned from the first few lines of the Lord's Prayer in Old English:

> Oure fadir that art in heuenes halwid be thi name;
>
> thi reume or kyngdom come to be.
>
> Be thi wille don in herthe as it is doun in heuene.
>
> (Our father that is in heaven, hallowed be thy name;
>
> Thy realm or kingdom come to be.
>
> Be thy will done in earth as it is done in heaven.)

The basic modern English vocabulary is dominated by words derived from Old English. Such words include **father**, **woman**, **sun**, **moon**, **water**, **dog**, **do**, and **be**.

In 1066 the **Normans** invaded Britain from France. The new Norman aristocracy spoke a German-influenced dialect of French called **Anglo-Norman**. Anglo-Norman gradually amalgamated with Anglo-Saxon as the upper classes began to lose their social and cultural ties to France. The resulting language, which emerged in the thirteenth century, is known today as **Middle English**. It includes many words of Latin origin that entered English via the French roots of Anglo-Norman. The best-known example of Middle English is Chaucer's *The Canterbury Tales*.

The vocabulary of most literate adults in the English-speaking world includes thousands of words of Latin origin that were incorporated into Middle English. Such words include **agree**, **appoint**, **opinion**, **security**, **chamber**, **entertain**, **mirror**, **restrain**, and **oppose**. Words with military, legal, or political meanings often have Norman roots; examples include **cavalry**, **bailiff**, **ordinance**, **county**, **jury**, **muster**, **legion**, **royal**, and **campaign**.

In the sixteenth century, the introduction of the **printing press** into Britain helped to inaugurate two major changes. First, the ready availability of books spread classical learning. Words derived from the late Latin of the clergy—such as **indicate**, **emphasis**, **item**, **legislator**, **translate**, **ultimate**, and **maximum**—thereby entered the language of the burgeoning middle class. Second, widespread literacy led to greater standardization of spelling. This more standardized English developed into the earliest form of **Modern English**. The works of **William Shakespeare**, **John Donne**, and **John Milton** are examples of literary texts from the period of early Modern English.

In the United States, **American English** borrowed many words from other languages. Examples include **ranch** and **canyon** (from Spanish), **bayou** and **prairie** (from French), **boss** and **cookie** (from Dutch), **okra** and **banjo** (from West African languages), and **opossum** and **squash** (from indigenous American languages). In America many spellings of English words were also modified; examples include **color**, **jail**, and **defense** (as opposed to the British spellings of *colour*, *gaol*, and *defence*).

Spoken American English is also characterized by **regional** differences. The best known of these regional variations is the difference in **vernacular** versions of the second-person plural pronoun: **y'all** is used in the southern United States, **youse** is sometimes heard in the Northeast, and **you guys** is used in the Midwest and West. Likewise, different regions often use different nouns for similar things; for example, the words **grinder** (New England), **hero** (New York), **po' boy** (Deep South), and **hoagie** (Pennsylvania) all refer to a **submarine** sandwich.

Structure and Form of Spoken and Written English

Both spoken and written English can be used at varying levels of **diction**. **Colloquial** diction is the language of everyday conversation and informal writing, including much electronic communication. **Formal** diction is used in academic, business, and journalistic writing. Formal diction is characterized by more rigorous rules of spelling, punctuation, grammar, and sentence structure than colloquial diction. **Technical** diction employs specialized vocabularies and usages, and is employed in many sciences, medicine, and law.

Linguistics studies the structure and use of language. Structural elements of language studied by linguists include **phonetics**, the properties of speech sounds; **morphology**, the structure of individual words; **syntax**, the ways words are ordered in statements; and **semantics**, the relationship of words to their meanings.

The **parts of speech** are categories that classify words by function according to the way they are used in sentences. In English, those categories are **nouns**, which name persons, places, things, or ideas; **pronouns**, which take the place of nouns, but do not name specific things; **verbs**, which express actions or states of being; **adjectives**, which modify nouns or pronouns; **adverbs**, which modify verbs, adjectives, or other adverbs; **conjunctions**, which link other sentence elements; and **interjections**, which express strong feelings on their own without naming things or modifying other words.

As in most languages, English **sentences** are composed of **subjects** and **predicates**. Subjects name the main thing or person acting in, or indicated by, the sentence; predicates name the subject's actions, relationships, or characteristics. Usually the first noun in a sentence is the subject: **The train** arrived at the station. However, sometimes **phrases** or **clauses** come before the subject: On Wednesday, **the director** released his report. Predicates may simply be verbs: The plane **landed**. However, they may also include modifiers, objects, or subject complements: (1) The athlete **ran swiftly**, (2) The judge **made his decision**, (3) Little Rock **is the capital of Arkansas**.

Sentences can also be thought of as consisting of **phrases** and **clauses**. Phrases are word groups that lack *either* a subject *or* a predicate. In the sentence "The boy who won the prize was from Mexico," the words "**The boy who won the prize**," which also form the subject of the sentence, constitute a **noun phrase**. In the sentence "Submit the report to the head of your department," "**the head of your department**" is also a noun phrase, but it is also part of the prepositional phrase "**to the head of your department**." Clauses, on the other hand, contain all the grammatical elements of a complete sentence; they may, however, be either **dependent** or **independent**. Independent (or main) clauses can stand alone logically as sentences, but dependent clauses cannot. For example, in the sentence "We went to the market because we needed supplies," "**We went to the market**" is an *independent* clause because it makes sense as a sentence. "**[B]ecause we needed supplies**" *is* a clause (not a phrase) because it contains a subject ("we") and a predicate ("needed supplies"); it is *dependent*, however, because it does not make sense by itself as a sentence.

Sentences may be either **declarative**, **imperative**, **interrogative**, or **subjunctive**. Declarative sentences make statements of fact or opinion. Imperative sentences express commands. Interrogative sentences ask questions. Subjunctive sentences express wishes, desires, doubts, or suppositions. Sentences may also be either **simple**, **compound**, **complex**, or **compound-complex**. Simple sentences are composed of a single independent clause; compound sentences are composed of two or more independent clauses; complex sentences are composed of an independent clause modified by one or more dependent clauses; compound-complex sentences are composed of two or more independent clauses modified by one or more dependent clauses.

History of Literature

0002 **Understand American literature and selected literature from classical and contemporary periods.**

For example: historically or culturally significant works, authors, and themes of U.S. literature; selected literature from classical and contemporary periods; literature of other cultures; elements of literary analysis (e.g., analyzing story elements, interpreting figurative language); and varied focuses of literary criticism (e.g., the author, the context of the work, the text, the response of the reader).

Classical Greece and Rome

The **canon** (list of important works) of Western (European) literature is often thought to begin with the works of ancient Greece and Rome. This canon has become more controversial in recent years, but classical Greek and Roman texts are still considered foundational for the literary tradition that has produced much of British and North American literature.

"Ancient Greece" is a broad, rather imprecise term that designates the early era of civilization around the Aegean Sea. The Greek **Archaic** period (c. 750–500 BCE, or Before Common Era) produced the works attributed to the poet **Homer**, which are thought to be transcriptions of much earlier oral epics, including the *Odyssey* and the *Iliad*. The poets **Hesiod** and **Sappho** lived during this era. The **Classical** (or **Hellenic**) period (c. 500–323 BCE) gave birth to the works of the dramatists **Sophocles**, **Aristophanes**, **Euripides**, and **Aeschylus**, the philosophers **Plato** and

Aristotle, and the historian **Herodotus**. The playwright **Menander** and the mathematician **Euclid** lived during the **Hellenistic** period (c. 323–30 BCE).

"Ancient Rome" includes the period of the **Republic** (509–27 BCE), which produced the speeches of **Cicero** and some of the epic poetry of **Virgil**. The literature of the **Roman Empire** (27 BCE–475 CE, or Common Era) includes Virgil's *Aeneid*, the poetry of **Horace** and **Ovid**, the works of **Seneca**, the history of **Tacitus**, and the philosophy of **Marcus Aurelius**.

British Literature

The earliest example of English literature is usually considered to be the **Anglo-Saxon** epic *Beowulf*, which was written anonymously sometime between 800 and 1000 CE. The most famous example of **medieval** British literature is Geoffrey Chaucer's collection of stories *The Canterbury Tales*, written at the end of the fourteenth century.

Literature of the British **Early Modern** period, considered to be the sixteenth through the seventeenth centuries, includes all the works of **William Shakespeare**, including his **sonnets**, **tragedies** (such as *Hamlet* and *Macbeth*), **comedies** (such as *As You Like It* and *Much Ado About Nothing*), and histories (such as *Henry V* and *Richard III*); the lyric poetry of **Ben Jonson**, **John Donne**, **Andrew Marvell**, and **George Herbert**; and the poetry of **John Milton**, including *Paradise Lost*.

The eighteenth and nineteenth centuries saw the emergence of **neoclassicism** and **Romanticism** in Britain. Neoclassical (or **Augustan**) poets include **Alexander Pope**, **John Dryden**, and **John Gray**. Romantic poets include **William Blake**, **William Wordsworth**, **Samuel Taylor Coleridge**, and **John Keats**. Important novelists of the period were **Daniel Defoe** (*Robinson Crusoe*), **Henry Fielding** (*Tom Jones*), **Jane Austen** (*Emma*), and **Mary Shelley** (*Frankenstein*).

Important British writers of the **Victorian** and **modernist** periods of the late nineteenth and early twentieth centuries include the poets **Alfred Lord Tennyson**, **Elizabeth Barrett** and **Robert Browning**, **Gerard Manley Hopkins**, **Thomas Hardy**, **T.S. Eliot**, and **Dylan Thomas**. Important British and Irish novelists and fiction writers of the same period are Hardy (*The Mayor of Casterbridge*), **George Eliot** (*Silas Marner*), **Joseph Conrad** (*Lord Jim*), **James Joyce** (*Ulysses*), **D.H. Lawrence** (*The Rainbow*), **Virginia Woolf** (*To the Lighthouse*), and **Katherine Mansfield** (*The Garden Party*).

American Literature

The anglophone literature of the **North American colonies** includes some texts that are also considered part of the British literature of the time. For example, the writings of the explorer and Virginia colonist **John Smith** could be considered part of both seventeenth-century British literature and colonial American literature, as could the writings of New England colonists **John**

Winthrop and **William Bradford**. Other important colonial-era writers include **Anne Bradstreet**, **Mary Rowlandson**, **Jonathan Edwards**, **William Byrd**, **Cotton Mather**, and **William Bartram**.

Important writers of the early nineteenth century in the United States include the poets **William Cullen Bryant** and **Henry Wadsworth Longfellow**, the novelists **James Fenimore Cooper** and **Edgar Allan Poe**, and the short-story writer **Washington Irving**. The **Transcendentalists**, who took their inspiration from the Massachusetts orator and philosopher **Ralph Waldo Emerson** (*Nature*), inaugurated a literary flowering now called the **American Renaissance**. Other transcendentalists were the New England writers **Henry David Thoreau** (*Walden*) and **Margaret Fuller** (**"Woman in the Nineteenth Century"**). Other writers who are considered part of the American Renaissance include Poe, **Nathaniel Hawthorne**, **Fredrick Douglass**, **Walt Whitman**, **Herman Melville**, and **Emily Dickinson**. Other styles and movements that grew in the antebellum era were the **sentimental novel**, the **slave narrative**, the **plantation novel**, and **frontier** or **southwestern humor**.

Movements such as realism, regionalism, and naturalism flourished after the U.S. Civil War. Important **realists** were **Mark Twain** (*Adventures of Huckleberry Finn*), **Henry James** (*The Bostonians*), **Abraham Cahan** (*The Rise of David Levinsky*), **William Dean Howells** (**"Editha"**), **Charles Chesnutt** (**"The Wife of His Youth"**), and **Edith Wharton** (*The House of Mirth*). Realist stories and novels sought to portray interior and social life accurately, emphasizing urban life and conflicts between the classes. **Regionalism** (or **local color**) portrayed the differences among U.S. regions in the years after the Civil War. Regionalist texts were written by Twain, Chesnutt, **Sarah Orne Jewett** (*The Country of the Pointed Firs*), George Washington Cable (*The Grandissimes*), **Hamlin Garland** (*Main-Travelled Roads*), and **Kate Chopin** (**"At the 'Cadian Ball'"**). American **naturalist** writers were influenced by the French novelist Émile Zola, and sought to present human beings as controlled by natural forces, history, chance, and instinct. Important U.S. naturalists were **Stephen Crane** (*The Red Badge of Courage*), **Jack London** (**"To Build a Fire"**), **Theodore Dreiser** (*Sister Carrie*), and **Frank Norris** (*The Octopus*).

In the U.S. during the early twentieth century, **modernist** writers often experimented with form and style, and addressed such themes as psychological alienation, the social changes brought about by technology, and the violence and uncertainty of the era. Important modernist writers of the years between World Wars I and II are the poets **T. S. Eliot** (who later emigrated to Britain), **William Carlos Williams**, **Marianne Moore**, **Robert Frost**, **Ezra Pound**, and **Hart Crane**. Important fiction writers of the era are **Sherwood Anderson** (*Winesburg, Ohio*), **William Faulkner** (*The Sound and the Fury*), **F. Scott Fitzgerald** (*Tender is the Night*), **Jean Toomer** (*Cane*), **Claude McKay** (*Home to Harlem*), **Ernest Hemingway** (*In Our Time*), **Djuna Barnes** (*Nightwood*), **Nella Larsen** (*Quicksand*), and **John Dos Passos** (*Manhattan Transfer*).

Recent and Contemporary Anglophone Literature

Important movements in literature since World War II are **Beat** and **confessional** poetry and **postmodern** fiction. Important recent writers from the U.S. include **Ralph Ellison**, **Robert Penn Warren**, **Elizabeth Bishop**, **Thomas Pynchon**, **J. D. Salinger**, **Sylvia Plath**, **Saul Bellow**, **Kurt Vonnegut**, **James Baldwin**, **Flannery O'Connor**, **Denise Levertov**, **Allen Ginsberg**, **Ishmael**

Reed, **Adrienne Rich**, **Gary Snyder**, **Leslie Marmon Silko**, **Louise Erdrich**, **Toni Morrison**, **Sandra Cisneros**, **Cormac McCarthy**, and **Paul Auster**. Other important anglophone writers include **Kingsley Amis**, **Graham Swift**, **Jeanette Winterson**, **Julian Barnes**, and **Salman Rushdie** from Britain, **Michael Ondaadje** and **Alice Munro** from Canada, **V. S. Naipaul** and **Arundhati Roy** from India, **Patrick White** and **Peter Carey** from Australia, **Chinua Achebe** from Nigeria, **Edna O'Brien** from Ireland, and **J. M. Coetzee** and **Bessie Head** from South Africa.

Literary Genres and Techniques

0003   **Understand literary genres, elements, and techniques.**

For example: basic literary terminology (e.g., flashback, foreshadowing); characteristics of different genres and types of literature (e.g., myths, folktales, fiction, nonfiction, drama, poetry); elements of fiction (e.g., plot, character, setting, theme, voice); types of poetry (e.g., lyric, narrative, haiku); characteristics of poetry and poetic techniques (e.g., meter, rhyme, alliteration, figurative language); and types of drama (e.g., comedy, tragedy) and common dramatic devices (e.g., suspense, soliloquy).

Genre

Genre refers to a distinctive type or "kind" of literary text. Genres include the **lyric poem**, the **epic poem**, the **novel**, the **literary sketch**, the **personal essay**, **tragic** drama, and **comic** drama.

Poetry is writing that uses such techniques as meter, rhyme, symbolism, and figurative language, and is intended to inspire the imagination or provoke reflection. Unlike **prose**, poetry is usually composed in short units such as lines and stanzas. **Epic** poems are lengthy and celebrate heroic deeds, philosophical ideas, and historical events. **Lyric** poems are short and express a poet's personal thoughts. **Ballads** are narrative poems that were originally sung, and continue to have a songlike structure. **Elegies** commemorate the life of someone who has died. **Sonnets** are lyric poems consisting of fourteen lines of **iambic pentameter**, a traditional form of meter and rhyme scheme. **Haiku** is a form of Japanese short poem, usually on the theme of nature, consisting of three lines and seventeen syllables. **Epigrams** are two-line satirical or witty poems.

Myths, **parables**, **fables**, **folktales**, and **legends** are traditional forms of oral narrations. Some written literature is based on these oral forms.

Fiction is narrative prose and is not necessarily concerned with events or characters from real life. The **literary sketch** is a very short narration, usually informal or humorous. A **short story** (before the twentieth century, sometimes called a **tale**) is, as the name suggests, a brief narration; it is longer than a sketch and usually contains a much greater degree of plot and character development. It began to achieve its current form around the end of the eighteenth century. The **novel** is a long work of fiction—usually over 50,000 words—with considerable plot and character development; the European novel as we know it originated in the seventeenth century.

Drama refers to texts written to be performed on stage. Theatrical productions date to the earliest civilizations, but the West traces its dramatic tradition to ancient Greece. Dramatic texts are traditionally considered to be either **comedies** or **tragedies**, although not all plays (and by no means all *modern* plays) fit into either category. **Comedy** is the dramatic genre that deals with everyday or amusing events; comedies usually have happy endings. Conversely, **tragedy** is characterized by solemn or heroic actions and usually ends unhappily for the **protagonist**, or main character.

Nonfiction includes all writing that is not fiction or poetry, including technical, academic, and journalistic writing. The **essay** is a form of nonfiction literature—usually more formal than journalism but less so than academic writing—that treats its subject matter thoughtfully, but from a personal point of view. The modern literary essay dates from the late sixteenth century.

Poetic Technique

Poetry (like much prose) uses various kinds of **figurative language**—that is, language used in ways that are not literal. Most poems (unlike prose) employ some kind of **prosody**, which designates various formal elements of poetry.

Figures of speech, sometimes called **rhetorical tropes**, include **metaphor**, **simile**, **metonymy**, **hyperbole**, **apostrophe**, **personification**, **litotes** (or **understatement**), and **oxymoron**. *Metaphor* is the comparison of two unlike things by calling one thing by the name of another. *Simile* is like metaphor, but compares two things using the words "like" or "as." *Metonymy* substitutes one word for another with which it is closely associated. *Hyperbole* is a fanciful or vivid exaggeration. In *apostrophe*, a speaker addresses a person who is absent or an inanimate thing or abstract idea. Similarly, *personification* attributes human characteristics to things or ideas. *Litotes*, the opposite of hyperbole, understates a thought or attribute of something. An *oxymoron* describes something using words with opposite meanings.

Elements of **prosody**, or poetic form, include **rhythm**, **meter**, and **rhyme**. The sound of poetry is further structured by formal techniques such as **alliteration**, and **assonance**. **Rhythm** means the regular alteration of stressed and unstressed syllables in a poem. **Meter** refers to a repeated pattern of stressed and unstressed syllables in each line of a poem (or **stanza**, a formal subdivision of a poem), as well as the length of lines in a poem. **Rhyme** means the repetition of vowel sounds at the ends of lines; **rhyme scheme** refers to the way rhyming sounds are patterned in a whole poem. **Alliteration** is the repetition of consonant sounds in a poem; **assonance** is the repetition of vowel sounds within lines or throughout a poem.

Elements of Fiction

A work of fiction often narrates a main series of events, known as the **plot**. These events may form not only the core of the work's content, but also the backbone of its structure or organization. **Foreshadowing** anticipates or hints at the future events or conclusion of a plot, while **flashbacks** are narrations of events in the past of the main narration.

A fiction's **narrator** is the person, or the imagined "voice," who is telling the story. A **first-person** narrator, or **first-person point of view**, is a narrator who is also actually a **character** in the narration; first-person narrators are only aware of events that a character would likely experience. Rarely used, a **second-person** narrator (or point of view) seems to describe events that the reader, or some person the narrator is addressing directly, is doing. A **third-person** narrator (or point of view) stands outside the action of the narration itself, and may be **omniscient**—that is, may know everything about the characters and events in the fiction—or **limited**, that is, they may only know the kinds of things the characters themselves know.

Voice is the degree of formality or informality, or of emotional involvement or distance, used by a narrator; voice is closely related to **tone**, which is the attitude a narrator seems to take toward his or her readers.

Characters are fictional persons. Their speech is called **dialogue**, while what the narrator says about characters is called **exposition**. **Round** characters are main characters who are thoroughly developed; **flat** characters are less well developed and often serve a minor function in the plot.

Setting is the place and time in which a narrative takes place.

A text's **theme** is the main idea or concept it deals with: the story's "problem."

Imagery, or **mimesis**, means vivid description, as opposed to narration in the strict sense. Imagery fleshes out the places and things in a fictional text.

Dramatic Devices

For both practical and traditional reasons, there are certain literary terms specific to dramatic literature. For example, while novels are often subdivided into **chapters** and poems are subdivided into **stanzas**, plays are usually subdivided into **acts** and **scenes**. Plays usually contain **stage directions**, or instructions for actors on stage as well as for production staff; they may indicate, for example, when characters should **enter** and **exit** scenes. Certain **conventions**, such as the **aside** and the **soliloquy**, are traditional dramatic techniques. In the *aside*, a character briefly speaks directly to the audience; in a *soliloquy*, a character utters his thoughts aloud at length. **Comic relief** consists of comic scenes or lines inserted into an otherwise serious play;

melodrama is a kind of popular drama with clear-cut heroes and villains; **stock characters**, who often appear in melodramas, are stereotyped characters.

Literature for Children

0004 **Understand literature for children, including genres, literary elements, and literary techniques.**

For example: major works and authors of children's literature; genres of children's literature and their characteristics; major themes associated with children's literature; analysis of rhetorical and literary devices (e.g., analogies, metaphors, symbolism) in children's literature; comparison of different styles and communicative purposes in children's literature; criteria for evaluating children's literature (e.g., reading level, literary quality, richness of vocabulary, appealing plot, interesting information, illustrations, gender preferences, variety of settings and characters); analysis of excerpts of children's literature in relation to style, theme, or voice; and uses of children's literature (e.g., providing exposure to high-quality language, enhancing other areas of the curriculum, fostering cross-cultural understanding).

Purposes of Children's Literature

Children's literature usually seeks to **entertain**. When literature entertains, it encourages children to master the skills of literacy and appreciate textuality.

Literature for children also often seeks to expand their ability to think in a **narrative** mode. This, in turn, helps develop the ability to understand cause and effect relationships, and thereby helps children learn to plan, evaluate, and judge.

Literature also develops ethical **values** by illustrating the consequences of wise and unwise actions. Similarly, children's literature seeks not only to deliver factual information to children but also to instruct them in matters of emotion, thereby fostering **empathy**.

Children's literature helps develop the **imagination**, along with spatial thinking, problem solving, and creativity.

Reading should help make children aware of **literate language** and **textuality**. While much children's literature may seek to imitate the spoken word, it should also accustom children to the special rhythms, diction, and conventions of written language.

Children's literature should make children aware of **universal** human experiences while also fostering **broadmindedness** and **curiosity** about the lives and cultures of others.

Literary Elements of Children's Literature

Themes in children's literature are often **didactic**; that is, they usually intend to teach a lesson. Common themes in children's literature are overcoming fear, learning empathy, facing new or unknown situations, learning a new skill or ability, gaining patience, and overcoming hardship.

Plots in children's fiction are usually simpler than in adult books, and rely less on flashbacks and other forms of counterintuitive sequencing. Often children's books follow a single plotline, although different plots are sometimes woven together. Mystery and suspense are used in children's books to maintain interest until the end of the narrative.

In children's books—especially those for younger children—**characterization** is often allegorical. Animals and fantastic characters stand for ideas or personality traits. These characters are often deliberately one-dimensional in order to make them recognizable to children as distinct personalities. Characterization in books for older children is usually more complex.

The literary **style** of books for young children relies on rhyme, repetition, and simple syntax. Children's books include more straightforward narration than description or authorial reflection. Again, literary style in books for older children is more like that of adult literature.

Genres of Children's Literature

Books for babies and **beginning readers** include **toy books**, which often include doors and flaps to open, special materials to be rubbed or patted, and electronic devices that play voices or sounds; an example is the popular **Pat the Bunny**. Books of **nursery rhymes** include easy-to-remember songs and poems; the most famous nursery rhyme books are the various editions of **Mother Goose**. **Alphabet** and **counting** books teach basic literacy and numeracy skills. **Concept books** list and describe the objects in an abstract class, such as animals, trees, or vehicles. **Wordless books** tell stories in pictures only.

Picture books for older children tell simple illustrated stories. Well-known picture books for older children include Maurice Sendak's **Where the Wild Things Are**, **Blueberries for Sal** by Robert McCloskey, **The Relatives Came** by Cynthia Rylant, and **Aunt Flossie's Hats (and Crab Cakes Later)** by Elizabeth Fitzgerald Howard.

Many children's books, including many picture books, adapt (or create anew) well-known **folktales**, **myths**, **legends**, and **fables** for children. Adaptations of **Aesop**, the stories collected by the **Brothers Grimm** and **Hans Christian Andersen**, and versions of **The Three Billy Goats Gruff** and *Puss in Boots* fall into this category, as do adaptations of the African-American **Uncle Remus** stories and the **Jack** stories of Appalachia. These tales usually feature magic, talking animals, a strong contrast between wise and foolish behavior, and repetition of words and events. Versions of the stories of **Robin Hood** and **King Arthur and the Knights of the Roundtable** are similar.

Fantasy literature for children includes such famous books as *Alice's Adventures in Wonderland* by Lewis Carroll, *The Wonderful Wizard of Oz* by L. Frank Baum, *The Hobbit* by J. R. R. Tolkien, and *The Lion, The Witch, and the Wardrobe* by C. S. Lewis. More recent fantastic books include *The Indian in the Cupboard* by Lynne Reid Banks, *James and the Giant Peach* by Roald Dahl, and the **Harry Potter** books by J. K. Rowling.

Realistic fiction for older children includes fiction with **contemporary** or **historical** settings. The stories in these texts plausibly portray life as it is lived today or in the past; realistic fiction does not usually include the adventures of supernatural beings, talking animals, or anthropomorphized objects. Realistic fiction may be concerned with the problems of growing up, elements of adult life, or the lives of important historical figures. Important examples of texts in this genre include *The Yearling* by Marjorie Kinnan Rawlings, *Where the Red Fern Grows* by Wilson Rawls, *My Side of the Mountain* by Jean Craighead George, *Island of the Blue Dolphins* by Scott O'Dell, *Roll of Thunder, Hear My Cry* by Mildred D. Taylor, *That Was Then, This Is Now* by S. E. Hinton, *Jacob Have I Loved* by Katherine Paterson, *The True Confessions Of Charlotte Doyle* by Avi, and *Out of the Dust* by Karen Hesse.

Nonfiction books for children may be concerned with scientific, historical, or biographical matters, or they may address the problems of childhood and adolescence. Important or award-winning children's nonfiction books include *Blizzard! The Storm That Changed America* by Jim Murphy, *The Wright Brothers: How They Invented the Airplane* by Russell Freedman, *Good Queen Bess: The Story of Elizabeth I of England* by Diane Stanley and Peter Vennema, *It's Perfectly Normal: Changing Bodies, Growing Up, Sex, and Sexual Health* by Robie H. Harris, and *When Marian Sang: The True Recital of Marian Anderson* by Pam Muñoz Ryan.

Poetry for children includes nursery rhymes and songs written for small children to learn and sing. Poetry written for older children is more complex than nursery rhymes, but usually simpler than adult poetry. Recent award-winning books of poetry for children include *All the Small Poems and Fourteen More* by Valerie Worth, *Joyful Noise: Poems for Two Voices* by Paul Fleischman, and *A Visit to William Blake's Inn: Poems for Innocent and Experienced Travelers* by Nancy Willard.

Evaluating Children's Literature

The **physical form** of children's books is much more important than that of books for adults. Books for very young children should be especially sturdy, and books for beginning readers should use a large, widely spaced **typeface**. Matte-finish paper cuts glare and is easier to read.

Books selected to be **read aloud** to young children should deal with familiar themes and have relatively simple storylines. Often, the best books for reading aloud are picture books.

Although some children's literature is didactic, children are often bored by **preachy** or **overly sentimental** books. Narrative books for all age levels should avoid letting thematic matters, especially direct address to the reader, overwhelm plot.

Many older books can be **culturally biased** or otherwise condescending to some readers. Books that insult children's cultural or social background should be avoided.

There are several **awards** presented for outstanding children's literature. The **John Newbery Medal**, the oldest award for children's literature, is awarded by the **Association for Library Service to Children** to the most outstanding author of a children's book in the previous year. The **Randolph J. Caldecott Medal** is awarded for the best illustrated book of the previous year. The **International Board on Books for Young People** awards the annual **Hans Christian Andersen Award** to a living author in recognition of his or her body of work. Lists of literary award winners can be helpful in choosing books for children.

Writing Skills and Strategies

0005   **Understand how to apply writing skills and strategies for various purposes.**

For example: knowledge and use of prewriting strategies, including techniques for generating topics and developing ideas (e.g., brainstorming, semantic mapping, outlining, reading and researching); formal elements of good writing (e.g., paragraphing, topic sentences, cohesive transitions); revising written texts to improve unity, coherence, and logical organization; editing written work to ensure conformity to conventions of edited American English (e.g., grammar, punctuation, spelling of homophones such as *there/ their/they're*); techniques and stylistic requirements for writing for various purposes (e.g., to respond, inform, analyze, persuade, entertain), including factors related to the selection of topic and mode of written expression; clarifying intended audience; and use of various techniques to convey meaning (e.g., precise vocabulary, figurative language, illustrations).

Purpose and Context of Writing

Traditionally, the purposes for writing have been defined as to **inform**, to **persuade**, and to **entertain**. More broadly, writing can seek to **explain**, to **praise** or to **condemn**, to **evaluate**, to **narrate**, to **express feeling**, or to **question**. Often, a particular written work will seek to accomplish more than one of these purposes; nevertheless, writers must determine the main purpose of the text before beginning to write.

Writers must consider their **audience** when determining their purposes for writing. Closely related to audience is the institutional context for the writing; writing may be done in a **creative**, **business**, **technical**, **personal**, or **academic** (or **scholarly**) context, among others.

Audience and context determine the appropriate **tone** of a writing project. Business, technical, and (especially) academic writing should strive for a **serious** and **objective** tone. Personal and creative writing may be more playful in tone, and may be more expressive of personal feelings. Condescension and rudeness should be avoided regardless of audience and context. Similarly, writers should strive for an appropriate and consistent level of **diction**, or word choice, in their writing. In academic writing, slang and regionalisms should be avoided; on the other hand, writers should avoid stilted, pretentious, and unnecessarily Latinate vocabulary and syntax in formal writing. In all cases, writers should aim for **clarity** and **concision**. Cliché, euphemism, biased or sexist language, wordiness, and vagueness should always—and especially in academic contexts—be avoided.

Formal Elements of Writing

Most academic and other formal writing calls for the writer to make an **argument**. For our purposes, an argument is a discourse on a subject about which people may disagree, that seeks to establish a position on that subject based on evidence and reason. Arguments, by definition, cannot be about a matter of universal agreement ("Triangles have three sides," "Ten is more than five"); nor can they be mere statements of personal opinion ("I like hip-hop better than jazz").

People sometimes talk about arguments in terms of **claims**, **evidence**, **reasons**, and **warrants**—a set of terms proposed by the philosopher Stephen Toulmin. **Claims** are broad statements that an argument seeks to establish. **Evidence** and **reasons** are, respectively, facts or authoritative opinions and more narrow assertions presupposed by the claim. **Warrants** lay out the logical principle by which the writer links claims to reasons and evidence. If I argue, for example, that a flight will be delayed because of a storm, my information confirming that it is, in fact, raining would constitute evidence and reasons. The warrant for the claim would be that, in general, we know that air travel can be affected by bad weather; hence, if it is raining, we can reasonably predict that the flight will be delayed.

In a formal paper, arguments are usually set out in a brief **thesis statement**; the rest of the paper seeks to develop the thesis. A thesis is almost always found in an **introduction**, which is one or several paragraphs (depending on the length of the whole paper) that explains what the paper will discuss and often provides basic knowledge for understanding the subject at hand.

Along with an introduction, a formal academic paper will be developed in its **body**. The **body** of the paper seeks to explain and support the thesis by making and elaborating subsidiary arguments. These arguments are made in a series of **paragraphs** that break the main argument into smaller logical and rhetorical units. The subsidiary arguments advanced in body paragraphs are usually stated in **topic sentences**, which serve the same purpose for body paragraphs that thesis statements serve for the paper as a whole.

Most papers will also have a **conclusion**. A concluding paragraph or paragraphs should tie all the subsidiary points of the paper together, often guiding the reader in drawing inferences from the paper and placing its argument in a broader context.

Well-written papers are characterized by **unity** and **coherence**. Keeping the paper's discussion within the bounds of the thesis and keeping paragraphs centered on their topic sentences ensures unity. Coherence can be achieved by making sure every element of the paper relates clearly to what precedes and follows it. Techniques used to make writing more coherent include **repetition** of key words or phrases, the use of **parallel** grammatical structures in lists and other logically parallel constructions, and the use of **transitional words and phrases** to indicate logical relationships between paragraphs and sentences. Important transitional words and phrases for linking sentences and paragraphs include **therefore**, **consequently**, **however**, and **moreover**.

The Writing Process

Preparing to write an academic paper involves techniques known as **prewriting**. Prewriting, also called **brainstorming**, is the process of narrowing down subject matter for writing and formulating a thesis. Such techniques include making impromptu **lists**; **clustering**, or making flowcharts, tree diagrams, or other graphic representations of the relationships between ideas; and **freewriting**, which, as the name suggests, is the writing down of whatever occurs to the writer. A more advanced kind of prewriting is **outlining** the structure of the paper.

Another technique for beginning a writing project is to perform some preliminary **research**. Reference books, the Internet, and serious periodicals can provide an overview of the subject matter at hand, and thereby help in formulating a thesis. The more advanced research required by university **research papers** calls for methodical gathering and organizing of existing information on a given topic. Students should be aware of the basics of performing library research (including the use of online library catalogs and databases), the purposes of **bibliographies** (including **annotated bibliographies**) and **notes**, and basics of **citation** (including the meaning and consequences of **plagiarism**).

The process of producing the first actual text of a writing project is called **drafting**. Experts stress the importance of drafting to develop the structure and argument of a paper; additional brainstorming or research can always be done after the drafting process begins, but it is important to begin writing so that the form of the final argument begins to take shape. A preliminary thesis should be produced as part of writing the first draft of a paper, but writers should be prepared to revise thesis statements later.

Revision is usually a multi-stage process. The first draft of a paper should first be closely revised for **content** and **organization**. One of the first tasks in revising is to ensure the overall coherence and unity of the draft. This process may entail deletion of extraneous passages and the further development of unclear or inadequate ones; first revision may also call for rearrangement of whole passages using a word processor's cut-and-paste or drop-and-drag functions. The thesis itself may need to be revised during the period of first revision, and the structure of the conclusion may not emerge until this stage. Secondary revision or **editing** of the draft may focus mainly on clarity of language. At this stage, such problems as **wordiness**, **vagueness**, and **stylistic** or **grammatical** errors should be found and corrected. Finally, a draft should be **proofread** for correct spelling, mechanics, punctuation, and format.

Mathematics

Objectives

0006   **Understand and apply number properties and number representations.**

For example: number sense; cardinal, ordinal, and negative numbers; properties of real numbers (e.g., commutative, distributive); the structure of the base ten number system (e.g., place value, decimal expansions); the expanded form of a number; the application of number concepts to count, compare, sort, order, and round numbers; equivalent forms of fractions, decimals, and percents; various equivalent symbolic representations of numbers (e.g., scientific notation, exponents); number theory concepts (e.g., prime and composite numbers); and the process of converting among graphic, numeric, symbolic, and verbal representations of numbers.

0007   **Understand and apply number operations to represent and solve problems.**

For example: relationships among mathematical operations (e.g., multiplication and division as inverse operations); order of operations; procedures for enhancing computational fluency; standard algorithms for basic arithmetic operations; the use of number properties to analyze nonstandard computational algorithms; proving number facts and relationships; representing operations using concrete models; multiple solutions; solving problems involving integers, fractions, decimals, ratios and proportions, and percents; strategies to estimate quantities (e.g., front end, rounding, regrouping); the relationships between number operations and algebra; and the use of mathematical reasoning to solve problems involving numbers and number operations.

0008   Understand and apply patterns, relations, algebra, and principles of geometry.

For example: recognizing and extending patterns using a variety of representations (e.g., manipulatives, figures, numbers, algebraic expressions); relationship between standard algorithms and fundamental concepts of algebra and geometry; the application of concepts of variable, function, and equation to express relationships algebraically; deriving algebraic expressions to represent real-world situations; the use of tables and graphs to explore patterns, relations, and functions; solving equations and inequalities; properties of lines and angles; attributes of two- and three-dimensional geometric figures; the application of the concepts of similarity and congruence to solve problems; geometric transformations; the classification of figures according to symmetries; and connections between algebra and geometry (e.g., the use of coordinate systems).

0009   Understand and apply concepts and methods of measurement, data analysis, statistics, and probability.

For example: the use of both standard and nonstandard units of measurement to describe and compare phenomena; appropriate instruments, units, and procedures for solving various measurement problems (e.g., problems involving time, length, area, angles, volume, mass, temperature); estimation and conversion of measurements within the customary and metric systems; the collection, organization, and communication of information using appropriate graphic and nongraphic representations (e.g., frequency distributions and percentiles); the use of measures of central tendency and spread to analyze data; problems involving simple probabilities; and predictions based on simulations, theory, or data from the real world.

Number Skills

Key properties of whole numbers (and some related terms) include the following:

The *Commutative Property for Addition and Multiplication* states that the order in which addends are added or factors are multiplied does not determine the sum or product. (6×9 gives the same product as 9×6, for instance.) Division and subtraction are not commutative.

The *Associative Property for Addition and Multiplication* states that "associating" three or more addends or factors in a different fashion will not change the sum or product. For example, $(3 + 7) + 5$ gives the same sum as $3 + (7 + 5)$. Division and subtraction are not associative.

The *Distributive Property of Multiplication over Addition* is shown hereafter in simple notation form:

$$a(b + c) = (a \times b) + (a \times c)$$

An illustration of the Distributive Property is this: multiplying 6 by 47 will give the same result as multiplying 6 by 40, multiplying 6 times 7, then *adding* the products. That is, 6 × (47) = (6 × 40) + (6 × 7).

Some pairs of operations are considered to be *inverse*. Addition and subtraction are inverse operations, as are multiplication and division. The operations can be thought of as "undoing" one another: Multiplying 4 by 9 gives 36; dividing 36 by 9 "gives back" 4.

The *Multiplicative Identity Property of One* states that any number multiplied by 1 remains the same. (34 × 1 = 34, for instance.) The number 1 is called the *Multiplicative Identity*.

The *Property of Reciprocals* states that any number (except for zero) multiplied by its reciprocal gives 1. (The *reciprocal* of a number is 1 divided by that number.)

Remember that dividing by zero is considered to have no meaning; avoid doing it when computing or solving equations and inequalities.

The *Additive Identity Property of Zero* states that adding zero to any number will not change the number (87 + 0 = 87, for instance). Zero is called the *Additive Identity*.

Division is *partitive* when you know the total and the number of parts or groups but you don't know how many are in each part. Consider: "You have 7 containers of bolts and a total of 98 bolts. How many bolts are in each container (assuming the same number in each)?" Arriving at the answer is an example of partitive division.

With *measurement division*, the number of groups is not known. Using the example above, if you knew that there were 14 bolts per container, and that there were 98 bolts altogether, finding the number of containers would require measurement division.

Rational Numbers, Fractions, and Decimals

A property of real numbers is the *Density Property*. It states that, given any two real numbers, there is always another real number between them. (Think of the number line: No matter how close two points are, there is always a point between them.)

Rational numbers are those that can be written as fractions. (This includes integers; 12, for instance, can be written as $\frac{12}{1}$.)

Decimals (or "decimal fractions"), which come to an end when represented exactly, are *terminating decimals* (2.125, for instance). *Repeating decimals* are those in which the digits repeat a pattern endlessly (3.333333 . . . , for example). To use shorthand notation to show repeating decimals, you can write the "repeating block" just once, putting a bar over it. The example above, for instance, can be shown as $3.\overline{3}$. (Both terminating and repeating decimals are rational numbers.)

Some numbers are real numbers, but cannot be accurately represented by fractions. The ratio of the length of the diameter of any circle to its circumference, or π, for instance, is irrational. There are useful approximations of π, such as 3.14159, but π cannot be "pinned down" in either fraction or decimal notation.

Fractions, decimal numbers, ratios, and percents can be thought of as different ways of representing values, and any given rational number can be shown any of those ways. It is useful to be able to convert from one to the other. The following are some conversion tips:

The practical method for changing a fraction into a decimal is by dividing the numerator by the denominator. For example, $\frac{1}{4}$ becomes 0.25 when 1 is divided by 4, as follows:

$$\begin{array}{r} .25 \\ 4\overline{)1.00} \\ \underline{8} \\ 20 \end{array}$$

Naturally, this can be done longhand or with a calculator. (If the decimal number includes a whole number, as with $2\frac{3}{5}$, you can ignore the whole number when doing the division.) The decimal number may terminate or repeat. Converting a simple fraction to a decimal number will never result in an irrational number.

To convert a non-repeating decimal number to a fraction in lowest terms, simply write the decimal as a fraction with the denominator a power of ten, and then reduce to lowest terms. For example, 0.125 can be written as $\frac{125}{1000}$, which reduces to $\frac{1}{8}$.

Any decimal number can be converted to a percent by shifting the decimal point two places to the right and adding the percent symbol. 0.135, for instance, becomes 13.5%. (If the number before the percent symbol is a whole number, there is no need to show the decimal point.)

A percent can be converted to a decimal number by shifting the decimal point two places to the left and dropping the percent symbol: 98% becomes 0.98 as a decimal.

A percent can be converted to a fraction simply by putting the percent (without the percent symbol) over 100, then reducing. In this way 20% can be shown as $\frac{20}{100}$, which reduces to $\frac{1}{5}$.

Ratio notation is simply an alternative method for showing fractions. For example, $\frac{2}{5}$ can be rewritten as "2 to 5." Ratio notation is commonly used when you want to emphasize the relationship of one number to another. Ratios are often shown as numbers with a colon between them; 2:5 is the same ratio as 2 to 5 and $\frac{2}{5}$.

To illustrate all of the above equivalencies and conversions at once, consider the fraction $\frac{19}{20}$. Shown as a ratio, it's 19 to 20, or 19:20. As a decimal, you have 0.95; as a percent, 95%.

The rules for performing operations on rational numbers (fractions) parallel in many ways the computational rules for integers. Just as adding –3 and –11 gives –14, adding $-\frac{1}{9}$ and $-\frac{5}{9}$ gives $-\frac{6}{9}$ (or $-\frac{2}{3}$ in reduced form.)

Problem Solving

The ability to render some real-life quandaries into mathematical or logical problems—workable via established procedures—is a key to finding solutions. Because each quandary will be unique, so too will be your problem-solving plan of attack. Still, many real-world problems that lend themselves to mathematical solutions are likely to require one of the following strategies.

1. **Guess and check** (not the same as "wild guessing"). With this problem-solving strategy, make your best guess, and then check the answer to see whether it's right. Even if the guess doesn't immediately provide the solution, it may help to get you closer to it so that you can continue to work on it. An example:

   Three persons' ages add up to 72, and each person is one year older than the last person. What are their ages?

   Because the three ages must add up to 72, it is reasonable to take one-third of 72 (24) as your starting point. Of course, even though 24 + 24 + 24 gives a sum of 72, those numbers don't match the information ("Each person is one year older . . . ") So, you might guess that the ages are 24, 25, and 26. You check that guess by addition, and you see that the sum of 75 is too high. Lowering your guesses by one each, you try 23, 24, and 25, which indeed add up to 72, giving you the solution. There are many variations of the guess and check method.

2. **Making a sketch or a picture** can help to clarify a problem. Consider this problem:

Mr. Rosenberg plans to put a four-foot-wide concrete sidewalk around his backyard pool. The pool is rectangular, with dimensions 12' by 24'. The cost of the concrete is $1.28 per square foot. How much concrete is required for the job?

If you have exceptional visualization abilities, no sketch is needed. For most of us, however, a drawing like the one shown below may be helpful in solving this and many other real-life problems.

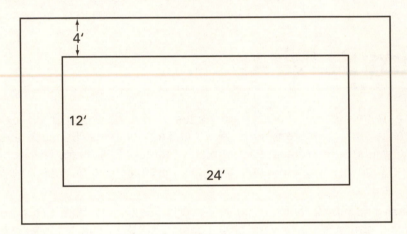

3. **Make a table or a chart.** Sometimes, *organizing* the information from a problem makes it easier to find the solution; tables and charts can be helpful.

4. **Making a list**, like making a table or chart, can help to organize information, and perhaps provide or at least hint at a solution. The strategy would work well for solving this problem: "How many different outcomes are there if you roll two regular six-sided dice?"

5. **Act it out.** Sometimes, literally "doing" a problem, with physical objects, your bodies, and so forth, can help produce a solution. A classic problem that could be solved in this manner is the following: "If five strangers meet, and if everyone shakes everyone else's hand once, how many total handshakes will there be?"

6. **Look for patterns.** This technique encourages you to ask, "What's happening here?" Spotting a pattern would be helpful in solving a problem such as:

Nevin's weekly savings account balance for 15 weeks are as follows: $125, $135, $148, $72, $85, $96, $105, $50, $64, $74, $87, $42, $51, $60, $70. If the pattern holds, (approximately) what might Nevin's balance be the next week?

7. Working a simpler problem means finding the solution to a different but simpler problem, hoping that you will spot a way to solve the harder one. *Estimating* can be thought of as working a simpler problem. If you need to know the product of 23 and 184, and no calculator or pencil and paper are handy, you could estimate the product by getting the exact answer to the simpler problem, 20 × 200.

8. **Writing an open math sentence** (an equation with one or more variables, or "unknowns"), then solving it, is often an effective strategy. This is sometimes called "translating" a problem into mathematics. Consider this problem: "Tiana earned grades of 77%, 86%, 90%, and 83% on her first four weekly science quizzes. Assuming all grades are equally weighted, what score will she need on the fifth week's quiz in order to have an average (or mean) score of 88%?" Using the given information, you can set up the following equation, which, when solved, will answer the question:

$$\frac{(77 + 86 + 90 + 83 + x)}{5} = 88$$

9. **Work backward.** Consider this problem: "If you add 12 to some number, then multiply the sum by 4, you will get 60. What is the number?" You can find a solution by *starting at the end*, with 60. The problem tells you that the 60 came from multiplying a sum by 4. When multiplied by 4, 15 equals 60, so 15 must be the sum referred to. And if 15 is the sum of 12 and something else, the "something else" can only be 3.

There are of course hybrid approaches. You can mix and match problem-solving strategies wherever you think they are appropriate. In general, attention to *reasonableness* may be most crucial to problem-solving success, especially in real-life situations.

Mathematical Communication and Mathematical Terminology, Symbols, and Representations

While a review of even basic mathematical terminology and symbolism could fill a book, there are some key points to keep in mind:

Mathematics is, for the most part, a science of precision. When working with math symbols and terminology, meticulousness is in order. For example, "less than" does not mean the same thing as "not greater than." The following two equations are *not* equivalent (both entire sides of the first equation should be divided by 6.)

$$6m + 2 = 18$$

$$\frac{6m}{6} + 2 = \frac{18}{6}$$

All of this matters, especially in real-life problem situations.

Certain mathematical concepts and terms are frequently misunderstood. Here are a few of the "repeat offenders":

Use care with *hundreds vs. hundredths, thousands vs. thousandths,* and so forth. Remember that the "th" at the end of the word indicates a fraction. "Three hundred" means 300, whereas "three hundredths" means 0.03.

Negative numbers are those less than zero. Fractions less than zero are negative numbers, too.

The *absolute value* of a number can be thought of as its distance from zero on a number line.

Counting numbers can be shown by the set (1, 2, 3, 4, . . .). Notice that 0 is not a counting number.

Whole numbers are the counting numbers, plus 0 (0, 1, 2, . . .).

Integers are all of the whole numbers and their negative counterparts (. . . –2, –1, 0, 1, 2, . . .). Note that negative and positive fractions are not considered integers (unless they are equivalent to whole numbers or their negative counterparts).

Factors are any of the numbers or symbols in mathematics that, when multiplied together, form a product. (The whole number factors of 12 are 1, 2, 3, 4, 6, and 12.) A number with exactly two whole number factors (1 and the number itself) is a *prime number*. The first few primes are 2, 3, 5, 7, 11, 13, and 17. Most other whole numbers are *composite numbers*, because they are *composed* of several whole number factors (1 is neither prime nor composite; it has only one whole number factor).

The *multiples* of any whole number are what are produced when the number is multiplied by counting numbers. The multiples of 7 are 7, 14, 21, 28, and so on. Every whole number has an infinite number of multiples.

Recall that *decimal numbers* are simply certain fractions written in special notation. All decimal numbers are actually fractions whose denominators are powers of 10 (10, 100, 1000, etc.) 0.033, for instance, can be thought of as the fraction $\frac{33}{1000}$.

There is an agreed-upon order of operations for simplifying complex expressions.

First you compute any multiplication or division, left to right. Then you compute any addition or subtraction, also left-to-right. (If an expression contains any parentheses, all computation within the parentheses should be completed first.) Treat exponential expressions ("powers") as multiplication. Thus, the expression $3 + 7 \times 4 - 2$ equals 29. (Multiply 7 by 4 *before* doing the addition and subtraction.)

Exponential notation is a way to show repeated multiplication more simply. $2 \times 2 \times 2$, for instance, can be shown as 2^3, and is equal to 8. (Note: 2^3 does *not* mean 2×3.)

Scientific notation provides a method for showing numbers using exponents (although it is most useful for very large and very small numbers.) A number is in scientific notation when it is shown as a number between 1 and 10 to a power of 10. Thus, the number 75,000 in scientific notation is shown as 7.5×10^4.

Addends (or *addenda*) can be thought of as "parts of addition problems." When addends are combined, they produce *sums*. Likewise, *factors* can be seen as "parts of multiplication problems." When factors are multiplied, they produce *products*. When two numbers are divided, one into the other, the result is a *quotient*.

Equations are not the same as mathematical *expressions*. $12 + 4 = 16$ and $2x + 7 = 12$ are equations. $(144 - 18)$ and $13y^2$ are expressions. Notice that expressions are "lacking a verb," so to speak (you don't say "is equal to" or "equals" when reading expressions). Inequalities are very much like equations, but "greater than" or "less than" are added, such as in $x \leq 7$.

A *trend* is a pattern over time.

Careful use of mathematical terms and ideas such as those noted above is essential to communicating mathematically.

Fast Facts

Careful use of mathematical terms and ideas is essential to communicating mathematically.

The ability to convert among various mathematical and logical representations (graphic, numeric, symbolic, verbal) is an important skill, and, as with problem solving, precision and care are keys to quality conversions. Consider this number line, which might represent ages of students who are eligible for a particular scholarship:

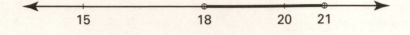

Are 21-year-old students eligible? No, because the conventional notation used on the number line shows a *circle* around the point at 21. That means that 21 is *not* included in the set. Converting the graphic representation to symbolism gives $18 < x < 21$.

Algebraic Concepts and Methods

An important skill is the ability to represent real problems in algebraic form, and the concept of the *variable* is key. A variable is simply a symbol that represents an unknown value. Most typically x is the letter used, although any letter can be used. By "translating" real problems to algebraic form containing one or more variables (often as equations or inequalities), solutions to many problems can be found mathematically.

Understanding the relationships among values, and being able to accurately represent those relationships symbolically is another key to algebraic problem solving. Consider the ages of two sisters. If you don't know the age of the younger sister, but know that the older sister is three years older, you can show the information symbolically as follows: The age of the younger sister can be shown as x, and the age of the older sister as $x + 3$. If you are told that the sum of the sisters' ages is, say, 25, you can represent that information via an equation:

$$x + (x + 3) = 25$$

which can be read as "the age of the younger sister plus the age of the older sister totals 25." This sort of translation skill is crucial for using algebra for problem solving.

Some helpful *translation* tips include the following: The word *is* often suggests an equal sign; *of* may suggest multiplication, as does *product*. *Sum* refers to addition; *difference* suggests subtraction; and a *quotient* is obtained after dividing. The key when translating is to make sure that the equation accurately matches the information and relationships given in the word problem.

Operations with algebraic expressions are governed by various rules and conventions. For instance, only *like* algebraic terms can be added or subtracted to produce simpler expressions. For example, $2x^3$ and $3x^3$ can be added together to get $5x^3$, because the terms are like terms; they both have a base of x^3. You cannot add, say, $7m^3$ and $6m^2$; m^3 and m^2 are unlike bases. (Note: To *evaluate* an algebraic expression means to simplify it using conventional rules.)

When multiplying exponential terms together, the constant terms are multiplied, but the exponents of terms with the same variable bases are *added* together, which is somewhat counterintuitive. For example, $4w^2$ multiplied by $8w^3$ gives $32w^5$ (not $32w^6$, as one might guess).

When like algebraic terms are divided, exponents are subtracted. For example,

$$\frac{2x^7}{5x^3}$$

becomes

$$\frac{2x^4}{5}$$

In algebra, you frequently need to multiply two *binomials* together. Binomials are algebraic expressions of two terms. The FOIL method is one way to multiply binomials. FOIL stands for "first, outer, inner, last": Multiply the first terms in the parentheses, then the outermost terms, then the innermost terms, then the last terms, and then add the products together. For example, to multiply $(x + 3)$ and $(2x - 5)$, you multiply x by $2x$ (the first terms), x by -5 (outer terms), 3 by $2x$ (inner terms), and 3 by 5 (last terms). The four products ($2x^2$, $-5x$, $6x$, and -15) add up to $2x^2 + x - 15$. If the polynomials to be multiplied have more than two terms (*trinomials*, for instance), make sure that *each* term of the first polynomial is multiplied by *each* term of the second.

The opposite of polynomial multiplication is factoring. Factoring a polynomial means rewriting it as the product of factors (often two binomials). The trinomial $x^2 - 11x + 28$, for instance, can be factored into $(x - 4)(x - 7)$. (You can check this by "FOILing" the binomials.)

When attempting to factor polynomials, it is sometimes necessary to factor out any factor that might be common to all terms first. The two terms in $5x^2 - 10$, for example, both contain the factor 5. This means that the expression can be rewritten as $5(x^2 - 2)$.

Factoring is useful when solving some equations, especially if one side of the equation is set equal to zero. Consider $2x^2 - x - 1 = 2$. It can be rewritten as $2x^2 - x - 3 = 0$. This allows the left side to be factored into $(2x - 3)(x + 1)$, giving equation solutions of $\frac{3}{2}$ and -1.

Consider all of the information above as the following problem is first "translated" into an equation, then solved.

> Three teachers who are retiring are said to have 78 years of experience among them. You don't know how many years of experience Teacher A has, but you know that Teacher B has twice as many as A, and Teacher C has two more years of experience than B. How many years of experience does each have?

You can start by calling Teacher A's years of experience *x*. You then consider the relationship to the other two teachers: You can call Teacher B's years of experience 2*x*, which allows you to call Teacher C's years of experience (2*x* + 3). You know that the teachers' years of experience add up to 78, allowing you to write:

$$x + 2x + (2x + 3) = 78$$

Using the rules for solving such an equation, you find that *x* = 15, meaning that the teachers' years of experience are, respectively, 15, 30, and 33 years.

Mathematical Reasoning Processes

Mathematical reasoning includes analyzing problem situations, making conjectures, organizing information, and selecting strategies to solve problems; evaluating solutions to problems; constructing arguments and judging the validity or logic of arguments; and using logical reasoning to draw and justify conclusions from given information.

Problem-solvers must rely on both formal and informal *reasoning processes*. A key informal process relies on *reasonableness*. Consider this problem:

> Center Town Middle School has an enrollment of 640 students. One day, 28 students were absent. What percent of the total number of students were absent?

Even if someone forgot how to compute percents, some possible answers could be rejected instantly: 28 is a "small-but-not-tiny" chunk of 640, so answers like 1%, 18%, and 25% are *unreasonable*.

There are also formal reasoning processes, such as *deductive reasoning*. Deductive reasoning is reasoning from the general to the specific, and is supported by deductive logic. Here is an example of deductive reasoning:

All ducks have wings (a general assertion). Donald is a duck; therefore Donald has wings (a specific proposition).

With *inductive reasoning*, a general rule is inferred from specific observations (which may be limited). Moving from the statement "All boys in this classroom are wearing jeans" (a specific but limited observation) to "All boys wear jeans" (a general assertion) is an example of inductive reasoning. Note that conclusions arrived at via deductive and inductive reasoning are not necessarily true.

Geometry

A fundamental concept of geometry is the notion of a *point*. A point is a specific location, taking up no space, having no area, and frequently represented by a dot. A point is considered one-dimensional.

Through any two points there is exactly one straight line; straight lines are one-dimensional. Planes (think of flat surfaces without edges) are two-dimensional. From these foundational ideas you can move to some other important geometric terms and ideas.

A segment is any portion of a line between two points on the line. It has a definite start and a definite end. The notation for a segment extending from point *A* to point *B* is $\overline{AB}$. A ray is like a straight segment, except it extends forever in one direction. The notation for a ray originating at point *X* (an *endpoint*) through point *Y* is $\overrightarrow{XY}$.

When two rays share their endpoints, an *angle* is formed. A *degree* is a unit of measure of the angle created. If a circle is divided into 360 even slices, each slice has an angle measure of 1 degree. If an angle has exactly 90 degrees it is called a *right* angle. Angles of less than 90 degrees are *acute* angles. Angles greater than 90 degrees are *obtuse* angles. If two angles have the same size (regardless of how long their rays might be drawn) they are *congruent*. Congruence is shown this way: $\angle m = \angle n$ (read "angle *m* is congruent to angle *n*").

A polygon is a closed plane figure bounded by straight lines or a closed figure on a sphere bounded by arcs of great circles. In a plane, three-sided polygons are *triangles*, four-sided polygons are *quadrilaterals*, five sides make *pentagons*, six sides are *hexagons*, and eight-sided polygons are *octagons*. (Note that not all quadrilaterals are squares.) If two polygons (or any figures) have exactly the same size and shape, they are *congruent*. If they are the same shape, but different sizes, they are *similar*.

Polygons may have lines of symmetry, which can be thought of as imaginary fold lines which produce two congruent, mirror-image figures. Squares have four lines of symmetry, and non-square rectangles have two, as shown later. Circles have an infinite number of lines of symmetry; several are shown on the circle.

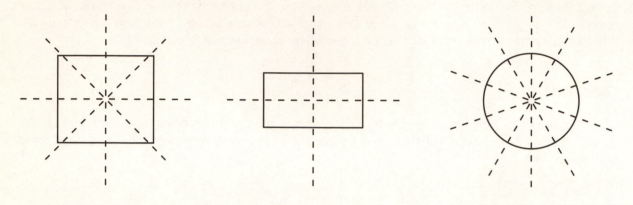

The *diameter* of a circle is a straight line segment that goes from one edge of a circle to the other side, passing through the center. The *radius* of a circle is half of its diameter (from the center to an edge). A *chord* is any segment that goes from one spot on a circle to any other spot (all diameters are chords, but not all chords are diameters).

The *perimeter* of a two-dimensional (flat) shape or object is the distance around the object.

Volume refers to how much space is inside of three-dimensional, closed containers. It is useful to think of volume as how many cubic units could fit into a solid. If the container is a rectangular solid, multiplying width, length, and height together computes the volume. If all six faces (sides) of a rectangular solid are squares, then the object is a cube.

Parallel and perpendicular are key concepts in geometry. Consider the two parallel lines that follow, and the third line (a *transversal*), which crosses them.

Note that among the many individual angles created, there are only two angle measures: 30° (noted in the figure) and 150° (180° − 30°).

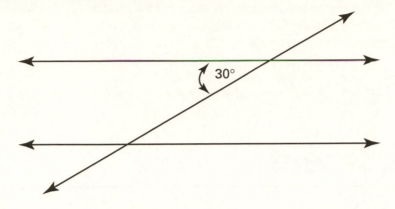

Triangles have various properties. One is that the sum of the measures of the three angles of any triangle is 180°. If, therefore, the measures of two angles are known, the third can be deduced using addition, then subtraction. The Pythagorean theorem states that in any right triangle with legs (shorter sides) a and b, and hypotenuse (longest side) c, the sum of the squares of the sides will be equal to the square of the hypotenuse. In algebraic notation the Pythagorean theorem is given as $a^2 + b^2 = c^2$.

Two important coordinate systems are the number line and the coordinate plane, and both systems can be used to solve certain problems. A particularly useful tool related to the coordinate plane is the Distance Formula, which allows you to compute the distance between any two points on the plane. Consider points C and D in the following figure.

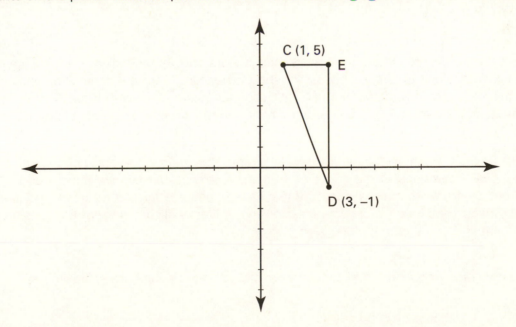

By finding the difference of the points' *x* coordinates (3 – 1, or 2) and the difference of their *y* coordinates (–1 – 5, or –6), you have found the lengths of the sides of triangle CED (2 units and 6 units—you can ignore the negative sign on the 6). You can now use the Pythagorean theorem to find the length of the hypotenuse of triangle CED, which is the same as the length from point C to D ($2^2 + 6^2 =$ 40, and the square root of 40 is approximately 6.3). Here is the distance formula in algebraic form:

$$d = \sqrt{(x_2 - x_1)^2 + (y_2 - y_1)^2}$$

Measurement

Measurement includes estimating and converting measurements within the customary and metric systems; applying procedures for using measurement to describe and compare phenomena; identifying appropriate measurement instruments, units, and procedures for measurement problems involving length, area, angles, volume, mass, time, money, and temperature; and using a variety of materials, models, and methods to explore concepts and solve problems involving measurement.

Here are some key measurement terms and ideas:

Customary units are generally the same as *U.S. units*. Customary units of length include inches, feet, yards, and miles. Customary units of weight include ounces, pounds, and tons. Customary units of capacity (or volume) include teaspoons, tablespoons, cups, pints, quarts, and gallons.

Metric units of length include millimeters, centimeters, meters, and kilometers. The centimeter is the basic metric unit of length, at least for short distances. There are about 2.5 centimeters to 1 inch. The kilometer is a metric unit of length used for longer distances. It takes more than 1.5 kilometers to make a mile. A very fast adult runner could run a kilometer in about three minutes.

Metric units of weight include grams and kilograms. The gram is the basic metric unit of mass (which for many purposes is the same as *weight*). A large paper clip weighs about 1 gram. It takes about 28 grams to make 1 ounce. Metric units of capacity include milliliters and liters. The liter is the basic metric unit of volume (or capacity). A liter is slightly smaller than a quart, so it takes more than four liters to make a gallon.

Here are some frequently used customary-to-metric ratios. Values are approximate.

1 inch = 2.54 centimeters

1 yard = 0.91 meters

1 mile = 1.61 kilometers

1 ounce = 28.35 grams

1 pound = 2.2 kilograms

1 quart = 0.94 liters

Metric-to-customary conversions can be found by taking the reciprocals of each of the factors noted above. For instance, 1 kilometer = 0.62 mile (computed by dividing 1 by 1.61).

An important step in solving problems involving measurement is to decide which area you are in. Generally, such problems will fall under one of these categories: length, area, angles, volume, mass, time, money, and temperature. Solving measurement problems will likely have you calling on your knowledge in several other areas of mathematics, especially algebra. The following is one example of a measurement problem that requires knowledge of several math topics:

Sophie's Carpet Store charges $19.40 per square yard for the type of carpeting you'd like (padding and labor included). How much will you pay to carpet your 9 foot by 12 foot room?

One way to find the solution is to convert the room dimensions to yards (3 yards by 4 yards), then multiply to get 12 square yards. Finally, multiply 12 by the price of $19.40 per square yard, for a total price of $232.80.

Statistics and Probability

Measures of central tendency of a set of values include *mean*, *median*, and *mode*. The mean is found by adding all the values, then dividing the sum by the number of values. The median of a set is the middle number when the values are in numerical order. (If there is an even number of values, and therefore no middle value, the mean of the middle two values gives the median.) The mode of a set is the value occurring most often. (Not all sets of values have a single mode; some sets have more than one.) Consider the following set.

6   8   14   5   6   5   5

The mean, median, and mode of the set are 7, 6, and 5, respectively. (Note: The mean is often referred to as the average, but all three measures are averages of sorts.)

Probability theory provides models for chance variations. The *probability* of any event occurring is equal to the number of desired outcomes divided by the number of all possible events. Thus, the probability of blindly pulling a green ball out of a hat (in this case the desired outcome) if the hat contains two green and five yellow balls, is $\frac{2}{7}$ (about 29%). *Odds* are related to probability, but are different. The odds that any given event *will* occur is the ratio of the probability that the event will occur to the probability that the event *will not* occur (typically expressed as a ratio). In the example above, the odds that a green ball will be drawn are 2:5.

Statistics is the branch of mathematics that involves collecting, analyzing, and interpreting data, organizing data to describe them usefully, and drawing conclusions and making decisions. Statistics builds on probability, and typically studies "populations," meaning quantifiable groups of things. Trends and patterns not otherwise noticed may be revealed via statistics.

One key statistical concept is that of *standard deviation*. The standard deviation of a set of values tells how "tightly" all of the values are clustered around the mean of the set. When values are tightly clustered near the mean, the standard deviation is small. If values are widespread the standard deviation is large. Here is one way to find the standard deviation of a set. Consider the set used earlier:

6   8   14   5   6   5   5

First find the mean (7). Next, find the difference of each value in the set and the mean (ignoring negative signs). This gives 1, 1, 7, 2, 1, 2, and 2. Now, you square each of those values, giving 1, 1, 49, 4, 1, 4, and 4. You next take the sum of those squares (64) and divide the sum by the number of values ($\frac{64}{7}$ = 9.14). Finally, you take the square root of 9.14, giving a standard deviation of 3.02. Think of 3.02 as the amount that the values in the set "typically" vary from the center.

History and Social Science

The MTEL History and Social Science section includes four test objectives. These objectives represent a broad range of integrated social sciences concepts from the content areas of history, geography, political science, and economics. Embedded within each broad objective are a number of essential social sciences concepts. A thorough understanding of each objective requires deep knowledge of the embedded concepts coupled with the ability to analyze and apply those concepts in a comparative analysis of Massachusetts, U.S., and world contemporary and historic society. For each objective an explanation of the embedded concepts is provided. Following the explanation is a set of practice test questions. Those questions are designed to give you an idea of the nature and type of questions included on the test.

When preparing for the social sciences portion of the test, you should review the embedded concepts enumerated within each objective. Once you think you have a thorough understanding of each concept, you should determine whether you can apply your understanding within the context of Massachusetts, U.S., and world contemporary and historic concepts.

0010   **Understand major developments in the history of the United States.**

For example: lives of indigenous peoples before the arrival of Europeans; European exploration and settlement of North America; the Revolutionary War and the formation of the national government; slavery; the Civil War and Reconstruction; the settlement of the West; the transformation from an agrarian to an industrial economy (e.g., immigration, the rise of entrepreneurship, the development of science and technology); the Progressive Era and the New Deal; the emergence of the United States as a world power (e.g., the era of U.S. overseas expansion, World War I, World War II, the Cold War); the Civil Rights movement; the Women's movement; the Vietnam War; the Persian Gulf War; the effects of the collapse of the Soviet Union and subsequent events on U.S. leadership in world affairs; and international terrorism.

0011   **Understand the governmental system of the United States; the principles, ideals, rights, and responsibilities of U.S. citizenship; and the fundamental principles and concepts of economics.**

For example: purposes of government; functions of federal, state, and local government in the United States; the branches of government and their roles; forms of local self-government in Massachusetts and the United States (e.g., town meeting, city government); how laws are enacted and enforced; the political process in the United States and the role of political parties; fundamental concepts and principles of capitalism (e.g., private property, wage labor, supply and demand, the global economy); democratic principles and values contained in the Declaration of Independence, the U.S. Constitution, and the Constitution of the Commonwealth of Massachusetts (e.g., the rule of law, due process, equal protection of the laws, majority rule, protection of minority rights); and responsibilities of U.S. citizens (e.g., respecting others' rights, obeying laws and rules, paying taxes, jury duty, voting).

0012   **Understand major developments in world history.**

For example: characteristics of early human civilizations; major eras, developments, and turning points in Western civilization (e.g., ancient Israel, the emergence of Greek civilization, the rise and fall of the Roman Empire, the Middle Ages, the Renaissance and Reformation, the Age of Discovery, the scientific revolution, the Enlightenment, the age of revolution, World Wars I and II); and the impact of industrialization, nationalism, communism, and religion on modern world history.

0013   **Understand basic geographic concepts, phenomena, and processes, and the major geographic features and regions of the United States and the world.**

For example: basic concepts of geography (e.g., location, place, movement); the use of globes, maps, and other resources to access geographic information; global features (e.g., continents, hemispheres, latitude and longitude, poles); major physical features and regions of Massachusetts, the United States, and world areas; and the relationship between geographic factors (e.g., climate, topography) and historical and current developments (e.g., human migrations, patterns of settlement, economic growth and decline).

U.S. History

Developing historical perspective includes knowledge of events, ideas, and people from the past. That knowledge encompasses an understanding of the diversity of race, ethnicity, social and economic status, gender, region, politics, and religion within history. Historic understanding includes the use of historical reasoning, resulting in a thorough exploration of cause-effect relationships to reach defensible historical interpretations through inquiry.

The American Revolution

The original 13 colonies came to be loosely divided along regional lines, with the northern colonies enjoying prosperity based on small farming and the southern colonies achieving less prosperity in an economy based on large farming operations and cheap labor. What the colonies had in common, though, was that they were fairly well organized, with a tradition of participation in local community affairs—at least on the part of the citizens with property. During the French and Indian Wars (1689–1763), the colonists came to depend less on the British Army and more on their own resources for self-defense. These wars, however, brought the British Empire deeply into debt. To defray these debts, Parliament took advantage of the colonies' resources by means of direct and indirect taxation.

Various attempts of the British authorities to tax and control the colonies were first met with restrained and tactful responses on the part of Americans who published petitions and pamphlets. These gradually gave way to resolutions, protests that turned violent, and the Stamp Act Congress (1765). This gathering showed that representatives of the colonies could work together and gave them a chance to get acquainted with one another. As Parliament continued passing heavy-handed legislation, more pamphlets and protests followed, along with boycotts and smuggling to avoid paying British taxes. This eventually led to the Boston Tea Party (1773), in which Bostonians threw imported tea overboard rather than pay even reduced taxes to the British.

Parliament responded by passing the Coercive Acts, which closed the port of Boston until the tea was paid for, increased the power of Massachusetts' royal governor, allowed royal officials accused of crimes to be tried in places where they would have a greater chance of acquittal, and allowed for the quartering of troops anywhere. The Americans called these acts the Intolerable Acts and called the First Continental Congress in 1774. Besides petitioning Parliament for relief, this body also passed resolutions denouncing the Intolerable Acts and calling for the preparation of local militias. By the time the Second Continental Congress met in 1775, the Battles of Lexington and Concord had taken place. Only gradually, though, did the Continental Congress move toward independence, which was declared July 4, 1776.

The Constitution

After the Revolutionary War was won, largely thanks to French support, the fledgling nation found that the Articles of Confederation afforded too loose a national structure. Shays' Rebellion (1786), a revolt of poor farmers in western Massachusetts, helped spur the development of a national Constitution at the Constitutional Convention (1787). The Constitution was signed in 1787 and ratified by nine states, as required, by June 21, 1788. The system of government it outlined began functioning in 1789.

Rather than enumerating specific laws, the Constitution describes broad principles to guide the actions of the legislative, executive and judicial branches of government. While controversies have arisen regarding how those principles are to be applied, provision is made for those controversies to be resolved within the three branches of government established by the Constitution and within the limits of power placed on each branch.

Early in the nation's history, two opposing viewpoints arose with regard to interpreting the Constitution. Those who favored a strong central government, mainly the business and financial groups in the commercial centers of the Northeast and the port cities of the South, interpreted the Constitution as having vested extensive powers in the federal government. These Federalists held the "broad interpretation" that the Constitution gave the government "implied powers," that is, all powers not expressly denied to it. On the other hand, the Democrat-Republicans, such as Jefferson and Madison, held the "strict interpretation" that any action not specifically permitted in the Constitution was prohibited. The Democrat-Republicans' main support came from the rural and frontier areas of the South and West. Based on the "strict interpretation," the Democrat-Republicans opposed the establishment of Hamilton's national bank.

The New Nation

The War of 1812 led to disruptions of maritime trade and the rise of local industry in the Northeast, which displaced dependence on British manufactures. To further assert the new country's dominance in the Western Hemisphere, President James Monroe declared the Monroe Doctrine in 1823, to the effect that the region was no longer to be considered subject to future colonization by European powers (who had lost their newly independent colonies in Latin America). Meanwhile, technology such as Eli Whitney's cotton gin spurred the development of both agriculture and industry. The country was also seeking to expand its territory westward, influenced by the idea of Manifest Destiny. The question of whether to allow slavery in newly settled territories led to the Missouri Compromise of 1820–1821. In this series of bills in Congress, Maine was admitted to the Union as a free state and Missouri as a slave state, to preserve the balance of slave and free states, while slavery was prohibited in all western territories north of the southern boundary of Missouri.

Sectional Conflict and the Causes of the Civil War

The discovery of gold in California in 1849 greatly expanded its population and led California to apply for admission as a state. Since it was to be a free state, a crisis was sparked that led to the Compromise of 1850, which allowed new territories to decide the matter of slavery for themselves, based on the principle of "popular sovereignty." In further debates over the expansion of slavery in the territories, Stephen A. Douglas argued that any territory desiring to exclude slavery could do so simply by declining to pass laws to protect it. Abraham Lincoln, while not advocating the abolition of slavery, argued that the country must restrict slavery's extension into the territories. The controversy was continued in the Kansas-Nebraska Act of 1854, which repealed the Missouri Compromise and allowed the people of those territories to decide for or against slavery by popular sovereignty. Fierce fighting later broke out in Kansas as pro- and anti-slavery forces battled for control. The nation's controversy over slavery was only heightened by the Dred Scott case (1857), in which the Supreme Court ruled that slaves who resided temporarily in free states or territories were still slaves and that Congress did not have the authority to exclude slavery from a territory.

The Civil War and Reconstruction

The secession of southern states from the Union in 1860 led to civil war when Confederate troops fired on Union-held Fort Sumter in Charleston, South Carolina, on April 12, 1861. After causing 600,000 casualties, the war ended with the surrender of Confederate General Robert E. Lee to Union General Ulysses S. Grant on April 9, 1865. Five days later, President Abraham Lincoln was assassinated. Meanwhile, the Southern states had been devastated, with little to replace the slavery-based plantation economy. This led to the period known as Reconstruction (1865–1877), in which the southern states were readmitted to the Union.

President Lincoln had already begun planning for reconstruction before the end of the war, beginning with the Emancipation Proclamation of 1862, which declared free all slaves in areas still in rebellion as of January 1, 1863. After Lincoln's death, Congress, dominated by Radical Republicans, divided the South into five districts ruled by military governors. Three amendments to the Constitution (the 13th, 14th, and 15th) were required to settle the question of the status and voting rights of black citizens.

Industrialism, War, and the Progressive Era (1877–1912)

The growth of cities, which had continued throughout the 19th century, became especially prominent in the period after Reconstruction. Internal and external migration led to the development of the industrial urban state. Clashes between labor and capital, between unions and management, also became common. After the American frontier was completely settled in 1890, economic expansionists began to look overseas to ensure continued political power and prosperity, leading to colonial expansion into Cuba and the Philippines in the Spanish-American War (1898). Reform movements at home aimed at specific social, economic, and political problems led to the presidency of Theodore Roosevelt from 1901 to 1909. Much of his work was aimed at restraining corporate monopolies and promoting economic competition. President Woodrow Wilson (1913–1921) advocated stronger measures to break up large corporations, whose leaders often sought to justify the unequal distribution of the nation's wealth by using the survival-of-the-fittest philosophy associated with Charles Darwin.

Wilson and World War I (1912–1920)

When World War I broke out in Europe, many Americans favored neutrality and staying out of the conflict. When Germany was seen as threatening U.S. interests, however, the U.S. entered the war on the side of England. The Espionage and Sedition Acts of 1917 and 1918, although they sounded reasonable, were applied in ways that trampled on civil liberties. After the war's end, President Wilson formulated a peace plan to make the world "safe for democracy." This led to the dismantling of the Austria-Hungarian Empire in Europe and the establishment of the League of Nations, forerunner of the United Nations.

The Roaring Twenties and Economic Collapse (1920–1929)

The post–World War I period was marked by prosperity based on increased sales of consumer goods, increased consumer credit and the growth of the advertising industry. For the first time in U.S. history, suburbs began to grow more rapidly than central cities. New technology, such as streetcars, commuter trains, and automobiles opened the suburbs to working-class families, along with easy credit for home construction. Large numbers of southern and rural African Americans also began migrating to northern cities to find jobs. Women also gained the right to vote in 1920, leading to a liberalization of divorce laws in many states. As the decade progressed, a depressed farm economy, the failure of over 5700 banks nationwide, great losses on broker's loans to buy stocks, a decline in new construction, sagging auto sales, and other factors culminated in the Great Depression after the stock market crash of October 29, 1929.

The Great Depression and the New Deal (1929–1941)

"New Deal" was the name given to President Franklin Roosevelt's program of domestic reform and relief from the Great Depression through programs of agricultural and business regulation, inflation, price stabilization, and public works. In the first phase, 1933–1934, Congress established various emergency programs, instituted farm relief, tightened banking and finance regulations, and founded the Tennessee Valley Authority. In its second phase, the New Deal continued with relief and recovery measures and provided for social and economic legislation to benefit the mass of working people, especially by establishing the Social Security system. The Supreme Court struck down some New Deal reforms as unconstitutional, and others met with growing resistance from Republicans opposed to huge government spending. Meanwhile, many Americans came to believe that U.S. involvement in World War I had been a mistake and favored isolationism in foreign affairs.

World War II and the Postwar Era (1941–1960)

The Lend-Lease Act of 1941 provided for U.S. support of Britain in World War II by promising supplies to Britain in return for goods and services after the war. This placed the U.S. on the Allied side, although in a non-combat capacity. Isolationism was broken, however, after the Japanese attack on Pearl Harbor, Hawaii, on December 7, 1941. Increased industrial output during the war stimulated the economy and helped the country pull out of the Depression.

After the war, President Harry Truman sought to enlarge and extend the New Deal by extending Social Security, rural electrification, and farm housing to more people. Cold War tensions led to a rise of anti-Communist sentiment, leading to imprisonments of leaders of the American Communist party and the Senate hearings led by Senator Joseph McCarthy to root out supposed Communists. In the 1950s, President Dwight Eisenhower sought to balance the budget and lower taxes without rolling back existing social and economic legislation. Slow economic growth, however, made balancing the budget difficult. During this time, however, the suburbs grew six times faster than the cities.

In the 1950s, the civil rights movement gathered momentum, beginning with the *Brown v. Board of Education* Supreme Court ruling in 1954 that "separate but equal" public schools were unconstitutional. This move toward desegregation was resisted in many parts of the South, with federal troops being sent in at times to enforce the Supreme Court's decision. The civil rights movement was emboldened after the *Brown v. Board* decision to end segregation entirely. The efforts of Dr. Martin Luther King, Jr. in organizing bus boycotts, along with sit-ins and freedom rides, eventually led to the passing of the Civil Rights Act and the Voting Rights Act.

Tensions with the Soviet Union during the postwar period also led to the division of Europe, known as the Iron Curtain, between Communist and democratic states. The struggle between Communism and capitalism led to the Truman Doctrine, which argued that the United States had to support populations who were resisting Communist movements, and the theory of "containment," a policy of U.S. opposition to the expansion of Communism in order to counterbalance pressure by the Soviet regime to expand its sphere of influence.

Vietnam and Social Upheaval (1960–1972)

After the defeat of French colonial forces in 1954, the U.S. originally supported the government of Ngo Dinh Diem in Vietnam by sending military advisors. Because the Communist Vietcong forces gained strength and Diem failed to implement promised reforms, the United States supported a military coup against Diem in 1963. In August 1964, after claiming that North Vietnamese forces had fired on American destroyers, President Lyndon Johnson pushed through Congress the Gulf of Tonkin Resolution, authorizing the use of military force in Vietnam. After a sustained bombing campaign in North Vietnam, combat troops were sent to South Vietnam. The war's supporters argued that if Vietnam should fall to the Communists, all Southeast Asia would eventually fall as well (the "domino theory"). Those opposed to the war rejected this theory and decried the war's toll in economic terms and in human lives. By 1967, antiwar demonstrations were already drawing large crowds.

American public opinion in general began turning against the war after the Vietcong scored a psychological victory with the Tet Offensive, a large-scale attack on numerous cities, towns, and American bases. President Richard Nixon advocated the building up of South Vietnamese forces while withdrawing U.S. troops, which he began to do in 1969. A peace agreement was signed in 1973, after which most U.S. troops were withdrawn. This agreement was part of a policy of relaxing tensions with the Communists, known as "détente." The collapse of the South Vietnamese armed forces in 1975 led to the withdrawal of all U.S. personnel and a victory for the North Vietnamese.

The 1960s also saw the rise of social movements such as Black Power and women's liberation. The civil rights movement had historically been supported by white as well as black activists, but in 1966 black activist Stokely Carmichael called for the civil rights movement to be "black-staffed, black-controlled and black-financed." Other movements, such as the Black Panthers, began to favor the exclusion of whites from organizations and efforts involving the African-American community, in favor of black self-determination and self-sufficiency.

The women's movement gained momentum in 1963 with the publication of Betty Friedan's *The Feminine Mystique*, which attacked the middle-class "cult of domesticity" and argued that society did not allow women to use their individual talents. The National Organization for Women (NOW), founded in 1966, called for equal employment opportunities and equal pay. It later advocated an Equal Rights Amendment to the Constitution, changes in divorce laws, and the legalization of abortion.

Watergate, Carter, and the New Conservatism

After being impeached in the House of Representatives, President Richard Nixon resigned in 1973 over a series of scandals involving the abuse of power, including political espionage by the Nixon reelection committee, illegal wiretapping of citizens by the administration, and corporate contributions to the Republican Party in return for political favors. Fallout from the scandal included widespread loss of confidence in public officials and an increased general suspicion of government agencies.

Nixon's successor in office, his vice president, Gerald Ford, was defeated in 1976 by Jimmy Carter, a Democrat whose common-sense appeal was soon overshadowed by increased Soviet aggression under his policy of détente, high inflation, and the Iran hostage crisis in 1979–1980. Carter was defeated after one term by Ronald Reagan, whose emphasis on "supply-side economics" was geared toward reducing taxes and the size of the federal government. Under Reagan's tax cuts, high-income individuals realized greater savings than middle- and low-income individuals. To reduce the size of the government, many social programs that had benefited poor and disadvantaged persons were cut. This, along with the appearance of crack cocaine in the

1980s, led to an increase in the urban underclass, heavily African-American, characterized by isolation in ghettoes, drug dealing, gang violence, and single-parent families.

Government and the Responsibilities of Citizens

The history and social science portion of the MTEL General Curriculum test requires comprehension of the ideals of American democracy, including a core set of values expressed in America's essential founding documents, the Declaration of Independence, the Articles of Confederation, the U.S Constitution, and the Bill of Rights. Those values include life, liberty, pursuit of happiness, common good, justice, equality, truth, diversity, popular sovereignty, and patriotism.

Furthermore, the ideals of American democracy include the following essential Constitutional principles: the rule of law, separation of powers, representative government, checks and balances, individual rights, freedom of religion, federalism, limited government, and civilian control of the military. Essential democratic principles include those principles fundamental to the American judicial system: the right to due process of law; the right to a fair and speedy trial, protection from unlawful search and seizure, and the right to decline to self-incriminate.

Comprehension of the rights and responsibilities of citizens of the United States involves understanding that it is essential for citizens to be active in order to maintain a democratic society. This activity includes participation in political activities such as voting, providing service to communities, and regulating oneself in accordance with the law.

> *Fast Facts*
>
> **It is essential for citizens to be active in order to maintain a democratic society.**

Diversity

Understanding the role of cultural diversity in shaping Massachusetts, the United States, and the world begins with knowledge of the commonalities and differences among such groups as African-Americans, Asian-Americans, Hispanic-Americans, and Native Americans. Commonalities and differences can be found when analyzing the role of language, education, religion, culture, and struggles for equality within and among groups. Understanding the role of cultural diversity in shaping Massachusetts, the United States, and the world should include an understanding of the struggles various groups undertake to gain equality and recognition within society.

A historical perspective of the role of cultural diversity in shaping the development of Massachusetts and the United States begins by gaining a sense of the types of people who came to Colonial America and their reasons for coming. This understanding can help one gain an appreciation for the diverse peoples that eventually won their independence from Great Britain. Following those people from the east during the various migrations westward can explain how various groups of people settled what today is the American West. Studies of Old Immigration (1830–1850) and New Immigration (1900–1920) further complete the picture of the settling of America that encouraged diverse peoples to come here. Within this historical understanding one should be able to identify examples of how immigrants sought to assimilate themselves into American culture, contributions of immigrant groups to American culture, and ways that immigrants have been exploited.

Diverse cultural groups have shaped world history. Diversity has both positive and negative results—from contributing to disputes over territories, creating alliances that eventually lead to world and regional conflicts, outsourcing of jobs, and relocation of companies from the United States to foreign countries, to more positive examples such as the economic specialization that enhances choice and the modern globalization that results in economic interdependence. The impact of cultural diversity on world history can be explored by careful analysis of the following events, among others: the origin and spread of Christianity and Islam; colonialism and exploration; the beginning of World War I; and contemporary conflict in the Middle East.

Economic and Political Principles

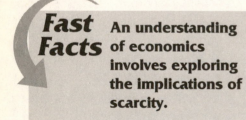

Fast Facts An understanding of economics involves exploring the implications of scarcity.

An understanding of economics involves exploring the implications of scarcity (the concept that wants are unlimited while resources are limited). Exploration of scarcity involves an understanding of economic principles spanning from personal finance to international trade. Economic understanding is rooted in exploring principles of choice, opportunity costs, incentives, trade, and economic systems. (For a definition of each of the economic principles see the Handy Dandy Guide [HDG] development by the National Council on Economic Education [1989]. For brief definitions based upon this guide see the Web site: *http://ecedweb.unomaha. edu/lessons/handydandy.htm.*) This exploration includes analysis of how those principles operate within the economic choices of individuals, households, businesses, and governments.

In addition, economic understanding includes knowledge of the role that price, competition, profit, inflation, economic institutions, money, and interest rates play within a market system. A complete understanding of markets includes knowledge of the role of government within an economic system, including how monetary and fiscal policy impacts the market. (These economic concepts are based upon the *National Content Standards in Economics* published by the National Council on Economic Education. A brief overview and complete list of standards can be found at *http://ncee.net/ea/standards/.*)

An understanding of various political systems involves the ability to compare different political systems, their ideologies, structures, institutions, processes, and political cultures. This requires knowledge of alternative ways of organizing constitutional governments from systems of shared power to parliamentarian systems. Systems of shared power include federal systems, where sovereign states delegate powers to a central government; a federal system, where a national government shares power with state and local governments; and Unitarian systems, where all power is concentrated in a centralized government.

Understanding local and state governments results from knowledge of the role of federal and state constitutions in defining the power and scope of state and local government. That knowledge should include comprehension of reserved and concurrent powers. Furthermore, an understanding of state and local government results from knowledge of the organization and responsibilities of such governments.

Understanding of the role of law in a democratic society results from a knowledge of the nature of civil, criminal, and constitutional law and how the organization of the judicial system serves to interpret and apply such laws. Essential judicial principles to know include comprehension of rights, such as the right of due process, the right to a fair and speedy trial, and the right to a hearing before a jury of one's peers. Additional judicial principles include an understanding of the protections granted in the Constitution, which include protection from self-incrimination and unlawful searches and seizures.

Understanding global interdependence begins with recognition that world regions include economic, political, historical, ecological, linguistic, and cultural regions. This understanding should include knowledge of military and economic alliances such as NATO, the G8 members, or cartels such as OPEC, and how their existence affects political and economic policies within regions. Knowledge of world regions and alliances leads to identification of issues that affect people in these areas. Common issues that affect people around the world include food production, human rights, resource use, prejudice, poverty, and trade.

A true sense of global interdependence results from an understanding of the relationship between local decisions and global issues. For example, consider how individual or community actions regarding waste disposal or recycling may affect worldwide resource availability. Fuel emissions standards may also affect air pollution or oil supply and gas prices.

World History

From earliest times, humans lived in hunter-gatherer societies, often nomadic and dependent on local natural resources such as edible plants and game animals. Over time, other forms of social organization developed, such as semi-nomadic livestock herding and subsistence farming, village-based subsistence farming, city-states, kingdoms, and empires. Societies have been classified by their level of technological development based on whether their tools were made of stone, bronze, iron, or more advanced materials. This has led to the designations Stone Age, Bronze Age, Iron Age, etc.

These designations have also applied to historical periods in Western civilization based on the level of technology in use at the time. During these periods, civilizations arose in the ancient Middle East to which modern Western civilization can trace its roots. These civilizations include Sumeria, Israel, Egypt, Assyria, Babylonia, and Medo-Persia. In these empires, writing systems and codes of laws were developed that represent the earliest origins of modern Western writing systems and law codes.

Of pivotal importance in Western history is the rise of the ancient Greek civilization, beginning with the conquest by Alexander the Great in the 4th century B.C.E. (before the Common Era) of much of the former territory of the previous Middle Eastern empires. This led to the spread of the Greek culture and language throughout the region. The presence of many words with Greek roots in modern European languages, including English, shows the lasting impact of ancient Greek civilization. Even after the fall of the political structures founded by Alexander the Great, ancient Greek learning in the arts, the sciences, philosophy, and political thought formed part of the basis of Western learning for centuries to come.

The civilization of Rome was strongly influenced by ancient Greece, but in time achieved greater dominance in the Middle East and the Mediterranean region. By conquering the Greek dynasty ruling over Egypt in 31 B.C.E., Rome became the undisputed regional power and in time went on to conquer much of the known world. Rome was the first empire to extend the ancient Middle Eastern and Greek cultures northward into Europe. In the first and second centuries C.E. (Common Era), the period known as *Pax Romana* (Roman Peace) saw the development of an extensive system of roads, as well as a postal system, that facilitated transportation and thus favored the expansion of trade. This was also favored by a relative absence of internal conflicts, enforced by Roman troops. The peace of this period led to a flourishing of the arts and higher learning, still influenced by classical Greek models.

Beginning in the third century, Rome began a long decline as the succession of emperors grew unstable and the army began to have trouble maintaining control over outlying provinces. In the fifth century, Rome was conquered by invading Germanic tribes. Remnants of imperial power survived, however, in the Eastern Empire with its capital in Constantinople and in the Roman Catholic Church. The Germanic invaders also preserved and adopted much of what was left of the Roman Empire.

Even after Rome's power was broken, its impact was still felt in its former territories in Europe. The vacuum of power resulting from Rome's fall was filled by the Church and the feudal system. In this system of social organization, the peasants, who worked the land, were ruled by nobles. Among the nobles, the less powerful swore oaths of loyalty to the more powerful, who promised them military protection in exchange for their loyal support. This system, with many variations, was the dominant system in Europe throughout the Middle Ages. The Holy Roman Empire was the foremost political organization of the feudal system in Europe.

The Middle Ages were also known as the Dark Ages because of political instability in the early centuries after Rome's fall. The sharp decrease in the spread of knowledge, widespread illiteracy and disasters such as the Black Plague of the fourteenth century contributed to the problems of the era. Stability was highly valued in the midst of such problems, and medieval world views emphasized finding security by accepting one's status in the great scheme of things. In time, however, increasing political stability and the growth of trade and commerce set the stage for the early modern era of Western history.

The modern era began with the period known as the Renaissance, meaning "rebirth," beginning around 1450. In this period, an increased interest in classical Roman and Greek learning led to advances in the arts. The growth of commerce, banking, and industry favored the spread of knowledge among the rising middle class. Around the time of the Renaissance, the Reformation also challenged the dominance of the Roman Catholic Church and led to the development of Protestantism, which more closely reflected the values of Northern European cultures and the middle class. The interest in discovering new knowledge, and the attitude of challenging traditional views, have continued until today. At this time England, Spain, and Portugal also began exploring the globe and founding overseas colonies.

The renewed interest in classical learning of the Renaissance spurred a great increase of scientific knowledge in the seventeenth century, which further challenged traditional views of humanity, earth, and the universe. This period was also marked by political change as the feudal system slowly gave way to the development of monarchies in Western Europe. In this form of government, power was centralized in the hands of the king rather than shared among the nobles. Advances continued in the fields of science, politics, education, and commerce; these advances further removed Europe from its medieval past and favored the growth of the middle class.

The eighteenth century saw the development of such ideals as rationality, reason, logic, and the application of scientific knowledge for the good of society. This period, known as the Enlightenment, further challenged medieval ideals of stability and order by championing progress and planned change. The growing pressures for progress caused strained relations between the ruling class and the middle class; the conflict eventually exploded in the French Revolution of 1789. In France this event led to the ascension of Napoleon I, who conquered much of Europe, and helped bring about the rise of nationalism that swept the entire world during the nineteenth century.

Meanwhile, the Industrial Revolution and colonialism were transforming the face of Europe and many other regions of the world. In the nineteenth century, the pressures for progress unleashed in the Enlightenment found expression in the unprecedented growth of industry and technology, and Western civilization expanded its power throughout the rest of the world. While Spain and Portugal were losing their colonies in the Americas, England, France, the Netherlands, and Germany expanded into Africa, Asia, and the Pacific, including areas that had never been colonized by Western nations before. The colonies were intended to serve as sources of cheap raw materials for Western industry and as markets for the manufactured goods it produced.

Patterns of Historical Development in Recent Times

The competition for the resources from overseas colonies was one of the major reasons for World War I, which, despite its name, was mainly a European war. Sparked by the assassination of the heir to the throne of Austria-Hungary, it soon claimed the lives of many more soldiers than any previous war. In addition, in countries such as Great Britain and Germany, the scale of the war meant for the first time that people from all walks of life—not just professional soldiers—became casualties of the war. In France, about half the men of an entire generation were killed, and in one battle (the battle of Sommes) the British suffered over 60,000 casualties on the first day alone.

Germany, the major instigator of World War I, fell far short in its attempt to expand its empire. At the end of World War I, the few colonies that Germany controlled fell into the hands of Great Britain and France, and Germany was a much poorer country than it had been before losing the war. Even though most of the world, especially Europe, was horrified over the carnage of World War I, Germany turned to a dictator who promised to restore the country's military might less than 20 years after the end of the first war. Adolf Hitler eventually failed in that mission, but he did temporarily make Germany a feared military power, killing 12 million people in concentration camps, including 6 million Jews, and 20 million Soviets while trying to conquer Europe. During World War II, which began in 1939 when Hitler invaded Poland, Germany was joined by Japan and Italy to form the Axis, which fought against the Allies—mainly Great Britain, the United States, and the Soviet Union. (France, perhaps remembering the dead of World War I, surrendered to Germany early in the war.) Although Great Britain was supposedly among the winners of the war, it expended so many resources in winning that it was no longer the dominant power in the world.

The Soviet Union was formed from Russia and other countries under Russian rule during World War I, by way of a Communist revolution. Communism had arisen during the nineteenth century, partly in response to the Industrial Revolution and the spread of capitalism. Its main theorist, Karl Marx, had expected revolution to come in one of the more industrially advanced countries, such as Britain or his native Germany, but the unpopularity of World War I helped create a power vacuum in Russia, where there had been plenty of misery among the poor along with relatively organized protest against the rich. The Communist Party under Vladimir Lenin took advantage of this to create a promised "worker's paradise." The Soviet Union was, however, beset by many problems from the beginning, and the Communist system was not well equipped to handle them. After Lenin's death in 1927, Josef Stalin took over the political machinery, and through disastrous policies and legal executions, Stalin was responsible for a tremendous amount of death and suffering. After Hitler invaded Poland in 1939, Stalin signed a non-aggression treaty with Germany, but Hitler nevertheless invaded the Soviet Union soon thereafter. The Soviets suffered far greater devastation than any other country during World War II, but they persevered and eventually drove the German armies all the way back to Germany and became one of the two main beneficiaries of the war.

Almost immediately after World War II, the Cold War began. The British Empire began to crumble. Its most important colony, India, broke away in 1948 under the famously nonviolent leadership of Mohandas Gandhi, and it was unable to prevent the establishment of the Jewish state of Israel in formerly British Palestine in the same year. Most of Britain's African colonies became independent in the 1950s and 1960s. In the meantime, Europe was divided by a figurative Iron Curtain between U.S.-dominated Western Europe and Soviet-dominated Eastern Europe.

In most of the rest of the world—what came to be known as the Third World—the two Cold War antagonists used both military might and peacefully persuasive means to gather as many countries as possible into their sphere. China, in which a Communist revolution under Mao Ze-Dong succeeded following the great devastation of Japanese occupation during World War II, was solidly in the Soviet camp for many years but was also rather independent during much of the Cold War. Japan, though not allowed to have a military as a condition of its defeat in World War II, became a U.S. ally and a dominant Asian economic power. The United States and the Soviet Union waged war through their allies in Korea (each side got half the country) and Vietnam (the Soviets got the whole country, but the United States succeeded in stopping the expansion of Soviet influence beyond Southeast Asia). The Cold War came to an end in 1989, when the Soviet Union essentially surrendered. It had never been a war between equals; the United States had emerged much stronger than had its rival, but the Soviet Union was able to keep up the appearance of equality by mimicking the U.S. development of weapon systems centered around nuclear devices. Even in that arena, however, the United States eventually wore down the Soviet Union, and the post–Cold War government soon gave independence to most of the non-Russian countries under its control and withdrew its troops from Eastern Europe.

The end of the Cold War did not, however, bring peace to the world. In the formerly Soviet-dominated state of Yugoslavia, long-buried ethnic rivalries (of which most Yugoslav citizens were barely aware) led to civil war, genocide, and an eventual split into three countries. In Africa, many of the countries that France and Britain had set up during the Colonial Period started to break apart along old tribal lines, occasionally leading to terrible bloodbaths, such as the Rwandan slaughter of the Tutsis. Although the South African revolution, led by Nelson Mandela, was a relatively peaceful victory for the people of that country, most of Africa is still subject to poverty, disease, and war. In the Middle East, the presence of Israel, along with the failure of the governments of the mostly Muslim countries of the region to defeat Israel or establish wealth for most of their citizens, has led to the spread of fundamentalist Islamist extremism. These extremist groups have wreaked much havoc in the world, most notably in the attacks on the World Trade Center and the Pentagon in 2001.

Geography

Understanding major geographic concepts involves comprehending both physical features of geography and the cultural aspects of geography. This would include knowledge of the five fundamental themes of geography, comprehension of the relationships within and between places, understanding interdependence within the local, natural, and global communities, and familiarity with global issues and events.

The five themes of geography are: place; human-environmental interaction; location; movement and connections; and regions, patterns, and processes. An understanding of these themes would include the ability to use them to analyze regions within Massachusetts, the United States, and the world to gain a perspective about interrelationships among those regions. The use of the five themes should also result in the ability to compare regions.

An understanding of the theme of location requires knowledge of both absolute and relative location. Absolute location is determined by longitude and latitude. Relative location deals with the interactions that occur between and among places. Relative location involves the interconnectedness among people because of land, water, and technology. For example, knowledge of the history of Boston includes an understanding of how its location at the mouth of the Charles River and its relationship to the Atlantic Ocean have contributed to its economic development and vitality.

An understanding of the theme of human-environmental interaction involves consideration of how people rely on the environment, how we alter it, and how the environment may limit what people are able to do. For example, knowledge of the shipping industry in Massachusetts' history includes an understanding of how the people of Massachusetts utilized the Charles River, Massachusetts Bay, and Atlantic Ocean to take their products to regional and world markets.

An understanding of the theme of location, movement, and connections involves identifying how people are connected through different forms of transportation and communication networks and how those networks have changed over time. This would include identifying channels of the movement of people, goods, and information. For example, the manufacturing industry in Boston had a profound impact on the movement patterns of ideas and people of both the Boston area and elsewhere in the state.

An understanding of the theme of regions, patterns, and processes include identifying climatic, economic, political, and cultural patterns within regions. Understanding why these patterns were created includes understanding how climatic systems, communication networks, international trade, political systems, and population changes contributed to a region's development. An understanding of regions enables a social scientist to study their uniqueness and relationship to other regions.

Understanding global issues and events includes comprehending the interconnectedness of peoples throughout the world. For example, knowledge of the relationship between world oil consumption and oil production would result in an understanding of the impact that increased demand for oil in China would have on the price of a barrel of oil, which in turn could affect the decisions of consumers of new vehicles in the United States.

Science and Technology/ Engineering

Scientific knowledge is a body of statements of varying degrees of certainty—some most unsure, some nearly sure, but none absolutely certain. . . . Now, we scientists are used to this, and we take it for granted that it is perfectly consistent to be unsure, that it is possible to live and not know.

Richard P. Feynman (1918–1988), Nobel Prize in Physics, 1965

Science education has as its goal the training of a scientifically literate public that fully participates in the economic, political, and cultural functions of our society. Scientifically literate individuals, students and teachers alike, must have knowledge that is connected and useful. The Massachusetts science curriculum, both for the preparation of pre-service teachers and for K–12 instruction, is guided by this principle.

An operational definition of the scientifically literate individual is one who uses scientific knowledge, constructs new scientific knowledge, and reflects on scientific knowledge. Such individuals have specific science content knowledge, they build upon that knowledge through their experiences and activities, and they can evaluate objectively and critically the value and limitations of that knowledge.

Life Science

I venture to define science as a series of interconnected concepts and conceptual schemes arising from experiment and observation and fruitful of further experiments and observations. The test of a scientific theory is, I suggest, its fruitfulness.

James Bryant Conant (1893–1978), Chemist and Educator

0014 **Understand and apply basic concepts and principles of life science to interpret and analyze phenomena.**

For example: basic characteristics and needs of living things; basic concepts and processes related to cells and organisms; plant structures, functions and processes (e.g., photosynthesis); the systems of the human body; basic principles of genetics and heredity; and how organisms interact with one another and their environments.

Cells

The concept of a cell is central to our understanding of the life sciences. Cells are the simplest living unit of life, just as atoms are the building blocks of molecules, and molecules of cells. Cell theory states that all organisms are composed of cells, that all cells arise from preexisting cells, and that the cell is the basic organizational unit of all organisms. Groups of specialized cells, or tissues, may have highly specialized characteristics and functions within an organism. A single organism may comprise only a single cell, or many billions of cells, and cells themselves range in size from the micron to many centimeters in dimension. Growth in most organisms is associated with cell division and replication, in addition to enlargement of the cells.

Classification

A dichotomous key is a tool of science that allows us to organize and classify objects by their observable traits and properties. In the life sciences, classification keys are widely used, and the simplest are based on the gross anatomy of all organisms, including plants, animals, fungi, protists, and two kingdoms of bacteria. Through comparison of the number of wings or legs, habitat, and eating habits, we begin, at the earliest levels, to understand patterns in nature, constructing our own understanding of the world around us, and practice the basic elements of scientific thought and discovery.

Scientific knowledge may be classified or organized by grouping similar types of knowledge into thematic concepts. Many concepts are so broad as to find application in multiple disciplines. Cycle, for example, is a powerful concept that has widespread application throughout science, useful for both explanation and prediction. Life cycles are central to the study of biology. The recurring pattern of events in the life cycle links birth, growth, reproduction, and death. The concept of a cycle is also evident in the carbon cycle, nitrogen cycle, Krebs cycle, hydrogeologic cycle, periodic table, and many other processes, including the transformations of energy needed to sustain life. The food chain represents the complex interdependency of all plants and animals on the energy from the Sun, and the recycling of nutrients from simple to complex organisms.

Heredity

The discussion of life cycles brings forward the concept that the offspring of one generation bears likeness to, but also variation from, the previous generation. Some characteristics of the individual parent are passed along, while others appear not to be. We observe the connections between the visible traits of the parents and children, connections evident in all sexually reproducing organisms. It is clear that the offspring of dogs are other dogs, which generally look much like the parent dogs. Details of how such traits are conveyed through genetics are important to understand; yet instruction in these topics is allocated to the curriculum of higher grades.

Evolution

The goal of science education is to develop a scientifically literate public. At the elementary level this involves an understanding of how physical traits promote the survival of a species, how environmental changes affect species that are not adapted to those new conditions, and the role of heredity in passing and modifying the traits of successive generations. There are ample examples available to illustrate these concepts to the elementary student. A rabbit whose coat regularly turns white before the snowfall is at a temporary disadvantage, and is therefore subject to a higher degree of predation. That rabbit may not live to produce other early-white-coated rabbits. Technology, the application of knowledge for man's benefit, includes activities that are designed to select those traits that are intended to lead to healthier, stronger, and more productive crops and animals.

While the tenets of evolution as scientific theory are widely accepted, particularly as they apply to the short-term changes and adaptations within a species, the subject continues to generate some debate. To place the discussion in its proper context, some discussion of the scientific use of terms is appropriate, because the common usage of a term may differ significantly from its scientific usage. A *scientific fact* is an observation that has been repeatedly confirmed. However, scientific facts change if new observations yield new information. Frequently, the development of new, more sophisticated or precise instruments leads to such new information. A *scientific hypothesis* is a testable statement about the natural world, and as such is the starting point for most scientific experimentation. A hypothesis can generally be proven wrong, but is seldom proven right. *Scientific theories*, like atomic theory and cell theory, are well-substantiated explanations of some aspect of the natural world. A scientific theory provides a unified explanation for many related hypotheses. While a theory is generally widely accepted (e.g., through much of human history, people accepted a flat Earth circled by a moving Sun), theories remain open to revision or even replacement should a better, more logical, more comprehensive or compelling explanation be found.

Not all issues of our human experience are subject to the analysis and rigors of scientific experimentation and validation. Our understanding of art, poetry, philosophy, and religion rely on ways of thinking and understanding that are not necessarily subject to repeated validation through the controlled scientific experiment, or which may rely more on personal values or deference to authority. The scientifically literate individual will distinguish the role and value of scientific thought from other ways of knowing, while maintaining respect and appreciation for the ways of thinking and understanding practiced in disciplines outside of science.

Ecology

Our surroundings are a complex, interconnected system in which the living organisms exist in relationship with the soil, water, and air, linked together through chemical and physical processes, and in states of continual change or dynamic equilibrium. *Ecosystem* is the term for all the living and nonliving things in a given environment and how they interact. Scientifically literate individuals are aware of their surroundings, the interdependence of each part, and the effects that man's activities can have on those surroundings. Mutualistic and competitive relationships also exist between the organisms in an ecosystem, defining how organisms rely upon each other, and exist in competition and conflict with each other.

Energy transformations are the driving force within an ecosystem. Many organisms obtain energy from light. For example, light drives the process of photosynthesis in green plants. Solar energy also provides necessary heat for cold-blooded animals. Organisms may also derive energy from other organisms, including other plants and/or animals. When one source of energy is depleted in an ecosystem, many organisms must shift their attention to other sources of energy. For example, a bear will eat berries, fish, or nuts depending on the season. The energy pyramid for an ecosystem illustrates these relationships and identifies those organisms that are most dependent on the other organisms in the system. Higher-order organisms cannot survive for long without the other organisms beneath them in the energy pyramid. The availability of adequate food within an ecosystem can be used to explain the system's functioning, the size of an animal's territory, or the effects of over-predation of a single species upon those organisms above it in the food chain.

Ecosystems change over time, both from natural processes and from the activities of man. The scientifically literate individual will be able to identify how the environment changes, how those changes impact the organisms that live there, and recognize the differences between long-term and short-term variation. Natural succession is observed when one community replaces another—for example, the colonies of fungus that grow, thrive, and then are replaced by different colonies on rodent droppings held under ideal conditions.

Physical Science

All of physics is either impossible or trivial. It is impossible until you understand it, and then it becomes trivial.

Ernest Rutherford (1871–1937), Physicist, Nobel Prize for Chemistry, 1908

0015   Understand and apply basic concepts and principles of physical and earth science to interpret and analyze phenomena.

For example: the composition and structure of matter (e.g., atoms, molecules); properties and states of matter; forms of energy (e.g., electrical, magnetic, sound, light); basic concepts related to the motion of objects (e.g., inertia, momentum); components and structure of the solar system; climate and weather; and forces that shape the earth's surface.

Matter & Energy

Broadly speaking, our experiences with the world involve interactions with and between matter and energy. The physical sciences give us a clearer understanding and appreciation of our surroundings and the way we interact with and affect those surroundings. Matter can be described and distinguished by its chemical and physical properties. Physical properties, such as color and density, are termed *intrinsic* when they do not change as the amount of matter changes. Properties like mass or volume do vary when matter is added or removed, and these are termed *extrinsic* properties. Mass is the amount of matter in an object, which is sometimes measured using a lever arm balance. Weight, although sometimes incorrectly used interchangeably with mass, is a measure of the force of gravity experienced by an object, often determined using a spring scale. An electronic scale may display an object's mass in grams, but it is dependent on gravity for its operation. Such a device is only accurate after using a calibration mass to adjust the electronics for the unique local gravitational force. While we may say an object is "weightless" as it floats inside the space shuttle, it is still affected by the gravitational forces from both the Earth and Sun, which keep it in orbit around each. The force of gravity is proportional to the product of the masses of the two objects under consideration divided by the square of the distance between them. Earth, being larger and more massive than Mars, has proportionally higher gravitational forces. This is the basis of the observation in H. G. Wells' *The War of the Worlds* that the Martian invaders were "the most sluggish things I ever saw crawl."

Density, the ratio of mass to volume, is an intrinsic property that depends on the matter, but not the amount of matter. Volume is defined as the amount of space an object occupies. The density of a 5-ton cube of pure copper is the same as that of a small copper penny. However, the modern penny is a thin shell of copper over a zinc plug, and the density of this coin is significantly lower than that of the older pure copper coin. Density is related to buoyancy. Objects sink, in liquids or gases alike, if they are denser than the material that surrounds them. Archimedes' principle, also related to density, states that an object is buoyed up by a force equal to the mass of the material the object displaces. Thus, a 160-lb concrete canoe will easily float in water if the volume of the submerged portion is equal to the volume of 20 gallons of water (water is approximately 8 lbs/gal × 20 gal = 160 lbs). Density is not the same as viscosity, a measure of thickness or flowability. The strength of intermolecular forces between molecules determines, for example, that molasses is slow in January, or that hydrogen bromide is a gas in any season.

All matter is composed of atoms, or combinations of atoms selected from among the more than one hundred elements. The atom is the smallest particle of an element that retains the properties of the element; similarly, the molecule is the smallest particle of a compound. Molecules cannot be separated into smaller particles (atoms or smaller) without a chemical change disrupting the chemical bonds that bind the molecule together. Physical separations, through the use of filter paper, centrifuge, or magnet, for example, do not affect chemical bonds. The scientific concept of a cycle, in this case without a time dependence, is evident in the fundamental makeup of matter and reflected in the structure of the periodic table. Mendeleev is credited with the development of the modern periodic table, in part for his predicting the existence of then-unknown elements based on the repeating trends in reactivity and physical properties. The concepts associated with atoms and molecules are not found in the elementary benchmarks, but they should be well understood by the elementary teacher nonetheless, as they provide the basis of all our understanding of matter and chemical change.

Energy is loosely scientifically defined as the ability to do work. Kinetic energy is the energy of motion ($KE = 1/2mv^2$), where m is the mass and v the velocity of an object. Chemical energy is stored in the bonds of our food, held for later conversion to kinetic energy and heat in our bodies. Potential energy is held in an icicle hanging off the roof ($PE = mgh$) where m is mass, g is the gravitational force constant, and h is the height. When the icicle falls, its potential energy is converted to kinetic energy, and then to sound energy as it hits the pavement, and additional kinetic energy as the fragments skitter off. At the elementary level, students need to be able to identify the types of energy involved in various phenomena and identify the conversions between types. In the popular Rube Goldberg competitions, students use a number of sequential energy conversions to perform a simple task like breaking a balloon or flipping a pancake. Energy is conserved in each of these normal processes, converted to less useful forms (e.g., heat) but not created or destroyed. Similarly, matter is never created or destroyed in a normal chemical reaction. Nuclear fusion is an obvious exception to both rules, following Einstein's equation $E = mc^2$; however, these reactions are generally not allowed in the classroom or school laboratory.

Students gain useful experience with energy conversions as they study simple electrical circuits and chemical dry cells. The dry cell produces electrical energy from chemical potential energy. The size of the dry cell is proportional to the amount of starting material, and thus the available current, but not the electromotive force or voltage, which is an intrinsic property. The D cell produces the same 1.5-volt potential as the AAA cell; the difference is in how long they can maintain the flow of current in the circuit. The battery is dead when one or more of the starting materials has been depleted, or when the essential electrolytic fluid leaks or dries out. The measured cell voltage depends on several factors: the oxidation and reduction potentials, the half-reactions involved, and the concentration of each chemical species. When a cell reaches equilibrium, the measured cell potential and free energy of the cell both reach zero.

Seldom do we find chemical reactants present in the precise quantities to match the stoichiometric ratio indicated by the chemical equation defining a reaction. In a battery, or any reaction for that matter, one of the chemicals will be depleted before the others. The concept of a limiting reactant is important in chemistry, whereby one reactant is consumed before the other, similar to a summer BBQ for which hot dogs are in packages of ten, but the buns are in packages of eight. In contrast, how quickly a battery drains is linked to the rates of chemical reactions (kinetics), dependent on temperature, concentration, and the presence of a catalyst. Many chemical reactions involve multiple steps, where one step, the rate-limiting step, controls the rate of the entire process. This is much like the child who is always the last one to get in the car when the rest of the family is in a hurry.

Simple dry cells do not pose a serious safety hazard—always an issue in hands-on activities—and are thus good for student experiments. A series connection linking dry cells in a chain increases the overall voltage, and thus the brightness of the bulb; a parallel connection with batteries placed in the circuit (like rungs in a ladder) increases the effective size of the cell but the voltage remains the same.

Changes in Matter

Scientific theories have their utility in providing a unified explanation for diverse and varied observations. Atomic theory, which views atoms and molecules as the fundamental building blocks of all matter, would be modified or abandoned if it didn't also explain other observations. Snow tracked into the kitchen quickly melts before either evaporating or being absorbed into someone's socks, which then must be hung by the fire to dry. In either of these changes the fundamental particles of water are the same, an assembly of three atoms held by covalent (shared electron) bonds in a bent molecular geometry associated with polar molecules. New attractions are possible between polar water molecules and the ions formed when some compounds are dissolved in solution. The relative strength of the new attractions to the water overcomes the attractions within the pure solid, allowing the solid to dissolve and in some cases dissociate in solution. Insoluble compounds do not dissolve because the strength of the attractions within the solid exceeds those available between the molecules and/or ions and the solvent.

Phase changes are also explained using atomic theory. Evaporation from a liquid occurs when individual molecules gain sufficient energy to break free from the intermolecular attractions in the liquid phase. The stronger the intermolecular attractions, the lower the vapor pressure and the higher the boiling point. The boiling point is the temperature at which the vapor pressure of molecules leaving solution equals the atmospheric pressure. Lowering the atmospheric pressure above a liquid makes it easier for the highest energy liquid molecules to escape, thus the boiling point is lower. Cooking while camping at high altitudes requires more time and, thus, more fuel because food cooks more slowly as a result of the lowered boiling temperature.

All matter has a temperature above the theoretical value of absolute zero because all matter is in continual motion. In a balloon filled with nitrogen gas, some molecules are moving relatively fast, others relatively slowly. The temperature of the gas is a measure of this motion, a measure of the average kinetic energy of the particles. Molecules are very small and fast moving, and there are vast empty spaces between them. The average speed of nitrogen molecules at 25°C is over 500 meters per second, whereas the lighter hydrogen molecules have an average speed in excess of 1,900 meters per second. One cubic centimeter of air at room temperature and normal pressure contains roughly 24,500,000,000,000,000,000 molecules (2.45×10^{19} molecules). The same quantity of water would contain roughly 3.34×10^{22} water molecules, while the same one cubic centimeter of copper would contain roughly 8.5×10^{22} copper atoms. The differences between these numbers are not nearly as large as the numbers themselves, yet the differences are readily observable. Gases have significant empty spaces between the molecules and thus can be compressed, whereas liquids and solids have less or no compressibility, respectively. If air enters the lines of hydraulic brake systems, the pedal depresses easily as the trapped gas compresses instead of having the non-compressible liquid transfer the motion into braking power.

While the atoms and molecules of all materials are in constant motion (vibrational energy), those in gases and liquids are also free to move about their own axes (rotational energy), and about the container (translational energy). Increasing the temperature of a solid imparts additional energy, which increases the vibrational energy. Once any particular atom or molecule gains sufficient energy to break free of the intermolecular attractions to the bulk solid or liquid, it will slip or fly away (melt or evaporate, respectively). Hotter atoms require more space in which to vibrate. For this reason wagon wheel rims are heated in the forge to expand the metal before slipping the rim onto the wheel, basketballs left outside on a cold night don't bounce well, and in thermometers the expansion of alcohol or mercury is used to indicate temperature.

Motion

The motion of atoms and molecules is essential to our understanding of matter at the molecular level, but we have many examples of motion readily available on the macroscopic level in the world around us. Many an idle moment can be passed with a young child timing small athletic feats, for example, "How long will it take you to run to that tree and back?" or "The time to beat is 8.65 seconds; who can do it faster?" These experiences provide an informal experience with measurements of motion that serve as the basis for more scientific descriptions of speed, direction and changes of speed.

We can use time and motion to evaluate other chemical and physical phenomena. The periodic motion of a pendulum can be timed to determine the period, and experiments devised to explore the effect of pendulum mass, string length or amount of initial deflection. Hook's law can be studied by timing the vibrations of a spring. Chemical kinetics can be studied by timing reactions and observing changes in absorbance, conductivity, or pH. The growth rates of seedlings can be studied as a function of soil, water and light conditions. Such activities provide a natural framework to teach the concepts of scientific exploration, control of variables, collection, and presentation of data.

Waves and Vibrations

Waves are one mechanism of transporting energy from one location to another. We experience waves directly in the form of light, sound, and water, and indirectly through radio and TV, wireless networks, and X-rays. Waves are periodic in their nature, and the concept of periodicity (cycles) is one of the key interdisciplinary concepts that include the motions of planets, the properties of elements, life cycles of plants and animals, and many other events. Energy is transmitted through a material in a translational wave when in water. For example, particles of water move perpendicular to the direction of energy travel. A wave with greater energy has greater amplitude. AM radio refers to amplitude modulation of the radio signal, where the carrier wave amplitude is modified by adding the amplitudes of the voice or music waves to create a cumulative and more complex wave form. The receiver must subtract from this complex waveform the simple sinusoidal waveform of the carrier to leave the voice or music.

Compressional waves, like sound, are characterized by having the media move along the same axis as the direction of energy travel. The speed of sound waves is dependent on the medium through which it travels, faster in denser materials like railroad track, and faster in water than through air, yet faster in warm air than colder air. Cold air is denser, but the gas molecules in warm air move faster and more quickly convey the sound energy. Sound cannot travel in a vacuum (referring to the absence of all matter in a given space) because, as a compressional wave, it needs to have particles to compress as it travels.

Light is energy, and darkness is the absence of that energy. A shadow is not "cast" by an object, but rather the stream of light energy is blocked by the object, leaving an area of darkness. A black light behaves like any other, giving off light energy, yet at frequencies too high and wavelengths too short for our eyes to see (thus the light appears black to us). Some objects held beneath a black light absorb the energy from the ultraviolet light, and reemit this light at slightly lower wavelengths that our eyes can see, giving them the appearance that they glow in the dark. Laundry soaps with whiteners and brighteners contain additives that do something similar, converting portions of the invisible UV radiation from the Sun into lower frequency near-UV and additional visible light to make your "whites whiter." Since deer are more sensitive to near-UV wavelengths than humans, hunters are careful to launder their camouflage hunting clothes with soaps that do not contain such whiteners.

White light comprises all the visible wavelengths. Color is a property that light already has. White light passing through a prism, raindrop, or spectroscope can be separated into its constituent colors. An object appears red because it, or the dye molecules it contains, reflects the red wavelengths constituent in the white light that strike it. If a red shirt is illuminated by a blue light, the shirt will appear black because there is no red light for it to reflect. Blue paint reflects blue light from a white source, and yellow paint reflects yellow. Mixing the paints gives a material that reflects blue and yellow light, and our eyes see the mixture as green. A blue filter placed before a white light allows only the blue light to pass, absorbing all other wavelengths. A red shirt, when viewed through a blue filter, will appear black because the shirt can only reflect red light, but the filter can only pass blue light. The phosphors of our TV screen are in sets of red, green, and blue, which release white light when illuminated together.

Earth and Space Science

One had to be a Newton to notice that the Moon is falling, when everyone sees that it doesn't fall.

Paul Valéry (1871–1945), French poet and philosopher

Geosphere

Scientifically literate individuals have an understanding and appreciation for the world around them. Rocks hold an early fascination, both for their utility as objects for throwing and skipping and also for their beauty, texture, and diversity. Physical landforms vary considerably across the face of the Earth, revealed to the observant and thoughtful eye in road cuts, and the scenic viewpoints everywhere. On a small scale, each puddle, rivulet, and mass of sand and gravel in a yard or parking lot reveals the same actions of erosion, deposition, and graded sorting of material by size and mass that are at work on a global scale to form and reform our physical environment. The scientifically literate individual continually constructs new knowledge by study of the geosphere through direct observation, through photographs, models and samples, and through graphical representations (maps). The geosphere is the source for many natural resources essential for modern life, and the recipient of pollution caused by man's activities.

Evidence of physical changes to the geosphere is abundant, and frequently newsworthy. Each landslide, earthquake, or volcanic eruption reveals something about the Earth and its structures. Fossils, preserved remnants of or marks made by plants and animals that were once alive, are one source of evidence about changes in the environment over time. Finding fossils of marine organisms in what is now a desert is an opportunity to discuss scientific ways of knowing, of how science forms and tests hypotheses, and how theories develop to explain the reasons behind observations. The scientifically literate individual understands the concepts of uncertainty in measurement and the basis of scientific theories. Such an understanding may lead the teacher in an elementary classroom to refer to fossils and rocks simply as "very old," to dinosaurs as "living long ago," and to occasionally preface statements of scientific theory with the observation that "many scientists believe . . ."

Hydrosphere

With about seventy-five percent of the Earth's surface covered with water, the hydrosphere defines our planet and its environment. Most people live near the ocean, but few people live on, or have even experienced, the vast reaches of the world's oceans. Closer to our daily lives, and important because of the fresh water necessary to sustain life and commerce, are the rivers and streams that are abundant and familiar to residents of Massachusetts. The hydrosphere includes not just the surface waters described, but the subsurface waters of aquifers, and the water vapor present in the atmosphere. Man has a significant impact on the hydrosphere through activities that contaminate, divert, and attempt to control the flow of water. These activities can benefit one part of the environment or society while harming another.

The scientific concept of cycle is also used to describe the movement of water through its various phases, and through each part of the environment. A climate chamber formed from discarded polyethylene soda bottles can easily demonstrate these changes, and when soil, plants, and small frogs are added, a nearly complete ecosystem is formed if we count the food we add for the frog each day. In this chamber the student can observe the water cycle as liquid water evaporates, then condenses again against an ice-filled chamber to fall back to the surface. Only two phases, solid and liquid, can be observed directly, since the individual molecules of water vapor are too small to be seen by the naked eye. The white cloud visible at the tip of the teakettle, like our breath when we exhale on a cold winter day and fog, are examples of condensed water vapor (liquid water). The supply of fresh water on the Earth is limited, and water is a reusable resource that must be carefully managed. With this in mind, we are grateful for the technology to treat and purify water, which has done much to extend the human lifespan and reduce disease by providing clean and reliable sources of water in some parts of the world.

Atmosphere

The atmosphere is the layer of gases held close to the Earth by gravitational forces. In size, it has been compared with the skin on an apple. The atmosphere is densest close to the surface, where gravity holds the heavier gases and the pressure is greatest. The atmosphere becomes less dense and pressure decreases exponentially as altitude increases. All weather is contained within the lowest layer of the atmosphere (troposphere), and the temperature decreases as one rises through this layer. We can often observe the top of this layer as clouds form anvil shaped tops when they cannot rise further than the height of the cold boundary between the lowest layer (troposphere) and the overlying layer (stratosphere).

The concept of cycle reappears in the discussion of the recurring patterns of weather and the progression of the seasons. The basis of the seasons has much to do with the angle of light striking the Earth and very little to do with the distance from the Sun. Classroom weather stations and weather charts are useful learning tools, and projects to build thermometers, hygrometers, and barometers are popular in classrooms.

Density variations related to temperature drive the movement of air. Heat energy warms the air and increases water evaporation, warm air expands and rises above cooler surrounding air, rising air cools and water vapor condenses to form clouds and precipitation. Cold, heavy air settles over the polar caps and flows toward the equator, generally leading to weather trends that bring cold northerly winds into Massachusetts for part of the winter. Temperature gradients and the resulting air movement are readily observed at home where the basement is cool, the upstairs warmer, and a draft is often felt when sitting near the stairway.

Space Science

The concept of cycle again finds application in the periodic movement of the Sun and planets. The size of objects, and distances between them, are difficult to represent on the same scale. The National Mall in Washington, D.C., contains a 1/10,000,000,000th-scale solar system model in which the Sun is the size of a grapefruit, and Pluto, located some 650 yards away, is the size of a poppy seed. The openness of space is mirrored at a much smaller scale by vast open spaces between atoms and between nuclei and their electrons.

A ball rolling down the aisle of a school bus appears, to observers sitting on the bus, to swerve to the right and hit the wall as the bus makes a left-hand turn. To an observer outside the bus, the ball continued its straight-line motion until acted upon by a force, often resulting from a collision with the wall. For centuries the best science available held that the Sun rose in the east and set in the west. As scientific instruments developed and improved (telescopes for example), scientists collected new information that challenged old theories. New theories are not always well received, a fact to which Galileo would attest. We now understand that the Sun is the gravitational center of the solar system, and that each planet's motions are defined by its path along an elliptical orbit defined by its speed and its continual gravitational attraction to the Sun.

Principles and Processes of Scientific Investigations

Happy is he who gets to know the reasons for things.

Virgil (70–19 BCE), Roman poet

0016   Understand the foundations of scientific thought, the historical development of major scientific ideas and technological discoveries, and the principles and procedures of scientific inquiry and experimentation.

For example: the development of scientific thinking (e.g., the process of observation, classification, and notation of evidence developed by the ancient Greeks, the scientific revolution of the seventeenth century, the concepts of uncertainty and relativity introduced in the early twentieth century) the history of major scientific and technological discoveries and inventions; cultural and historical factors that have promoted or discouraged scientific discovery and technological innovation; basic concepts of scientific experimentation (e.g., hypothesis, control, variable, replication of results); and health and safety measures related to scientific inquiry and experimentation.

Tools of Science

From the pencil and field notebook to modern instruments in the laboratory, science involves the tools of observation, measurement, and computational analysis. The microscope and telescope each extend the range of human observation beyond human physiology. The spectroscope separates visible light into its component colors, and the spectrophotometer measures the selective absorption of those colors as a function of some property of a solution, solid, or gas. Mathematics is a tool to evaluate the results of our observations and to organize large quantities of data into averages, ranges, and statistical probabilities.

All measurements are limited by the fundamental uncertainty of the measuring device. The concept of significant figures is derived from the simple assumption that calculations on measurements cannot generate results that are more precise than the measurements themselves. If we divide one pie into three pieces the calculator might report that each piece is 0.33333333 (depending on the number of digits on the calculator display). We know from experience that there will be crumbs left in the pan and that no amount of care in dividing the pieces will result in the level of accuracy the calculation suggests. Every measuring device is presumed to be accurate to the smallest of the subdivisions marked, and every measurement with such a device should include one additional estimated digit. Measurements made with a ruler whose smallest divisions are one centimeter apart should be recorded to the tenth of a centimeter, the smallest measured digit plus one estimated digit. When scientists read the results of measurements made by others they therefore presume that the recorded values include a final digit that is an estimate based on the inherent accuracy of the instrument or device.

Technology

Compared to the goose quill, the modern mechanical pencil is a dramatic advancement in the technology of written communication. However, neither replaces the critical, analytical, and creative act of authorship. Many tools are available to assist in the observation, collection of data, analysis, and presentation of scientific information, yet none replace the role of the investigator who must formulate meaningful questions that can be answered using the tools of science. It is through the application of technology that we have the tools upon which all of modern science is based. We make some of these tools available in our classrooms to give students the opportunity to participate firsthand in the process of inquiry and discovery. The technology we employ in this context must facilitate student learning, remove barriers to understanding, and not create new barriers to delay and obscure the scientific concepts that we want to teach.

Scientific process skills, including the proper and accurate use of laboratory equipment, are an important component of science education. Instruction is necessary to guide the effective use of each measurement or observational tool: rulers, microscopes, balances, laboratory glassware, and so forth. As students develop these skills, they move from simple observations and confirmatory activities to using these tools to find answers to questions that they develop themselves.

Health and Safety

Through active, hands-on activities, science instruction is made a richer and more meaningful experience. From simple observations and activities at early grades, through detailed controlled experiments at higher grades, students who do science to learn science understand science better. While students are engaged in the process of discovery and exploration, the teacher must be engaged in protecting the health and safety of these students. The hazards vary with the discipline, and thoughtful planning and management of the activities will significantly reduce the risks to students. In all cases, students must utilize appropriate personal hygiene (hand washing) and wear personal protective equipment (goggles, gloves) while engaged in laboratory or field activities. Substitution of less hazardous materials whenever possible is a high priority. For example, in the physical sciences, replace mercury thermometers with alcohol or electronic, replace glass beakers and graduated cylinders with durable polyethylene, and eliminate or reduce the use of hazardous chemicals. In the earth sciences, rocks and minerals used in class should not contain inherently hazardous materials, students should not be allowed to taste the minerals, and reagents like HCl used for identification of carbonate minerals should be dispensed from spill-proof plastic containers. In the life sciences, special care should be given to topics such as safe practices for sharps, safe handling of living organisms, and care and use of microscopes. Experiments or activities involving the collection or culture of human cells or fluids should be discouraged, and proper sterilization procedures followed to prevent the growth or spread of disease agents. When they are possible, outdoor, museum, and other field activities can bring a valuable enrichment to the science curriculum in all disciplines. They also bring additional responsibilities for the safe planning and implementation of activities that increase student learning while maintaining the health and safety of the students.

Experimental Design

It is a capital mistake to theorise before one has data. Insensibly one begins to twist facts to suit theories instead of theories to suit facts.

Sherlock Holmes, the fictional creation of
Arthur Conan Doyle (1859–1930), British
physician and novelist

When a bat bites Gilligan, first mate of TV's ill-fated *SS Minnow*, he is convinced that he will turn into a vampire. Seemingly, no amount of reassurance by the Professor will convince him otherwise because, he claims, he saw the movie three times and it always came out the same way. We trust the results of experiments, both formal and informal, to help us understand our surroundings. Unfortunately, without proper control of the variables and a sound experimental design, our observations may lead us to entirely wrong-headed or incorrect conclusions.

Scientific Method

The scientific method is not a specific six-step method that is rigorously followed whenever a question arises that can be answered using the knowledge and techniques of science. Rather, it is a process of observation and analysis that is used to develop a reliable, consistent, and non-arbitrary representation and understanding of our world. We can use the scientific method (observation and description, formulation of hypotheses, prediction based on hypotheses, and tests of predictions) for many, but not all, questions. The approach is best applied to situations in which the experimenter can control the variables, eliminating or accounting for all extraneous factors, and perform repeated independent tests wherein only one variable is changed at a time.

Controlling Variables

The science fair project is a common tool for instruction in the scientific method. Many formal and informal sources, often Web based, provide lists of suggested science fair topics, but not all are experiments. For the youngest students it is appropriate and useful for the focus to be upon models and demonstrations—for example, the solar system model, volcano, or clay cross-section of an egg. Later the students should move to true experiments where the focus is on identifying a testable hypothesis, and the control of all experimental variables but the one of interest. Many projects may be elevated from model or demonstration to experiment. A proposal to demonstrate how windmills work can be made an experiment when the student adds quantitative measurements designed to measure one variable while varying only one other and while holding all other variables constant. For example, using an electric fan, the number of rotations per minute can be measured as a function of the fan setting (low, medium, or high). However, while keeping the fan setting constant, several different experiments could vary any one of the following variables: number of fins, size of fins, or shape of fins while in each case measuring the rotational speed.

Collecting and Presenting Data

The male has more teeth than the female in mankind, and sheep and goats, and swine. This has not been observed in other animals. Those persons which have the greatest number of teeth are the longest lived; those which have them widely separated, smaller, and more scattered, are generally more short lived.

Aristotle (384–322 BCE), Greek philosopher

Scientifically literate individuals have detailed and accurate content knowledge that is the basis of their scientific knowledge. They do not strive to recall every detail of that knowledge, but build conceptual frameworks upon which prior knowledge, as well as new learning, is added. From this framework of facts, concepts, and theories, the scientifically literate individual can reconstruct forgotten facts and use this information to answer new questions not previously considered. The scientifically literate individual is a lifelong learner who asks questions that can be answered using scientific knowledge and techniques.

Science is based upon experimentation, but not all knowledge is derived daily from principles first. The scientifically literate individual is informed by existing knowledge and is knowledgeable about the sources, accuracy, and value of each source. Not every source is equally reliable, accurate, or valid. Classroom teachers are advised to use trusted educational Web sites.

Scientifically literate individuals must be able to evaluate critically the information and evidence they collect, and the conclusions or theories to which that information and evidence leads. Such analysis incorporates an understanding of the limitations of knowledge in general, and the limitations of all measurements and information based on the quality of the experimental design. The literate individual can evaluate claims for scientific merit, identify conflicting evidence and weigh the value and credibility of conflicting information. He or she can also recognize that not every question can be answered using scientific knowledge, valuing the contributions of other cultures and other ways of knowing, including art, philosophy, and theology.

Scientific information is communicated to nonscientific audiences in order to inform, guide policy, and influence the practices that affect all of society. This information is presented through text, tables, charts, figures, pictures, models, and other representations that require interpretation and analysis. Scientifically literate individuals can read and interpret these representations and select appropriate tools to present the information they gather.

Interdisciplinary Science

All theoretical chemistry is really physics; and all theoretical chemists know it.

Richard P. Feynman (1918–1988), Nobel Prize in Physics, 1965

The separation of the natural sciences into life, physical, and earth sciences is relatively arbitrary. Many school curricula, and state-level science standards, are based on the cross-disciplinary integration of science based on key concepts rather than individual disciplines. The science concept of cycle is one of many concepts that find application, and can be used to understand science content, in more than one scientific discipline. This approach to science instruction is viewed as important for several reasons. It is consistent with the goals of scientific literacy and of developing science content knowledge upon which students build and extend their own understanding. Science knowledge is constantly developing and expanding in a continuous process made more meaningful through the development of an organizing framework. Scientific concepts, which often have application in contexts outside the laboratory, help us see similarities and recognize patterns, which allow us to better function within society.

Science concepts can serve as organizers, often unifying disparate topics in the process of learning science. Examples of key interdisciplinary science concepts include: cause-effect, model, cycle, equilibrium, population, and gradient. As an example, the concept of model is among the most ubiquitous in all of science. Models are tentative schemes or structures that relate to real-world objects or phenomena. Our explanations of many phenomena rely on models, descriptions of electricity, atoms, tectonics, and genetics. Like a model airplane, a scientific model will bear a certain resemblance to the real object that is useful at some level to represent, but not fully replicate, the real object. Models are used when the phenomenon or object of interest cannot be used directly. Models may be constructed to scale, but often are not, in order to emphasize some portion of the object. An artistic drawing is a model, as is a three-dimensional, cross-sectional plastic casting, or a computer-rendered animation. Each has its limitations, and its beneficial function, to extend our understanding of the object or phenomenon. Models can limit our understanding when they are treated as statements of descriptive fact or when the limitations of the physical model are confused with the characteristics of the real object or phenomenon.

Science, Technology, and Society

It is unworthy of excellent men to lose hours like slaves in the labor of calculation which could be relegated to anyone else if machines were used.

Gottfried Wilhelm von Leibniz (1646–1716), German polymath

Science disciplines hold to certain central values that unify them in their philosophy and methodology. Science relies on evidence collected in verifiable experiments, on conclusions validated by replication, and on theories that explain observations and that are capable of making testable predictions. Much, but far from all, modern scientific thought traces a significant portion of its development to the work of Western European scientists. It is important to recognize the contributions made by all peoples and cultures to the development of scientific knowledge. Men and women from all continents and races continue to make meaningful contributions to the advancement of science in all disciplines. Examples are readily available for enrichment and instruction from online resources.

Technology can be loosely defined as the application of science for the benefit of mankind. For both political and economic reasons, not all peoples have the same ready access to clean, safe water supplies or to adequate food supplies, in spite of the technological capabilities that basic science has provided. Science certainly can benefit society, but it too, arguably, can harm mankind and our environment. Science gives us the knowledge and tools to understand nature's principles and that knowledge can often be applied for some useful purpose. Few would debate the benefits of the wheel and axle, the electric light, the polio vaccine, or plastic. The benefits of science and technology become more complicated to evaluate when discussing the applications of gene splicing for genetically modified foods, of cloning, of nuclear energy to replace fossil fuels, or of the application of atomic energy to weapons of mass destruction. Science can tell us how to do something, not whether we should.

Scientific literacy helps us participate in the decision-making process of our society as well-informed and contributing members. Real-world decisions have social, political, and economic dimensions, and scientific information is often used to both support and refute these decisions. Understanding that the inherent nature of scientific information is unbiased, and based on experimental evidence that can be reproduced by any laboratory under the same conditions can help us all make better decisions, recognize false arguments, and participate fully as active and responsible citizens.

Child Development

Children develop in several domains that are of interest to teachers. They grow and mature physically, of course, but they also develop intellectually or cognitively, socially in how they interact with others, psychologically, and linguistically as they learn to express themselves through language.

Over the decades, a number of theories of how children develop and how they learn have evolved out of the systematic observation of children and the ocean of experiences of teachers everywhere. These theories have shaped educational philosophy and have important implications for classroom teaching.

Major Child Development Theories

0017   Understand child development from birth through the elementary years.

For example: major theories of child development; characteristics and processes of cognitive, language, physical, social, and emotional development during the elementary years; developmental progressions and ranges of individual and cultural variation in cognitive, language, physical, social, and emotional development; factors that may facilitate or impede a child's development in various domains; major learning theories; processes by which children acquire knowledge and construct meaning; interrelationships between cognitive development and other developmental domains; and principles and procedures for promoting students' cognitive, language, physical, social, and emotional development.

Stages of Cognitive Development (Piaget)

Jean Piaget (1896–1980) was a Swiss biologist who applied the scientific method to the study of how children grow and learn. He concluded that children develop through a series of four major stages. The rate of progress varies from individual to individual, but they will each progress through the following stages in sequence:

1. Sensory-motor intelligence (birth to 2 years): The child develops actions such as sucking, grasping, and hitting to deal with the immediate world. No thinking as such.

2. Preoperational thought (2 to 7 years): The child learns to speak and understand; rapid conceptual development. Begins to use symbols and think of objects in the immediate environment.

3. Concrete operations (7 to 11 years): The child begins to use logical thought to solve concrete problems. Thinks systematically.

4. Formal operations (11 to 15 years): The child develops the ability to think systematically on an abstract or hypothetical plane. Uses language creatively.

Implications for the Classroom

Piaget's insights reveal what teachers can expect children at the various stages or ages to be able to understand. Instruction can then be geared to the appropriate level. For instance, until they are ready for abstract concepts in the fourth stage, children learn more effectively through concrete examples. That does not mean, however, that children cannot be challenged. Also, curriculum and instruction can be set up with the understanding that learning is a process of spontaneous discovery best gained by letting the child explore the environment, including the subject matter of the particular classroom.

Moral Reasoning (Kohlberg)

Lawrence Kohlberg (1937–1987), an American psychologist, applied and expanded Piaget's concepts to "moral development." He believed that what he called moral reasoning evolved through three major phases, each containing two stages:

1. Preconventional level: The child is responsive to cultural concepts of right and wrong. *Stage 1. Punishment and obedience*: Physical punishment or rewards determine what is good and bad. *Stage 2. Instrumental-relativist*: Right is what satisfies one's own needs. Deals can be made.

2. <u>Conventional level</u>: The values of one's family or group are "good" regardless of consequences. *Stage 3. Interpersonal relationships*: Living up to expectations of family and community is "good." *Stage 4. Law and Order*: Living by the fixed rules of society is "good." Doing one's duty is "right."

3. <u>Postconventional Level</u>: The child defines what is right or moral independently of authority or groups. *Stage 5. Social contract*: What is "right" has been defined and agreed to by the individual independent members of society. *Stage 6: Universal principles*: Right is defined by an individual's social consciousness, according to that individual's chosen ethical principles.

Implications for the Classroom

Children do not automatically progress through Kohlberg's stages of moral maturation. Nor can children be "taught" through them as such. Rather, individuals progress through their own thinking. Parents and teachers can help by exposing children to the next level of moral reasoning, by posing problems or situations that reveal the limitations of their current level, and by inviting dialogue between individuals at different levels and of different views. The rise of moral reasoning thus encompasses cognitive, linguistic, and social development.

A Hierarchy of Needs (Maslow)

The work of psychologist Abraham Maslow (1908–1970) suggests that children's development can be influenced by how well their biological, social, cognitive, and personal needs are met. Maslow's concept is that the basic needs must be satisfied *before* higher level needs can be successfully addressed.

Think of the hierarchy as a pyramid with the base consisting of the four so-called "deficiency needs" (from the bottom): physiological needs; then safety needs; then belongingness and love needs; then, at the top of the base, esteem needs. As these deficiency needs are met, the motivation to satisfy them decreases, and the individual can move up the pyramid to the "being or growth needs."

The first of these is the need to know and understand; then up to aesthetic needs (to create and appreciate beauty), and finally, at the top, the need for self-actualization. This level could be defined as the ability to use one's talents to the fullest. In contrast to the lower half of the pyramid, the higher needs continue to motivate as they are met. Thus, we continue to seek to grow, to achieve, to become more than we are now.

Implications for the Classroom

Recognizing students' levels of needs helps schools and teachers motivate them to greater achievement. At the base level, that is why we provide breakfast and lunch for the economically deprived, counsel those with inadequate emotional support, nurture those with family difficulties, and try to provide a safe learning environment for all our children.

Psychosocial Development (Erikson)

Erik Erikson (1902–1974) was born to Danish parents in Germany and trained there as a Freudian psychoanalyst. His study of child development came after he moved to the United States. Erikson describes 8 to 9 stages of development ranging from infancy to old age. Each is defined by a psychosocial crisis central to the individual's emotional and social growth. Eventually, all of us, if we live long enough, must go through these stages. However, stages 3–5 are the ones of particular relevance to the educational system:

Stage 3. Play Age (3–6 years): Conflict is initiative vs. guilt. The child learns control and seeks independence.

Stage 4. School Age (6–12 years): Conflict is industry vs. inferiority. The child becomes more assertive and takes more initiative.

Stage 5. Adolescence (13–adult): Conflict is identity vs. role confusion. The child forges an identity and deals with peer relationships.

Implications for the Classroom

Educators can use Erikson's insights to help them recognize the psychosocial vulnerability of children and adolescents as they struggle for feelings of competence and belonging and strive to establish their own identities. Teachers can also facilitate that development in the following ways:

- Letting students take risks and make mistakes

- Assigning challenging but doable tasks

- Having realistic but high expectations

- Giving praise more than criticism

- Respecting students' dignity

- Teaching and modeling critical thinking

- Providing a safe and structured learning environment

Major Learning Theories

Behaviorism and Operant Conditioning (Skinner)

American psychologist B. F. Skinner (1904–1990) enlarged upon the behaviorist work of Ivan Pavlov (the salivating dogs) and John Watson. He developed a comprehensive model of shaping behavior know as operant (or type R) conditioning. Essentially, one person establishes a desired behavior in another by rewarding (reinforcing) it as close to immediately as possible. Conversely, one discourages (extinguishes) an undesired behavior by withholding rewards, or, if necessary, punishing. Skinner believed that positive reinforcement was more powerful than punishment and could be coupled with extinguishing responses (withholding reward) to effectively modify behavior.

Skinner's emphasis on learning and development through the manipulation of behavior is at odds with other theorists who focus on a child's seemingly self-generated psychological and cognitive growth. Thoughts and feelings are less important to Skinner than behaviors. Skinner and his followers would question the validity of the "stages" proposed by Piaget, Erikson, and others.

Implications for the Classroom

Rewarding appropriate behavior and extinguishing attention-seeking disruptive behavior have become a central part of modern parenting and classroom management. If a teacher's or fellow student's smiles, verbal approval, or active encouragement can reinforce something a student should do, then denying those reactions can discourage the student from things he/she shouldn't do. Teachers need to be systematic, timely, and, above all, consistent in their responses to make operant conditioning succeed.

Modeling and More (Bandura)

Albert Bandura (1925–), a Canadian psychologist, became interested in how people learn in social situations. In contrast to Skinner and the Behaviorists' insistence on incremental learning, Bandura believed people (children in particular) can learn a collection of behaviors quickly through observation of others. This process is cognitive learning through modeling. We also learn through symbolic models such as books, television, and verbal instruction.

Bandura's observational learning process occurs in four steps:

1. <u>Attention</u>: The model (person being observed, book, etc.) must be distinctive to attract and hold our interest.

2. <u>Retention</u>: The behaviors or information of the model must be associated with visual or verbal codes that we can reference later.

3. <u>Motor reproduction</u>: After seeing, or reading, or hearing about how something is done, we must do it ourselves to acquire the behavior.

4. <u>Reinforcement and motivation</u>: To retain the behavior, skill, or information, we must get the desired reaction of others or achieve self-satisfaction from learning it.

Modeling the practices and heeding the verbal instructions of others is the process of socialization. As the child matures, externals give way to internals; that is, the self-regulation of behavior occurs. At this point, we are motivated by performing and behaving to meet our own goals; we give ourselves what Bandura called *self-efficacy appraisals*. He came to believe that these self-efficacy appraisals are more important to learning than modeling.

Implications for the Classroom

Modeling is a powerful tool in the teaching of children. Verbal instructions are reinforced by actions and vice versa. Teachers, administrators, and parents who want children to act in a certain way (teamwork, sharing, civility, respect for others) must both practice and preach. Competent, self-contained teachers lead to competent, self-contained students.

Pedagogically, educators can apply the four stages of learning—attention, retention, reproduction, reinforcement—in classroom settings to teach skills as well as behaviors.

Bandura believed that such common school practices as ranking of students and competitive grading undermines self-efficacy and makes children feel inadequate. It would be better, he felt, if children could work cooperatively and judge their own progress according to their own self-assessment rather than against the standards of other students.

Constructionism (Vygotsky)

A more recent movement in education focuses on how children construct understanding of new material based on what they already know. This notion is based on the rediscovered work of Russian psychologist L. S. Vygotsky (1896–1934), who attempted to forge a theory of learning that encompassed both the inner resources of the child and environmental factors. He concluded that children learn best with assistance—sometimes carefully structured, sometimes not—that gives them a framework for self-discovery, which he called a *scaffolding* for their cognitive construction.

Implications for the Classroom

A constructionist teacher would begin by eliciting what the students know about the subject and use that information as a starting point of instruction. Teachers would then respond to the students' attempts to master the material—*learning about students' learning*. Students would then be guided to use their information and/or skills, perhaps by teaching others. This process is sometimes called *reciprocal teaching*.

The constructionist goal is for the teacher to provide just enough support to allow students to discover for themselves. That means carefully reading students' cues to be sensitive to the areas where the student needs "scaffolding" support. These areas where students need—and can use—more assistance, Vygotsky called *zones of proximal development*.

Information Processing

The computer is the metaphor for human learning that involves using long- and short-term memory to access information and solve problems. Proponents such as psychologist Anita Woolfolk (contemporary) assert that the human mind encodes, stores, and retrieves information much as a computer does, all guided by a central control process.

Implications for the Classroom

According to Woolfolk, teachers who apply information processing to learning begin where all theories begin: first get the student's attention. That done, the teacher's tasks are to

- Help students focus on the most important information

- Help students connect the new information to what they already know

- Present the new material in a clear, organized, and concrete way

- Repeat and review information; practice skills

- Focus on meaning, not memorization

Students with Exceptionalities

0018   Understand child development and learning in students with exceptionalities.

For example: types of disabling conditions, developmental delays, indices of advanced academic or artistic talent; effects of exceptionalities on cognitive, physical, social, and emotional development and functioning; significance of various exceptionalities for learning; identification of students with exceptionalities; criteria and procedures for selecting, creating, and modifying materials and equipment to address students' exceptionalities; legal requirements for providing education to students with disabling conditions; and purposes and procedures for developing and implementing Individualized Education Plans (IEPs) or 504 Accommodation Plans.

Students are considered *exceptional* for categorization purposes when they have physical attributes or learning abilities/disabilities that are far enough above or below the norm to require a specialized, adaptive program to meet their needs. Students with *disabilities* have some physical problem that restricts their capacity to learn. A *handicap* is any impediment to functioning within a certain environment. A disability is only a handicap, therefore, if the environment (such as a school or classroom) is not adapted (or adaptable) to allow the person (student) to function normally. Some physical adaptations are simple and easy to make. Others are more complex and require the ongoing intervention of trained educational professionals.

Types of Disabling Conditions

The exact number of students with disabling conditions is difficult to pin down because of definitions that vary from state to state and student assessments that vary from school district to school district. However, federal statistics indicate over five (and perhaps six) million students nationwide receive special education services yearly. Approximately a dozen categories of disability are commonly recognized.

Learning Disabilities

The broadest category and the hardest to define is *learning disabilities*, which describes more than half of the students served in the United States. Generally, students are considered learning disabled (LD) if they (1) exhibit a large gap between their ability and their actual achievement, (2) have learning problems that cannot be attributed to other disabilities, and (3) need special education services to succeed in school. Usually, such students are average or above in intelligence but have information processing problems that make it difficult for them to read, write, and/or compute. Dyslexia has become the umbrella term for these problems, but it constitutes only a small part of the range of LD conditions.

Other conditions associated with LD students are *attention deficit disorder* (*ADD*) and *attention deficit hyperactive disorder* (*ADHD*). Both are commonly diagnosed, but criteria seem to vary as much as the LD designation itself. Both can be treated with medication and behavior modification. It is important to note that these disorders are *not* learning disabilities by themselves.

Speech and Language Impairments

This category is the second largest, encompassing about one-fifth of the students receiving services. It applies to students with extraordinary difficulties in communicating with others, especially articulation and fluency problems.

Mental Retardation

These students (more than 10% of those receiving services) have significant limitations in cognitive ability. They learn at a slower pace and level off sooner. The once common terms of *educable mentally retarded* (*EMR*) and *trainable mentally retarded* (*TMR*) are not used much today because they seem to prescribe limits.

Emotional Disturbance

When students have sufficient social or emotional problems to interfere with learning, they are said to have *emotional disturbance* (*ED*). More than just "bad behavior" problems, ED students have great difficulty relating to other people and functioning in a social setting. They represent slightly less than 10% of those served.

Other Impairments

The remaining categories represent about 10% of the students served. In approximate order of their frequency, they are: chronic or acute illness, multiple disabilities, hearing impairments, orthopedic impairments, autism, visual impairments, traumatic brain injury, deaf-blindness.

Legal Issues

Various pieces of civil rights-related legislation from the 1970s through the 1990s have established obligations and procedures for educating students with disabilities. For instance, *Section 504* of the Vocational Rehabilitation Act of 1973 prevents discrimination in public schools, thus giving disabled students equal opportunity to participate. The various manifestations of the *Individuals with Disabilities in Education Act* (*IDEA*) require states to locate, identify, and evaluate all children with disabilities. Further, the identification and evaluation must be nondiscriminatory. Education must be provided at public expense.

Mandated as well is education in the *least restrictive environment* (see next page). Parents' participation in the evaluation and their consent are required for the student's *individual education program* or *IEP* (see below). Schools are also encouraged through grants to provide programs for preschoolers. Finally, the law requires schools to provide necessary *related services* (e.g., transportation, physical therapy) and *assistive technology* (specialized equipment) to disabled students.

Identification and Screening

The majority of students who receive special education are identified by the time they reach the elementary grades. However, students can be found eligible at any time during their school careers. Often, a teacher in the early grades will notice a pattern of poor and inconsistent achievement, behavior and socialization problems, as well as physical and/or sensory deficiencies. Those students are brought to the attention of an administrator or counselor. The student is then screened by a special team or specially trained individual. Assessment is carried out in the best-case scenario by a multidisciplinary team, including consultation with the classroom teacher and the parent(s). What formal procedures for testing they employ depend on the nature and severity of the disability.

Individual Education Programs (IEPs)

The IEP is a team effort. Participants include the parent(s) or surrogate, general education teacher(s), special education teacher(s), special education administrator, and (if over age 14) the student. The team is put together for any student identified as needing special services. It meets to produce a plan that will include several statements that (1) define the student's current levels of performance, (2) enumerate measurable goals and objectives, (3) delineate which services will be provided and when, (4) explain to what degree the student will participate in regular classes and activities, (5) establish to what extent the student will be subject to state and district assessments, and (6) identify how the student's progress towards the goals or objectives will be determined and conveyed to the parents.

The IEP is generated every year for each student receiving services or being considered for services. It is also mandated by law and is arguably the centerpiece of the special education process.

Implications for the Classroom

The federally mandated goal for teaching students with disabling conditions is to place them in the *least restrictive environment* (*LRE*); that is, a setting most like that of nondisabled peers in which the student can be supported and succeed. For most disabled students, that means full-time or nearly full-time attendance in a regular classroom with periods of help from a specially trained teacher. Disabled students participating in regular classroom activities (with or without assistance) are said to be *mainstreamed*. How much time they can spend in a regular classroom depends on the nature and severity of the disability.

While mainstreaming often refers to at least a physical presence in the classroom, the concept of *inclusion* is meant to convey a more thorough integration of the disabled student into the social and instructional aspects as well. Advocates of inclusion believe it mandates a focus on students' abilities rather than their disabilities. Regardless of the conceptual terminology applied, teachers still face the concrete reality of doing their job for all their students.

Once the IEP has placed this student in the LRE, how does the classroom teacher meet the now-defined learning objectives? The best general answer is to work closely with the special education teacher(s) who have experience in working with disabled students. Together, the teachers might do any of the following: (1) rearrange the classroom's physical organization, (2) modify instructional methods, (3) offer a variety of ways to complete assignments and test progress, and (4) identify the student's academic skills and limitations, as well as any socio-emotional and behavioral issues.

Special education professionals are invaluable resources with training and expertise in helping disabled students both cope and succeed. They offer additional assistance to students on their caseload and are in regular communication with parents to seek to work out academic and behavioral problems. Their presence in the school and in classrooms is not to help underachieving students "get away with things" but to help them get on with things—to learn what they can, and to progress in school.

Students Who Are Gifted or Talented

Students who are designated as gifted or talented are those who have demonstrated either exceptional intellectual ability or creativity and proficiency in the visual or performing arts. They also possess a high level of commitment to tasks in their areas of excellence. Precise definitions for these designations, as in many aspects of special education, are elusive. Various states have identified as low as 1% or as high as 15% of their students as "gifted" or "talented." Most experts would say a reasonable number is between 3–5%—which is distributed across all socioeconomic, ethnic, and racial groups.

Locating and identifying these special students is also an inexact science. To be sure to find all the possible candidates from as many diverse backgrounds as there might be, data and impressions need to be gathered from a variety of sources. Authorities advise school districts to: (1) accept referrals from peers, parents, teachers, and persons outside the educational mainstream, (2) examine work with a creative eye, and (3) look for people from all groups, girls as well as boys, and from the learning and physically disabled. Inclusion is better than exclusion when seeking talent. Gifts can be found in unexpected places.

Implications for the Classroom

Because these students are so able, achievement oriented, driven, and creative, they put a strain on any educational system not willing or able to accommodate their special needs. On the plus side, gifted and talented students tend to express themselves well, be eager to learn, seek new ways to accomplish tasks, make original contributions in class, require little repetition, and complete assignments quickly. On the other hand, they can be glib rather than knowledgeable, dominate discussions, be impatient with others, struggle against regulations, and become bored and frustrated with a too-slow pace.

Educational approaches to developing the gifted and talented as fully as their abilities allow include:

- Acceleration: Children who are ready can enter school early, skip grades, telescope subject matter—particularly in the lower grades. Later, they can take AP courses or enroll concurrently (or early) in college.

- Self-directed or independent study: Gifted and talented students are often self-motivated and work well at their own pace with minimal supervision.

- Enriching the curriculum: Bringing in material from outside the traditional disciplines, perhaps via new technologies, can expand educational horizons.

- Alternative or magnet schools: Larger school districts have dedicated schools for specific disciplines (science, math, the arts) that serve the gifted and talented population by creating a community of learners.

Though not mandated by federal law, schools can set up IEPs for gifted and talented students to design educational programs that meet their needs—perhaps by including some of the strategies listed above, as well as other creative approaches teachers and students might envision. Special students deserve special accommodations, whatever their exceptionalities.

Integration of Knowledge and Understanding

0019   **Prepare an organized, developed analysis on a topic related to one or more of the first five elementary subareas (Language Arts, Mathematics, History and Social Science, Science and Technology/Engineering, and Child Development).**

- (Refer to objectives 0001 through 0018 and associated descriptive statements.)

In the final part of General Curriculum test, you will be asked to write two constructed responses. That is, you will be asked to prepare a written response of approximately 150 to 300 words to each question. Each open-response item will typically include both of the following:

1. Contextual or background information that presents the topic of the open-response item

2. One or more specific directions or assignments that advise you of the elements that you are expected to provide in your response

The components of a typical open-response item are as follows:

- The first paragraph introduces the topic of the assignment.

- The second paragraph, and accompanying bulleted instructions, describe the writing task you must undertake and what elements to include in your response.

Unlike the constructed responses that ask you to formulate an argument and write a structured essay on other tests, knowledge of standard English is *not* a critical part of your score.

The Assignment

You will typically be given a question or questions that pertain to one or more of the first 18 test objectives. The four criteria by which you will be graded are

- Purpose—the extent to which your response fulfills the purpose of the assignment

- Subject matter knowledge—the accuracy and appropriateness with which you apply your knowledge of the subject

- Support—the quality and relevance of your supporting details

- Rationale—the soundness of your arguments and the degree of understanding you demonstrate

Of these four criteria, the most important is "support": you cannot get high scores in either "subject matter knowledge" or "rationale" unless you use the information you are given to marshal examples that will support whatever your argument is.

Here is a sample assignment. Read it through carefully.

Hiru is a fifth grader. His teacher has analyzed his performance on a fifth-grade-level passage that he has read aloud to her. She did this by keeping a running record of his miscues while reading. His accuracy rate was 88%, which is usually considered to be just below a student's instructional level (90%). He read the passage with expression (usually correctly inflected) and enthusiasm. Hiru was able to talk about the passage, but not always accurately, and he was able to make some simple predictions about what might happen next.

He did not self-correct on any of the words he misread. Here is a list of the words he substituted for:

Text	Student
shall	will
tired	tie-red
lie	lay
scratch	scrap
stretched	streaked
radiator	radio
returned	retired

In addition, the teacher had to tell him the word "admonition," and he omitted a "now" and an "and."

Using your knowledge of how to teach word identification and fluency, write a response in which you

- Analyze Hiru's pattern(s) of miscues and his overall reading fluency and cite specific examples to back up your analysis.

- Describe at least two different types of activities that might improve Hiru's reading fluency and explain why these types of activities might work.

Preparing to Write

Writing Process for the Open Response

- Prewriting
  - o   Jot notes, make diagrams
  - o   Outline
  - o   Reread the questions
  - o   Adjust outline to questions if necessary
- Writing
- Revising
  - o   Did you answer the questions?
  - o   Do you have support for all the assertions you make?
  - o   Is your writing clear?
  - o   Is your writing free of grammatical/spelling mistakes?

For this open response, it is not necessary to frame your answer with a strong, creative opening and closing; the best strategy here is simply to begin your **prewriting** stage by jotting down notes.

Because the questions in this type of constructed response will typically be rather specific, you should begin by writing down anything that will help you answer each question—in order, if possible. For instance, the first thing you will want to do with this assignment is to organize the facts you need in order to *analyze* the pattern of misreadings. You can use the table that is already provided for you; you might add columns that are headed by "Similar Meaning," "Graphophonically Similar," and "Syntactically Acceptable" and put checkmarks in the table cells that apply. You would have checkmarks under Similar Meaning for the first and third words, and checkmarks under Graphophonically Similar for all but the first word. You would also have checkmarks under Syntactically Acceptable for four of the seven words. (That is, the substitution is the same part of speech as the actual word in the text.) At this point, you're well on the way to answering the first two questions.

Now you want to turn your prewriting attention to what types of activities will help this fifth grader improve his reading and why. His problem seems to be word recognition rather than syntactic comprehension. In addition, he seems to have mastered phonics, at least at the beginnings of words. Thus, he could be given lessons or mini-lessons, either by the teacher or by a peer, on basic word-identification strategies: phonic analysis (beyond the initial sounds), analogies (i.e., making associations with known words), syllabic analysis, and morphemic analysis (i.e., study of roots). Hiru needs to learn to recognize words that an average fifth grader knows in order to make use of his ability at comprehension so that he can read at grade level or above, so you should choose two strategies/activities that you are most familiar with in order to do that.

Now you are ready to outline. Outlining should not take much time, because the assignment makes a rough outline for you. You do have some choices, though; for example, you could combine the first two questions so that you can present one element of your analysis, along with your reasoning, followed by another element and your reasoning, and so on, rather than simply making an analysis and then going back to your reasons. With this assignment, it is probably better to present your reasons along with each analytic statement. You could use the same kind of organization with questions three and four: for instance, a paragraph on teaching syllabic analysis and a paragraph on giving Hiru extra morphemic analysis work. Thus, your outline might look something like this:

I. Analysis and reasoning

    A. Good overall comprehension—answers questions and reads with enthusiasm, and most errors are nevertheless syntactically correct

    B. Will be at frustration level with fifth-grade texts—too many words he doesn't know

    C. Needs to improve word recognition—although he has a rough understanding of phonics, his ability to recognize words is below grade level

II. Strategies

    A. Lessons on syllabic analysis—miscues show Hiru needs to look beyond initial sounds

    B. Lessons on morphemic analysis—returned–retired pair and scratch–scrap pair have different roots

    Conclusion: Hiru needs to learn to recognize words that an average fifth grader knows in order to make use of his ability at comprehension so that he can read at grade level or above, so you should choose two strategies/activities that you are most familiar with in order to do that.

Writing and Revising

This outline will give you a good start. Now is the time for **writing**: get the ideas down as clearly and as coherently as you can. In your **revising** stage, you should look at what you've written, making sure that you have indeed answered the questions clearly, that you have good examples for everything you wrote, and (even though standard English is not one of the grading criteria) that your writing is free of spelling and grammatical errors.

Open Responses for Mathematics

It is very likely that you will be given a mathematical problem to solve in an open response. If you are asked to do so, you will also have to explain the mathematical concepts involved and how you applied them to the solution of your problem. For example, you might get a problem like the following:

> Suppose that you want to create an enclosed rectangular play area and you have only 120 feet of fence.
> What length and width would give you the most area? What would the maximum area be?

Use your knowledge of mathematics to create a response in which you analyze and solve this problem. In your response you should:

- describe two prerequisite mathematical skills necessary for solving this problem;

- identify two mathematical concepts involved in solving this problem; and

- solve the given problem, showing your work and justifying the steps you used in arriving at your solution.

For mathematical problems, your **prewriting** strategy will be somewhat different from what it is in the other types of open-response prompts. Your first task for this type of prompt is to **solve the problem**, keeping track of everything you do to solve it. For example, you may know that a square will be the rectangle of a given perimeter that gives you the maximum area, but even if you do, you should develop a strategy that shows you can prove this fact to a classroom of students.

1. Fence length of an enclosed area is another way of saying *perimeter*.

2. Try some lengths and widths that add up to 120: for instance, length of 45 and width of 15 produces an area of 675 square feet; length of 40 and width of 20 produces an area of 800 square feet; and length of 50 and width of 10 gets you an area of 500 square feet.

3. If you put these values into a table, you'll see that area increases as length gets closer to width. If you make your rectangle a square (a square is a form of a rectangle), you get an area of 900 square feet. There is no way to get a larger area.

4. What did you have to know to do this problem? First, you had to know the formulas for areas and perimeters of rectangles: perimeter = 2 × length + 2 × width and area = length × width. You had to know strategies for solving problems: in this case, you used the guess-and-check strategy, and you also constructed a table of values. You might also have drawn a picture, although without graph paper it might not have helped much.

5. You had to know how to solve simple equations, e.g., 120 = 2 × 45 + 2 × w in order to find the width when the length is 45.

Thus, you have already solved the problem, and you can now jot down the answers to the first two questions: (1) two mathematical skills necessary for solving this problem are knowledge of formulas for area and perimeter of a rectangle and knowledge of problem-solving strategies; and (2) two mathematical concepts involved in solving this problem include understanding the effect how increasing or decreasing lengths of the sides of a rectangle has on its area, and understanding how to solve equations for adding or subtracting the same value from both sides or dividing both sides by the same value.

If you do know that a square using the 120 feet of fencing will maximize the area, you can prove it by mathematical induction, but doing so is probably not the best response here. By going through the basic steps that you might expect an elementary student to follow in order to solve the problem, given the skills you would expect that student to have, you demonstrate how you would teach, in addition to how well you can think and write. Knowledge of mathematical induction would be beyond the educational background of most elementary students.

One last word about the outline for the mathematical open response: your best outlining strategy is to present the solution first, followed by the listing of mathematical skills and concepts. If your solution is correct and presented well, you will already have earned at least 3 points for subject matter knowledge, support, and rationale. Also, the response will be easier for the grader to follow if you present a concrete solution procedure before going into the more abstract and general areas of mathematical skills and concepts.

Scoring the Open Responses

All responses to the General Curriculum test open-response assignments are scored using scales that describe varying levels of performance. These scales were approved by committees of Massachusetts educators.

Each response is scored by multiple scorers according to standardized procedures during scoring sessions held immediately after each administration of the test. Scorers with relevant professional backgrounds are oriented to these procedures before the scoring session and are carefully monitored during the scoring sessions.

MTEL

General Curriculum

Practice Test 1

This practice test for the MTEL is also on CD-ROM in our special interactive MTEL TEST*ware*®. It is highly recommended that you first take this exam on computer. You will then have the additional study features and benefits of enforced timed conditions and instantaneous, accurate scoring. See page xi for guidance on how to get the most out of our MTEL book and software.

Practice Test Directions

Time:　4 hours

This test contains two sections: (1) a multiple-choice section and (2) an open-response item assignment section. You may complete the sections of the test in any order you choose. Directions for the open-response items appear before that section.

Each question in the first section is a multiple-choice question with four answer choices. Read each question carefully and choose the ONE best answer. Record your answer on the answer sheet in the space that corresponds to the question number. Completely fill in the space having the same letter as the answer you have chosen. *Use only a No. 2 lead pencil.*

Sample Question:

1.　What is the capital of Massachusetts?

　　A.　Worcester

　　B.　New Bedford

　　C.　Boston

　　D.　Springfield

The correct answer to this question is C. You would indicate that on the answer sheet as follows:

1.　Ⓐ Ⓑ ● Ⓓ

Try to answer all questions. In general, if you have some knowledge about a question, it is better to try to answer it. You will NOT be penalized for guessing.

The second section consists of two constructed-response items. You will be asked to provide a written response to the assignment. Directions for completing your written response to the open-response items appear immediately before the assignment.

Answer Sheet

1. Ⓐ Ⓑ Ⓒ Ⓓ	26. Ⓐ Ⓑ Ⓒ Ⓓ	51. Ⓐ Ⓑ Ⓒ Ⓓ	76. Ⓐ Ⓑ Ⓒ Ⓓ
2. Ⓐ Ⓑ Ⓒ Ⓓ	27. Ⓐ Ⓑ Ⓒ Ⓓ	52. Ⓐ Ⓑ Ⓒ Ⓓ	77. Ⓐ Ⓑ Ⓒ Ⓓ
3. Ⓐ Ⓑ Ⓒ Ⓓ	28. Ⓐ Ⓑ Ⓒ Ⓓ	53. Ⓐ Ⓑ Ⓒ Ⓓ	78. Ⓐ Ⓑ Ⓒ Ⓓ
4. Ⓐ Ⓑ Ⓒ Ⓓ	29. Ⓐ Ⓑ Ⓒ Ⓓ	54. Ⓐ Ⓑ Ⓒ Ⓓ	79. Ⓐ Ⓑ Ⓒ Ⓓ
5. Ⓐ Ⓑ Ⓒ Ⓓ	30. Ⓐ Ⓑ Ⓒ Ⓓ	55. Ⓐ Ⓑ Ⓒ Ⓓ	80. Ⓐ Ⓑ Ⓒ Ⓓ
6. Ⓐ Ⓑ Ⓒ Ⓓ	31. Ⓐ Ⓑ Ⓒ Ⓓ	56. Ⓐ Ⓑ Ⓒ Ⓓ	81. Ⓐ Ⓑ Ⓒ Ⓓ
7. Ⓐ Ⓑ Ⓒ Ⓓ	32. Ⓐ Ⓑ Ⓒ Ⓓ	57. Ⓐ Ⓑ Ⓒ Ⓓ	82. Ⓐ Ⓑ Ⓒ Ⓓ
8. Ⓐ Ⓑ Ⓒ Ⓓ	33. Ⓐ Ⓑ Ⓒ Ⓓ	58. Ⓐ Ⓑ Ⓒ Ⓓ	83. Ⓐ Ⓑ Ⓒ Ⓓ
9. Ⓐ Ⓑ Ⓒ Ⓓ	34. Ⓐ Ⓑ Ⓒ Ⓓ	59. Ⓐ Ⓑ Ⓒ Ⓓ	84. Ⓐ Ⓑ Ⓒ Ⓓ
10. Ⓐ Ⓑ Ⓒ Ⓓ	35. Ⓐ Ⓑ Ⓒ Ⓓ	60. Ⓐ Ⓑ Ⓒ Ⓓ	85. Ⓐ Ⓑ Ⓒ Ⓓ
11. Ⓐ Ⓑ Ⓒ Ⓓ	36. Ⓐ Ⓑ Ⓒ Ⓓ	61. Ⓐ Ⓑ Ⓒ Ⓓ	86. Ⓐ Ⓑ Ⓒ Ⓓ
12. Ⓐ Ⓑ Ⓒ Ⓓ	37. Ⓐ Ⓑ Ⓒ Ⓓ	62. Ⓐ Ⓑ Ⓒ Ⓓ	87. Ⓐ Ⓑ Ⓒ Ⓓ
13. Ⓐ Ⓑ Ⓒ Ⓓ	38. Ⓐ Ⓑ Ⓒ Ⓓ	63. Ⓐ Ⓑ Ⓒ Ⓓ	88. Ⓐ Ⓑ Ⓒ Ⓓ
14. Ⓐ Ⓑ Ⓒ Ⓓ	39. Ⓐ Ⓑ Ⓒ Ⓓ	64. Ⓐ Ⓑ Ⓒ Ⓓ	89. Ⓐ Ⓑ Ⓒ Ⓓ
15. Ⓐ Ⓑ Ⓒ Ⓓ	40. Ⓐ Ⓑ Ⓒ Ⓓ	65. Ⓐ Ⓑ Ⓒ Ⓓ	90. Ⓐ Ⓑ Ⓒ Ⓓ
16. Ⓐ Ⓑ Ⓒ Ⓓ	41. Ⓐ Ⓑ Ⓒ Ⓓ	66. Ⓐ Ⓑ Ⓒ Ⓓ	91. Ⓐ Ⓑ Ⓒ Ⓓ
17. Ⓐ Ⓑ Ⓒ Ⓓ	42. Ⓐ Ⓑ Ⓒ Ⓓ	67. Ⓐ Ⓑ Ⓒ Ⓓ	92. Ⓐ Ⓑ Ⓒ Ⓓ
18. Ⓐ Ⓑ Ⓒ Ⓓ	43. Ⓐ Ⓑ Ⓒ Ⓓ	68. Ⓐ Ⓑ Ⓒ Ⓓ	93. Ⓐ Ⓑ Ⓒ Ⓓ
19. Ⓐ Ⓑ Ⓒ Ⓓ	44. Ⓐ Ⓑ Ⓒ Ⓓ	69. Ⓐ Ⓑ Ⓒ Ⓓ	94. Ⓐ Ⓑ Ⓒ Ⓓ
20. Ⓐ Ⓑ Ⓒ Ⓓ	45. Ⓐ Ⓑ Ⓒ Ⓓ	70. Ⓐ Ⓑ Ⓒ Ⓓ	95. Ⓐ Ⓑ Ⓒ Ⓓ
21. Ⓐ Ⓑ Ⓒ Ⓓ	46. Ⓐ Ⓑ Ⓒ Ⓓ	71. Ⓐ Ⓑ Ⓒ Ⓓ	96. Ⓐ Ⓑ Ⓒ Ⓓ
22. Ⓐ Ⓑ Ⓒ Ⓓ	47. Ⓐ Ⓑ Ⓒ Ⓓ	72. Ⓐ Ⓑ Ⓒ Ⓓ	97. Ⓐ Ⓑ Ⓒ Ⓓ
23. Ⓐ Ⓑ Ⓒ Ⓓ	48. Ⓐ Ⓑ Ⓒ Ⓓ	73. Ⓐ Ⓑ Ⓒ Ⓓ	98. Ⓐ Ⓑ Ⓒ Ⓓ
24. Ⓐ Ⓑ Ⓒ Ⓓ	49. Ⓐ Ⓑ Ⓒ Ⓓ	74. Ⓐ Ⓑ Ⓒ Ⓓ	99. Ⓐ Ⓑ Ⓒ Ⓓ
25. Ⓐ Ⓑ Ⓒ Ⓓ	50. Ⓐ Ⓑ Ⓒ Ⓓ	75. Ⓐ Ⓑ Ⓒ Ⓓ	100. Ⓐ Ⓑ Ⓒ Ⓓ

Practice Test Answer Sheets

Begin Essay 1 on this page. If necessary, continue on the next page.

_____

_____

_____

_____

_____

_____

_____

_____

_____

_____

_____

_____

_____

_____

Continue on the next page if necessary.

Continuation of your essay from previous page, if necessary.

Begin Essay 2 on this page. If necessary, continue on the next page.

Continue on the next page if necessary.

Continuation of your essay from previous page, if necessary.

Practice Test 1

1. Six employees at a circuit board factory—strangers to each other—are chosen to compose a new work team. So that the workers might get to know each other better, they are asked to arrange short, one-on-one introductory meetings with each other. If every worker meets individually with each of the other team members, how many one-on-one meetings will there be?

   A. 12

   B. 36

   C. 15

   D. 18

2. The distance from Tami's house to Ken's house is 3 miles. The distance from Ken's house to The Soda Depot is 2 miles. Which of the following statements are true?

   I. The greatest possible distance between Tami's house and The Soda Depot is five miles.

   II. The greatest possible distance between Tami's house and The Soda Depot is six miles.

   III. The shortest possible distance between Tami's house and The Soda Depot is one mile.

   IV. The shortest possible distance between Tami's house and The Soda Depot is two miles.

   A. I and III only

   B. I and IV only

   C. II and III only

   D. II and IV only

3. Use the figure to answer the question that follows.

    ```
    ┌─────────────────┐
    │  75 MPH         │
    │  MAXIMUM        │
    │                 │
    │  40 MPH         │
    │  MINIMUM        │
    └─────────────────┘
    ```

    Which inequality describes the allowable speeds indicated by the speed limit sign?

    A. $75 \le x \le 40$

    B. $75 < x > 40$

    C. $40 \le x \le 75$

    D. $40 < x > 75$

4. Which types of graphs or charts would be appropriate for displaying the following information?

    Favorite lunch foods of 40 surveyed 6th graders

Pizza	18
Chicken Nuggets	12
Macaroni and Cheese	4
Tacos	4
Hamburgers	2

    I.   bar graph
    II. circle (pie) chart
    III. scatter plot
    IV. broken-line graph

    A. I and II only

    B. III and IV only

    C. I and III only

    D. II and IV only

5. Which of the following illustrates the Distributive Property?

    A. Multiplying 23 by 16 gives the same product as multiplying 16 by 23.

    B. 65, 70, and 12 can be added together in any order; the sum will always be the same.

    C. The sum of 102 and 9 is the same as the sum of 9 and 102.

    D. The product of 3 and 42 is the same as the sum of the products 3×2 and 3×40.

6. Which of the following words is derived from Latin roots?

    A. learning

    B. explain

    C. dynamic

    D. choreograph

Read the passage below; then answer the question that follows.

NOW when the child of morning, rosy-fingered Dawn, appeared, Telemachus rose and dressed himself. He bound his sandals on to his comely feet, girded his sword about his shoulder, and left his room looking like an immortal god. . . . Aegyptius, a man bent double with age, and of infinite experience, the first to speak. His son Antiphus had gone with Ulysses to Ilius, land of noble steeds, but the savage Cyclops had killed him when they were all shut up in the cave . . .

(**Odyssey**, Book II, Homer)

7. In the passage, figures of speech such as epithets (rosy-fingered Dawn, land of noble steeds) and similes (like an immortal god) are used in order to:

        I. add vivid and lifelike detail to the narrative.
      II. highlight the author's originality of style.
    III. make the oral recitation of the poem more understandable to a largely illiterate audience.

    A. I and III

    B. II only

    C. II and III

    D. I, II and III

8. The literary technique of foreshadowing is often used

    A. in novels, short stories and drama to manifest the characters' emotions by reflecting them in the natural world.

    B. in novels, short stories and drama to hint at future developments in the plot.

    C. in lyric poetry to manifest the speaker's emotions by reflecting them in the natural world.

    D. in myths and ballads to hint at future developments in the plot.

9. Which line on the chart best matches the resources with the historical question that is being asked?

Line	Historical Research Question	Source of Information
1	How many people were living in Boston, MA, during the time of the American Revolution?	Historical atlas
2	What role did Fort Mackinac fulfill during the American Revolution?	Encyclopedia article
3	How did the average temperatures and snowfall during the winter of 1775–1776 compare with previous winters?	Historical almanac
4	When was the first U.S. treaty signed and what were the terms of the treaty?	Government publication

A. line 1

B. line 2

C. line 3

D. line 4

DIRECTIONS: Use the passages below, adapted from Herodotus's *Histories*, to answer the two questions that follow.

Passage A: I think, too, that those Egyptians who dwell below the lake of Moiris and especially in that region which is called the Delta, if that land continues to grow in height according to this proportion and to increase similarly in extent, will suffer for all remaining time, from the Nile not overflowing their land, that same thing which they themselves said that the Hellenes would at some time suffer: for hearing that the whole land of the Hellenes has rain and is not watered by rivers as theirs is, they said that the Hellenes would at some time be disappointed of a great hope and would suffer the ills of famine. This saying means that if the god shall not send them rain, but shall allow drought to prevail for a long time, the Hellenes will be destroyed by hunger; for they have in fact no other supply of water to save them except from Zeus alone. This has been rightly said by the Egyptians with reference to the Hellenes: but now let me tell how matters are with the Egyptians themselves in their turn.

Passage B: If, in accordance with what I before said, their land below Memphis (for this is that which is increasing) shall continue to increase in height according to the same proportion as in the past time, assuredly those Egyptians who dwell here will suffer famine, if their land shall not have rain nor the river be able to go over their fields. It is certain however that now they gather in fruit from the earth with less labour than any other men and also with less than the other Egyptians; for they have no labour in breaking up furrows with a plough nor in hoeing nor in any other of those labours which other men have about a crop; but when the river has come up of itself and watered their fields and after watering has left them again, then each man sows his own field and turns into it swine, and when he has trodden the seed into the ground by means of the swine, after that he waits for the harvest, and when he has threshed the corn by means of the swine, then he gathers it in.

10. Which of the following best states the main issues being discussed in the above passages?

   A.   Ancient Egyptians were so dependent upon the Nile River that one's location determined one's prosperity.

   B.   The Nile River was so important to the prosperity of ancient Egyptians that it determined where many Egyptians settled.

   C.   Egyptians who depend upon the Nile River for irrigation will not suffer from famine as those who depend upon rain.

   D.   Egyptians settling in the Delta were dependent upon religion because irrigation from rain was more unpredictable than the Nile.

11. Herodotus, in passage A, could best support assertions made in the passage by presenting which of the following types of evidence?

   A.   Data showing the productivity of Egyptian farmers in both the Delta and Memphis regions.

   B.   Data showing the average rainfall in the Delta as compared to average rainfall in Memphis.

   C.   Data showing the cycle of flooding along the Nile as compared to the cycles of rainfall in the Delta.

   D.   Data showing the wealth of Egyptians in the Delta as compared to the wealth of Egyptians in Memphis.

DIRECTIONS: Use the information below to answer the three questions that follow.

An experiment is planned to test the effect of microwave radiation on the success of seed germination. One hundred corn seeds will be divided into four sets of twenty-five each. Seeds in Group 1 will be microwaved for one minute, seeds in Group 2 for two minutes, and seeds in Group 3 for ten minutes. Seeds in Group 4 will not be placed in the microwave. Each group of seeds will be soaked overnight and placed between the folds of water-saturated newspaper.

12. When purchasing the seeds at the store, no single package contained enough seeds for the entire project; most contain about thirty seeds per package. Which of the following is an acceptable approach for testing the hypothesis?

    I.   Purchase one packet from each of four different brands of seed, one packet for each test group.

    II.   Purchase one packet from each of four different brands of seed and divide the seeds from each packet equally among the four test groups.

    III.   Purchase four packets of the same brand, one packet for each test group.

    IV.   Purchase four packets of the same brand, and divide the seeds from each packet equally among the four test groups.

    A.   I and II only

    B.   II and IV only

    C.   III and IV only

    D.   IV only

13. During the measurement of seed and root length, it is noted that many of the roots are not growing straight. Efforts to manually straighten the roots for measurement are only minimally successful, as the roots are fragile and susceptible to breakage. Which of the following approaches is consistent with the stated hypothesis?

    A.   At the end of the experiment, straighten the roots and measure them.

    B.   Use a string as a flexible measuring instrument for curved roots.

    C.   Record the mass instead of length as an indicator of growth.

    D.   Record only the number of seeds that have sprouted, regardless of length.

14. In presenting the results of this experiment, which of the following could be used to present the data to confirm or refute the hypothesis?

  I. A single bar graph with one bar for each test group indicating the number of days until the first seed sprouts.

  II. A pie chart for each test group showing the percent of seeds in that group that sprouted.

  III. A line graph plotting the total number of sprouted seeds from all test groups vs. time (experiment day).

  IV. A line graph plotting the number of germinated seeds vs. the minutes of time exposed to the microwave.

  A. I only

  B. II only

  C. II and IV only

  D. III and IV only

15. A hot-air balloon rises when propane burners in the basket are used to heat the air inside the balloon. Which of the following statements correctly identifies the explanation for this phenomenon?

  A. Heated gas molecules move faster inside the balloon; their force striking the inside causes the balloon to rise.

  B. Hot gas molecules are themselves larger than cool gas molecules, resulting in the expansion of the gas.

  C. The amount of empty space between gas molecules increases as the temperature of the gas increases, resulting in the expansion of the gas.

  D. The combustion of propane releases product gases that are lighter than air which are trapped in the balloon, causing it to rise.

16. A marble and a feather are both released at the same time inside a tube that is held at very low pressure (a near vacuum). Which of the following correctly links the observation to the explanation?

  A. The marble falls faster because it is heavier.

  B. The marble falls faster because it has less air resistance.

  C. Both fall at the same rate because there is no air resistance in a vacuum.

  D. Both fall at the same rate because the forces of gravity are different in a vacuum.

17. One advantage of using interactive CD-ROM technology is that students have the opportunity to actually observe demonstrations of how such phenomena as sound waves work. Teaching students by allowing them to see the natural phenomenon of sound waves taking place instead of merely offering complex theoretical descriptions of sound waves is most important for students at what stage of development?

    A.   Piaget's sensorimotor stage

    B.   Piaget's concrete operational stage

    C.   Piaget's formal operational stage

    D.   Piaget's interpersonal concordance stage

18. Objectives given to a class for student mastery

    A.   should be tailored to students at all levels.

    B.   should be expected to be achieved only by certain students.

    C.   should be ignored when assessing whether a student learned the material.

    D.   are generally unnecessary.

19. Piaget's theory of cognitive development states that

    A.   children should be able to understand complex directions.

    B.   younger children are unable to understand complex language.

    C.   younger children will be unable to understand directions, even in simple language.

    D.   directions should not be given to young children.

20. Children under the age of eight

    A.   are unable to answer questions.

    B.   process information more slowly than older children.

    C.   can answer the same questions as slightly older children.

    D.   cannot learn in a cooperative environment.

21. What does it mean that multiplication and division are *inverse operations*?

    A.   Multiplication is commutative, whereas division is not. For example, 4×2 gives the same product as 2×4, but $4 \div 2$ is not the same as $2 \div 4$.

    B.   Whether multiplying or dividing a value by 1, the value remains the same. For example, 9×1 equals 9; $9 \div 1$ also equals 9.

    C.   When performing complex calculations involving several operations, all multiplication must be completed before completing any division, such as in $8 \div 2 \times 4 + 7 - 1$.

    D.   The operations "undo" each other. For example, multiplying 11 by 3 gives 33. Dividing 33 by 3 then takes you back to 11.

22. One day, 31 students were absent from Pierce Middle School. If that represents about 5.5% of the students, what is the population of the school?

    A. 177

    B. 517

    C. 564

    D. 171

23. Which of the following are equivalent to 0.5%?
    I. One-half of one percent
    II. 5%
    III. 1/200
    IV. 0.05

    A. I and III only

    B. I and IV only

    C. II and III only

    D. II and IV only

24. The United States Constitution defines the powers of the United States Congress and the states. The U.S. Constitution reserves powers to the states in the 10th Amendment, while Article I, Section 8 of the U.S. Constitution delegates powers to the federal government. Some powers are shared concurrently between the states and federal government. Which of the following powers are concurrent powers?
    I. Lay and collect taxes
    II. Regulate commerce
    III. Establish post offices
    IV. Borrow money

    A. I and II only

    B. II and III only

    C. III and IV only

    D. I and IV only

25. The United States has a two-party system while several European governments have a multiparty system. Which of the following statements is true about political parties in the United States but not true about political parties in multiparty European governments?

    A. Political parties form coalitions in order to advance their policy initiatives through Congress.

    B. Single-member district voting patterns clearly identify candidates for seats in political offices.

    C. Parties provide candidates for office and organize campaigns to get the candidate elected.

    D. Political parties are linked to religious, regional, or social class groupings.

26. The Pacific Northwest receives the greatest annual precipitation in the United States. Which of the following statements best identifies the reason that this occurs?

   A. The jet stream moving south from Canada is responsible for pushing storms through the region.

   B. The region's mountains along the coast cause air masses to rise and cool, thereby reducing their moisture-carrying capacity.

   C. Numerous storms originating in Asia build in intensity as they move across the Pacific Ocean and then dump their precipitation upon reaching land.

   D. The ocean breezes push moisture-laden clouds and fog into the coastal region, producing humid, moist conditions that result in precipitation.

27. Light is refracted when it passes across a boundary between media with different densities. This can occur between solids, liquids, gases, or can result from differences within the same phase. The longer wavelengths of light are refracted less than the shorter wavelengths. Which of the following correctly places the colors of the visible spectrum in order from lowest extent of refraction to highest?

   A. Blue/Violet – Green – Orange – Yellow – Red

   B. Blue/Violet – Green – Yellow – Orange – Red

   C. Red – Yellow – Green – Orange – Blue/Violet

   D. Red – Orange – Yellow – Green – Blue/Violet

28. Around the time of World War II, the chemical industry developed several new classes of insecticide that were instrumental in protecting our soldiers from pest-borne diseases common to the tropic regions they were fighting in. These same insecticides found widespread use at home to increase production of many agricultural crops by reducing the damage from insects like cotton weevils and grasshoppers. While farmers continued to use the same levels of insecticide, over time it was found that the insect population was increasing. Identify the best explanation for this observation:

   A. Insecticides, like most chemicals, lose their potency when stored.

   B. The insect population was increasing to reach the carrying capacity of a given ecosystem.

   C. The initial doses of pesticide were too low to effectively kill the insects.

   D. Insects with a tolerance to insecticide survived the initial doses and lived to produce insecticide-resistant offspring.

29. Under the right conditions of temperature and pressure, any type of rock can be transformed into another type of rock in a process called the Rock Cycle. Which of the following processes is not a part of the Rock Cycle?

   A. the drifting and encroachment of sand at the edge of a desert

   B. the melting of rock beneath the surface to form magma

   C. the erosion of sedimentary rocks to form sand

   D. the eruption of a cinder cone volcano

30. Every good children's nonfiction book should have which *one* of the following features?

    A. a timeline

    B. engaging characters

    C. a useful index

    D. tables and charts

31. Lois Lowry's *Number the Stars* is an example of

    A. historical fiction.

    B. epic poetry.

    C. fantasy.

    D. nonfiction.

32. Picture books can be used, even in upper elementary grades, to

    I.   subtly affirm classroom members' cultural values.
    II. help younger students predict what will happen next.
    III. pronounce difficult words.
    IV. help children identify with a main character's point of view.

    A. I and III only

    B. II and IV only

    C. I, II, and IV only

    D. I, II, III, and IV

33. In the lines from his poem "Stopping by Woods on a Snowy Evening" Robert Frost used what literary device in these lines: "My little horse must think it queer / To stop without a farmhouse near"?

    A. personification

    B. metaphor

    C. simile

    D. alliteration

34. Which equation could be used to answer the following question?

    Together, a pen and a pencil cost $2.59 (ignoring tax). The pen cost $1.79 more than the pencil. What was the cost of the pencil?

    A. $x = (2.59 - 1.79) \times 2$

    B. $2.59 = x - 1.79$

    C. $2.59 = x + (x + 1.79)$

    D. $x = 2.59 - 1.79$

35. Use the figure to answer the question that follows.

    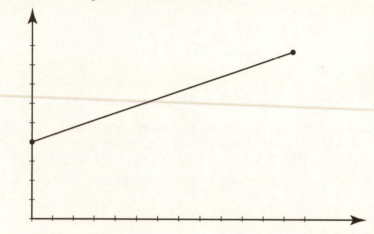

    Which of the following situations might the graph illustrate?
    - I.   The varying speed of an experienced runner over the course of a 26-mile race.
    - II. The number of households a census taker still has to visit over the course of a week.
    - III. The value of a savings account over time, assuming steady growth.
    - IV. The changing height of a sunflower over several months.

    A. I and II only

    B. III and IV only

    C. II, III, and IV only

    D. I, III, and IV only

36. Which of the following best describes the western, or Pacific, region of Canada comprising British Columbia and the Yukon?

    A. The area contains many uninhabitable areas, including a mix of arid desert-like terrain and rugged mountain ranges that hinder rail and car transportation, resulting in minimal population settlement.

    B. The area contains arid deserts and vast grasslands that are ideal for cattle farming and oil production.

    C. The area contains the vast majority of Canada's natural resources and the majority of Canada's population.

    D. The area contains fifty percent of Canada's population, resulting in seventy percent of Canada's manufacturing.

DIRECTIONS: Read the following passage and answer the question that follows.

The Police believed that Dollree Mapp was hiding a person suspected in a crime. The police went to her home in Cleveland, Ohio, knocked, and requested entry. Mapp refused. After more officers arrived on the scene, police forced their way into Mapp's house. During the police search of the house they found pornographic books, pictures, and photographs. They arrested Mapp and charged her with violating an Ohio law against possession of pornographic materials. Mapp and her attorney appealed the case to the Supreme Court of Ohio. The Ohio Supreme Court ruled in favor of the police. Mapp's case was then appealed to the Supreme Court of the United States. Mapp and her attorney asked the Supreme Court to determine whether or not evidence obtained through a search that violated the Fourth Amendment was admissible in state courts. The U.S. Supreme Court, in the case ***Mapp v. Ohio***, ruled that evidence obtained in a search that violates the Fourth Amendment is not admissible. The majority opinion states, "Our decision, founded on reason and truth, gives to the individual no more than that which the Constitution guarantees him, to the police officer no less than that to which honest law enforcement is entitled, and, to the courts, that judicial integrity so necessary in the true administration of justice."

37. The excerpt above best illustrates which of the following features of judicial proceedings in the United States?

    A. due process of law

    B. a fair and speedy trial

    C. judicial review

    D. the exclusionary rule

38. Which of the following statements are true about economic activity in Massachusetts?
    I. Military spending has indirectly stimulated the manufacturing sector of Massachusetts' economy in the past 25 years.
    II. Agriculture remained a vibrant force in Massachusetts well into the mid-19th century.
    III. Massachusetts is in the top 20 states in terms of gross state product.
    IV. The tourism industry and service sector in Massachusetts employ fewer people than the printing and publishing industry.

    A. I and II only

    B. I and III only

    C. II and III only

    D. II and IV only

39. Which of the following statements best defines the role of the World Trade Organization (WTO)?

    A. It resolves trade disputes and attempts to formulate policy to open world markets to free trade through monetary policy and regulation of corruption.

    B. It is an advocate for human rights and democracy by regulating child labor and providing economic aid to poor countries.

    C. It establishes alliances to regulate disputes and polices ethnic intimidation.

    D. It regulates trade within the United States in order to eliminate monopolistic trade practices.

40. The drought of the 1930s that spanned an area from Texas to North Dakota was caused by
    I. overgrazing and overuse of farmland.
    II. natural phenomena, such as below-average rainfall and wind erosion.
    III. environmental factors, such as changes in the jet stream.
    IV. the lack of government subsidies for new irrigation technology.

    A. I and II only

    B. II and III only

    C. I and III only

    D. II and IV only

41. The atmospheres of the Moon and some planets were studied using telescopes and spectrophotometers long before the deployment of interplanetary space probes. In these studies, scientists examined the spectral patterns of sunlight that passed through the atmosphere of distant objects to learn what elements make up those atmospheres. Which of the following explains the source of the black-line spectral patterns?

    A. When an element is excited, it gives off light in a characteristic spectral pattern.

    B. When light strikes an object, some wavelengths of light are absorbed by the surface and others are reflected to give the object its color.

    C. When light passes through a gas, light is absorbed at wavelengths characteristic of the elements in the gas.

    D. The black lines are the spectra of ultraviolet light, which is called black light because it cannot be seen with human eyes.

42. We may be told to "gargle with saltwater" when we suffer from a sore throat. Which of the following phenomena would be used to explain this advice?

    A. lowering of vapor pressure

    B. increasing osmotic pressure

    C. increasing boiling point

    D. decreasing freezing point

43. An IEP for a student with a learning disability might do all of the following EXCEPT

    A. state responsibilities of the parent for the child's learning.

    B. establish to what extent the student will be subject to state and district assessments.

    C. enumerate measurable learning goals and objectives.

    D. state what kind of services will be provided, how often, and by whom.

44. Which one of the following statements concerning the *least restrictive environment* (LRE) is false?

    A. The LRE may be a general classroom for part of the day and a special education room for the rest of the day.

    B. An LRE for an emotionally disturbed student could include a very highly structured behavior management plan, even though other students are not governed by exactly the same plan.

    C. The LRE rarely includes significant time in a general classroom.

    D. The LRE always involves at least some time in a general classroom.

DIRECTIONS: Read the story, and then respond to the two questions that follow.

BESSIE

I began my days as a cow. Well, a calf, to be more precise. I was born to the world a soft tawny color, with liquid brown eyes and soft, floppy ears that begged to be touched. My days were simple. I spent all my time in the company of other bovine females, most especially my mother. She was a prized breeder, my mother; as a result it was my misfortune to be weaned earlier than most other calves.

Only hours after my weaning, a miraculous event changed the course of my life. Princess Georgette happened to be riding by on her shaggy little pony, alongside her nanny, when she heard my lows of despair and turned.

"Whatever could be making that pitiful noise?" she asked aloud.

One of the farmers called out to her, "'Tis only a wee calf, Highness. She'll not be at it long, I assure you."

"I shall see the creature at once," she ordered, pulling her pony up against the rail and dismounting.

At this point, I had moved hopefully toward the commotion, and, as I inched my tender nose out of the barn to investigate, I came face-to-face with the oddest-looking creature I had seen so far in my somewhat short existence. She had outrageous red curls rioting all over her head, and tumbling down over her shoulders. The thing I noticed most, though, was her hopelessly freckled nose, which, at that moment, was uncomfortably close to my own. So close, in fact, that I decided to remedy my discomfort, and did so by lowing rather loudly in her petulant little face. To my astonishment, she giggled with delight at my rudeness, and reached out to stroke my furry forehead. I found myself nuzzling up to her small chest. "Oh Nan, I must have it. Such a funny furry thing must be kept in my garden where I might entertain myself endlessly with it."

So that is how I became a member of the royal household.

My days fell into an odd sort of routine. I spent my mornings cropping on the lawns and shrubs until Georgette would appear, luring me into the hedge ways with a handful of cresses nipped from the kitchen. As soon as I got close enough and started to nibble, she would shriek, and startle me into a canter, at which she would chase me into the hedges until I was so thoroughly lost, I would have to low helplessly until Georgette found me.

Tragically, calves do not stay calves forever. As the seasons passed, her interest in our games began to wane. The gardeners had, at this time, gotten very tired of working around me as I lumbered through the hedges. They communicated up through the chain of command, straight to the king himself, their wish to be rid of me. He dismissed the problem with an order to have me put down.

Georgette pouted at this and stamped her foot, but her father would not budge an inch. "Now, don't get missish with me, Georgette. I've given the order, and I'll see it done as I've dictated whether you like it or not."

Georgette, during this speech, had become thoughtful. After a long pause, she proposed: "Well, if I must see my Bessie put down as you've said, mightn't I get a handbag and boots out of her at least?"

"Very well," sighed her father.

For my part, it was a stroke of luck that this conversation had taken place just on the other side of the hedge where I had been, only moments before, contently munching on the last bit of clover to be found this season. Naturally, I took exception to being discussed in such a candid manner. In fact, I could not believe my furry, floppy ears. I felt myself slipping into a sort of self-pity, and walked away. When I passed the westernmost gate, it occurred to me that I might not have to face my doom. This door, that was normally latched and guarded, stood open. I was out that gate and on the lane nearby in an instant.

I wandered aimlessly for hours, when I abruptly came upon a little clearing. A stream ran through it, past the coziest of tiny cottages. I trotted straight over to the stream and began drinking in long draughts. After several moments of such behavior, I became aware of another presence nearby. It was a small, old man, leaning toward me in a strange sort of furry robe, and balancing himself on the most incredibly gnarled staff, and holding a silver bucket that steamed and hissed, yet smelled overwhelmingly delicious.

"Hello," he said in a pleasant tone. "I'm happy you have finally arrived. I read it in *The Book*. Would you care to drink from my bucket?" he asked. . . .

45.   This is the beginning of a story. To what genre does it belong?

   A.   poetry

   B.   historical fiction

   C.   nonfiction

   D.   fantasy

46.   If you were going to ask the children to finish this story as a writing activity, what would you do next?

   A.   Have them complete a worksheet about the vocabulary words.

   B.   Ask them to diagram the first sentence.

   C.   Ask them to form small groups and talk about what might happen next.

   D.   Have them complete a Venn diagram about Bessie and a real cow.

47.   The invention of the printing press led indirectly to the standardization of English spelling because

   A.   more and more people could afford to buy dictionaries.

   B.   the need for standardized spelling became more apparent as material written in English became more widely available and literacy increased.

   C.   the publication of Latin and Greek classics resulted in the development of English dictionaries.

   D.   people became more literate by reading religious literature.

Read the sentence below; then answer the question that follows.

The artist's growing fascination with African sculpture, and his interest in mysterious and enigmatic themes, were evident not only in the bold contours of his later paintings but also in the juxtaposition of unexpected elements.

48. The above sentence is an example of formal diction rather than colloquial diction because

    A. its structure is governed by rigorous rules.

    B. it contains a "not only . . . but also" construction.

    C. it uses words such as "unexpected" and "mysterious."

    D. it talks about an academic subject such as the fine arts.

49. The poetic genres of epic poetry, elegies, and ballads can be distinguished in that

    A. elegies and epic poems celebrate heroic deeds or philosophical ideas; ballads have a songlike structure.

    B. ballads commemorate the life of someone who has died; elegies and epic poems have a narrative structure.

    C. epic poems may consider philosophical ideas; elegies and ballads usually consider lively or comical subjects.

    D. elegies commemorate the life of someone who has died; ballads and many epic poems have a narrative structure.

50. Use the figure to answer the question that follows.

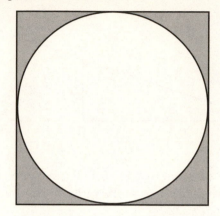

What is the approximate area of the shaded region, given that:

    a.   the radius of the circle is 6 units

    b.   the square inscribes the circle

A.   106 square units

B.   31 square units

C.   77 square units

D.   125 square units

51. How many lines of symmetry do all non-square rectangles have?

A.   0

B.   2

C.   4

D.   8

52. Use the figure to answer the question that follows.

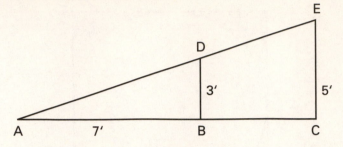

The figure above is a sketch of a ramp. Given that the two ramp supports (DB and EC) are perpendicular to the ground, and the dimensions of the various parts are as noted, what is the approximate distance from point B to point C?

A. 4.7 feet

B. 4.5 feet

C. 4.3 feet

D. 4.1 feet

53. Bemus School is conducting a lottery to raise funds for new band uniforms. Exactly 1000 tickets will be printed and sold. Only one ticket stub will be drawn from a drum to determine the single winner of a big-screen television. All tickets have equal chances of winning. The first 700 tickets are sold to 700 different individuals. The remaining 300 tickets are sold to Mr. Greenfield.

Given the information above, which of the following statements are true?

  I. It is impossible to tell in advance who will win.
  II. Mr. Greenfield will probably win.
  III. Someone other than Mr. Greenfield will probably win.
  IV. The likelihood that Mr. Greenfield will win is the same as the likelihood that someone else will win.

A. I and II only

B. I and III only

C. II and IV only

D. III and IV only

54. Which of the following would be considered a primary source in researching the factors that influenced U.S. involvement in the Korean War?

      I.   The personal correspondence of a military man stationed with the 5th Regimental Combat Team (RCT) in Korea.

      II.   A biography of Harry S. Truman by David McCullough, published in 1993.

      III.   A journal article about the beginning of the Korean War by a noted scholar.

      IV.   An interview with Secretary of Defense George Marshall.

    A.   I and II only

    B.   II and IV only

    C.   II and III only

    D.   I and IV only

55. Which of the following was *not* a major Native American tribe that resided in or near Massachusetts before the 1700s?

    A.   the Iroquois

    B.   the Niantic

    C.   the Pequot

    D.   the Wampanoag

56. Which of the following best describes a major difference between a state government and the federal government?

    A.   State governments have more responsibility for public education than the federal government.

    B.   State governments are more dependent upon the personal income tax for revenue than the federal government.

    C.   State governments are more dependent upon the system of checks and balances than the federal government.

    D.   State governments are subject to term limits, whereas federal government representatives serve unlimited terms.

57. Identify the incorrect statement from the following:

    A.   Heredity is the study of how traits are passed from parent to offspring.

    B.   The chemical molecule that carries an organism's genetic makeup is called DNA.

    C.   Sections of the DNA molecule that determine specific traits are called chromosomes.

    D.   The genetic makeup of an organism is altered through bioengineering.

58. Which of the following sources of energy is nonrenewable?

    A. hydrogen-cell

    B. geothermal

    C. nuclear

    D. hydroelectric

59. To move a heavy book across a tabletop at a constant speed, a person must continually exert a force on the book. This force is primarily used to overcome which of the following forces?

    A. The force of gravity

    B. The force of air resistance

    C. The force of friction

    D. The weight of the book

60. Which of the following best explains why the boiling point of water is reduced and cooking times are increased at high altitudes?

    A. At high altitudes there is greater atmospheric pressure than at sea level.

    B. At high altitudes there is less oxygen than at sea level.

    C. At high altitudes the vapor pressure of water is reduced because of the reduced atmospheric pressure.

    D. At high altitudes water boils at a lower temperature because of the reduced atmospheric pressure.

61. Which line in the table below correctly matches a major learning theorist with the view of learning commonly associated with his work?

Line	Theorist	Description
1	Piaget	The moral/behavioral dimension of learning is of paramount importance; children's intellectual progress cannot overtake their moral development.
2	Kohlberg	All learning can be associated with a hierarchical pyramid.
3	Bandura	Young children learn through models in four stages: attention, retention, reproduction, and reinforcement.
4	Vygotsky	Students are best taught by peers at about the same level of intellectual development.

    A. Line 1

    B. Line 2

    C. Line 3

    D. Line 4

62. Because advocates of the information processing model of learning believe human minds function much like computers, they believe which of the following should be a feature of classroom learning?

    A.   Emphasize memorization

    B.   Let students first learn information through their own reading

    C.   Help students connect the new information to what they already know

    D.   Draw mathematical connections among facts taught

63. The "zone of proximal development" is a concept introduced by

    A.   Piaget

    B.   Skinner

    C.   Bandura

    D.   Vygotsky

64. The novel *The Adventures of Huckleberry Finn*, by Mark Twain, has been a subject of controversy because:

    A.   it contains graphic descriptions of violence considered unsuitable for young readers.

    B.   it challenged attitudes toward race in America.

    C.   it portrays a hostile relationship between a young boy and an escaping slave.

    D.   it was thought to have influenced the outcome of the Civil War.

65. The Japanese form of poetry called haiku is known for its

    A.   brevity and concision.

    B.   elaborate and flowery description.

    C.   logic and directness of statement.

    D.   humor and lifelike detail.

66. Which author wrote: "What's in a name? That which we call a rose/ By any other name would smell as sweet"?

    A.   Christopher Marlowe

    B.   Ben Johnson

    C.   William Shakespeare

    D.   Geoffrey Chaucer

67. Contemporary writers of world literature, such as Chinua Achebe, have emphasized which of the following themes?

    A.   imperialism and the impact of Western culture on traditional societies

    B.   conflicts between traditional and modern ways of life

    C.   the living conditions and problems of everyday life in developing nations

    D.   all of the above

Read the poem below; then answer the question that follows.

When I heard the Learn'd Astronomer
Walt Whitman

> WHEN I heard the learn'd astronomer;
> When the proofs, the figures, were ranged in columns before me;
> When I was shown the charts and the diagrams, to add, divide, and
>   measure them;
> When I, sitting, heard the astronomer, where he lectured with much
>   applause in the lecture-room,
> How soon, unaccountable, I became tired and sick;
> Till rising and gliding out, I wander'd off by myself,
> In the mystical moist night-air, and from time to time,
> Look'd up in perfect silence at the stars.

68. This poem

    A.   is an example of lyric poetry because it reveals the speaker's personal thoughts.

    B.   explicitly emphasizes the superiority of higher learning over personal experience.

    C.   makes extensive use of alliteration and assonance.

    D.   highlights the psychological alienation and uncertainty characteristic of the Modernist movement.

69. Matt earned the following scores on his first six weekly mathematics tests: 91%, 89%, 82%, 95%, 86%, and 79%.

    He had hoped for an average (mean) of 90% at this point, which would just barely give him an A– in math class on his first report card. How many more total percentage points should Matt have earned over the course of those six weeks to qualify for an A–?

    A.   87

    B.   3

    C.   90

    D.   18

70. Ms. Williams plans to buy carpeting for her living room floor. The room is a rectangle measuring 14 feet by 20 feet. She wants no carpet seams on her floor, even if that means that some carpeting will go to waste. The carpeting she wants comes in 16-foot-wide rolls. What is the minimum amount of carpeting that will have to be wasted if Ms. Williams insists upon her no-seams requirement?

    A.   40 square feet

    B.   60 square feet

    C.   80 square feet

    D.   100 square feet

71. Use the figure to answer the question that follows.

    Consider this sequence of calculator keystrokes:

    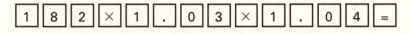

    That sequence would be useful for finding which of the following values?

    A.   The total distance an automobile travels if it covers 182 miles one day, but only 1.03 and 1.04 miles over the next two days.

    B.   The amount of money in a savings account after the original deposit of $182 earns 3% and then 4% simple annual interest over two years.

    C.   The total distance an automobile travels if it covers 182 miles one day, 103 miles the next day, and 104 miles the third day.

    D.   The amount of money in a savings account after the original deposit of $182 grows by $1.03 and $1.04 in interest over two days.

72. The Silk Road did not connect to which of the following countries?

    A.   China

    B.   Greece

    C.   Iran

    D.   India

73. The characteristics of fascism include all of the following EXCEPT

    A.   democracy.

    B.   totalitarianism.

    C.   romanticism.

    D.   militarism.

74. The industrial economy of the nineteenth century was based upon all of the following EXCEPT

    A. the availability of raw materials.

    B. an equitable distribution of profits among those involved in production.

    C. the availability of capital.

    D a distribution system to market finished products.

75. The term "Trail of Tears" refers to

    A. the Mormon migration from Nauvoo, Illinois, to what is now Utah.

    B. the forced migration of the Cherokee tribe from the southern Appalachians to what is now Oklahoma.

    C. the westward migration along the Oregon Trail.

    D. the migration into Kentucky along the Wilderness Road.

76. When a member of the House of Representatives helps a citizen from his or her district receive federal aid to which that citizen is entitled, the representative's action is referred to as

    A. casework.

    B. pork barrel legislation.

    C. lobbying.

    D. logrolling.

77. Which of the following observations explains the geologic instability surrounding the Pacific Ocean known as the "Ring of Fire"?

    A. Similarities in rock formations and continental coastlines suggest that the Earth's continents were once one landmass.

    B. The Earth's plates collide at convergent margins, separate at divergent margins, and move laterally at transform-fault boundaries.

    C. Earthquakes produce waves that travel through the Earth in all directions.

    D. Volcanoes form when lava accumulates and hardens.

78. The Earth's Moon is

    A. generally closer to the Sun than it is to the Earth.

    B. generally closer to the Earth than to the Sun.

    C. generally equidistant between the Earth and Sun.

    D. closer to the Earth during part of the year, and closer to the Sun for the rest of the year.

79. Which of the following statements is not true?

    A. Infectious diseases are caused by viruses, bacteria, or protists.

    B. Cancers and hereditary diseases can be infectious.

    C. Environmental hazards can cause disease.

    D. The immune system protects the body from disease.

80. Which one of the following statements about gifted and talented students is NOT generally true?

    A. They can become impatient with others.

    B. They are more likely to come from higher-level socioeconomic groups.

    C. They often make original contributions in class.

    D. If not pushed toward higher achievement, they can become glib rather than knowledgeable.

81. Which line in the table below DOES NOT correctly match a disability with a true statement about the disability?

Line	Condition	Statement
1	Mental retardation	Indicates significant limitations in cognitive ability
2	Learning disability	Is hard to define but accounts for over 50% of students receiving special educational services nationwide
3	Emotional disturbance	Is often treated with a very structured reward/ punishment system
4	Speech and hearing impairment	Accounts for less than 10% of students receiving special educational services nationwide

    A. Line 1

    B. Line 2

    C. Line 3

    D. Line 4

82. Which one of the following statements about IEPs is true?

    A. IEPs are advisory only; they do not define a teacher's responsibility.

    B. Although assessment methods are on the IEP, the special education teacher or administrator can unilaterally change the assessment method during the year if it is not working out well.

    C. Children under the age of 14 do not have to be present when the IEP is formulated.

    D. IEPs are difficult for all involved; generally the students would be better off without them.

83. According to Bandura's theory of the "self-efficacy appraisal," teachers should

    I. reinforce every new skill learned with repetition and assessment.
    II. allow students to work cooperatively as much as possible.
    III. model respect for others in all aspects of classroom behavior.
    IV. let students know where they stand by frequently ranking them.

    A. I, II, and III only

    B. I and III only

    C. I, II, and IV

    D. I, II, III, and IV

84. The floor of a rectangular room is to be covered in two different types of material. The total cost of covering the entire room is $136.00. The cost of covering the inner rectangle is $80.00. The cost of covering the shaded area is $56.00.

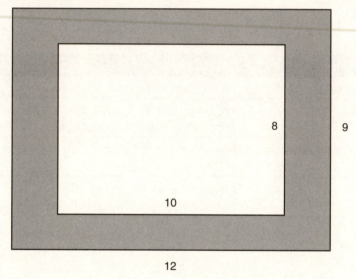

We wish to determine the cost of material per square foot used to cover the shaded area. What information given below is unnecessary for this computation?

    I. The total cost of covering the entire room.
    II. The cost of covering the inner rectangle.
    III. The cost of covering the shaded area.

    A. I only

    B. II only

    C. I and II

    D. I and III

85. The distribution of a high school chorus is depicted in the graph below. There is a total of 132 students in the chorus.

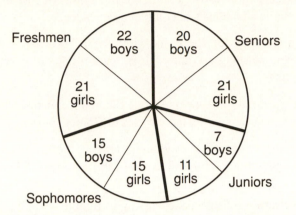

Which of the following expressions represents the percentage of freshman and sophomore girls in the chorus?

A. $\dfrac{21+15}{132} \times 100$

B. $\dfrac{21+15}{132} + 100$

C. $\dfrac{21+15}{132}$

D. $\dfrac{21+15}{100} \times 132$

86. In announcing the Emancipation Proclamation, Lincoln's immediate purpose was to

A. free black slaves in all of the slave states.

B. free black slaves in only the border slave states that had remained loyal to the Union.

C. let the Southern states know that whether or not they chose to secede from the Union, slavery would not be tolerated by his administration once he took office.

D. rally Northern morale by giving the war a higher moral purpose than just preserving the Union.

87. In its decision in the case of ***Dred Scott v. Sanford***, the U.S. Supreme Court held that

A. separate facilities for different races were inherently unequal and therefore unconstitutional.

B. no black slave could be a citizen of the United States.

C. separate but equal facilities for different races were constitutional.

D. Affirmative Action programs were acceptable only when it could be proven that specific previous cases of discrimination had occurred within the institution or business in question.

88. Thomas Paine's pamphlet *Common Sense* was significant in that it

    A. emotionally aroused thousands of colonists to the abuses of British rule, the oppressiveness of the monarchy, and the advantages of colonial independence.

    B. rallied American spirit during the bleak winter of 1776, when it appeared that Washington's forces, freezing and starving at Valley Forge, had no hope of surviving the winter, much less defeating the British.

    C. called for a strong central government to rule the newly independent American states and foresaw the difficulties inherent within the Articles of Confederation.

    D. asserted to its British readers that they could not beat the American colonists militarily unless they could isolate New England from the rest of the American colonies.

89. Mr. Rodriguez has two learning-disabled students in his middle-school world history class. Both have difficulty staying on task during lectures and have difficulty figuring out what to write down. Which one of the following procedures might best help these students learn?

    A. Supplement the lessons by having the two learning-disabled students read fourth-grade textbooks during study time.

    B. Present a partially completed outline to the entire class when presenting new material.

    C. Give the two students rewards such as candy and chips if they improve their test scores.

    D. Ask them to take notes when new material is presented and share it with each other.

90. If a student is usually quick to attempt answers to questions, but very often blurts out the wrong responses, the teacher's best response to the student is to

    A. say, "Wrong answer, but better luck next time."

    B. say, "Well, not exactly. But you're close."

    C. say nothing, but smile and call on someone else.

    D. say, "Why don't I give you another minute to think about that answer?"

91. Which of the following types of pollution or atmospheric phenomena are correctly matched with their underlying causes?
    I. global warming – carbon dioxide and methane
    II. acid rain – sulfur dioxide and nitrogen dioxide
    III. ozone depletion – chlorofluorocarbons and sunlight
    IV. aurora borealis – solar flares and magnetism

    A. I and II only

    B. II and III only

    C. I and IV only

    D. I, II, III, and IV

92. Which of the following characteristics of a sound wave is associated with its pitch?

      I.   Amplitude
     II.   Frequency
    III. Wavelength
    IV. Speed

A. I only

B. II only

C. II and III only

D. IV only

93. Which of the following statements correctly describes each group of vertebrates?

      I.   Amphibians are cold-blooded, spending part of their life cycle in water and part on land.
     II.   Reptiles are generally warm-blooded, having scales that cover their skin.
    III. Fish are cold-blooded, breathing with gills, and covered by scales.
    IV. Mammals are warm-blooded with milk glands and hair.

A. I and IV only

B. I, III, and IV only

C. IV only

D. I, II, III, and IV

94. The needle on the dial points most nearly to which reading?

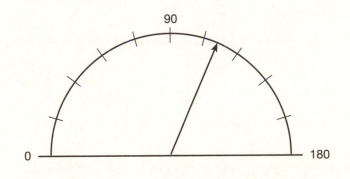

A. 108

B. 128

C. 114

D. 117

95. How many ten thousands are there in one million?

    A. 100

    B. 10

    C. 1,000

    D. 10,000

96. Hamlet's "To be or not to be" speech, in the play by William Shakespeare, is an example of the dramatic technique known as

    A. aside.

    B. dialogue.

    C. soliloquy.

    D. comic relief.

Read the passage below; then answer the three questions that follow.

[1]The pillaging of the human past is a problem the world over, hardly limited to the Mediterranean. [2]To reduce it, all countries that have antiquities at risk should police their historical sites effectively and create programs that teach citizens the value and community importance of local remains. [3]The international trade can also be discouraged by import bans. [4]The UNESCO convention allows the United States to sign bilateral agreements with countries where pillaging is rampant, banning entire categories of objects at risk. [5]Nine such agreements are now in force with countries in Central and South America, Africa, the Mediterranean and Asia. ([6]The agreement with Italy is up for renewal.)

(Bell, Malcolm III, "The Getty Museum's Italian Job," *New York Times*, November 28, 2005.)

97. The above passage uses

    A. a serious tone, to persuade lawmakers to take action to reduce the pillaging of historical artifacts.

    B. a formal tone, to inform newspaper readers of a Unesco convention.

    C. a didactic tone, to instruct students in international policy.

    D. an urgent tone, to convince business leaders of the need for immediate action.

98. A sentence that could be removed without affecting the passage's unity and coherence is

    A.   Sentence 1.

    B.   Sentence 3.

    C.   Sentence 4.

    D.   Sentence 6.

99. Which of the following statements is NOT true regarding the passage?

    A.   In an essay, it could be preceded by reasons and evidence as to why historical artifacts should not be pillaged, and followed by other steps that could be taken to prevent this problem.

    B.   Sentences 2 and 3 mention steps that should be taken to combat the problem of the pillaging of historical artifacts, and Sentences 4 through 6 mention examples of how such steps are being taken.

    C.   The passage has a compare-and-contrast structure.

    D.   The passage would not be the first paragraph of an essay.

100. Which of the following statements about the writing process is not true?

    A.   Prewriting can lay the groundwork for the structure of a paper by organizing ideas and data.

    B.   Research and the formulation of the thesis should always be finished when drafting begins.

    C.   Multiple revisions allow for refining the paper's coherence and unity.

    D.   Final editing should focus on how clearly the paper's wording or style conveys its thesis.

Directions for the Open-Response Item Assignments

This section of the test consists of two open-response item assignments that appear on the following pages. You will be asked to prepare a written response of approximately 150 to 300 words (1 to 2 pages) for each assignment. **You must write responses to both of the assignments.**

For each assignment, read the topic and directions carefully before you begin to work. Think about how you will organize your response.

As a whole, your response to each assignment must demonstrate an understanding of the knowledge of the field. In your response to each assignment, you are expected to demonstrate the depth of your understanding of the subject area by applying your knowledge rather than by merely reciting factual information.

Your response to the assignment will be evaluated based on the following criteria:

- **PURPOSE**: the extent to which the response achieves the purpose of the assignment

- **SUBJECT KNOWLEDGE**: appropriateness and accuracy in the application of subject knowledge

- **SUPPORT**: quality and relevance of supporting evidence

- **RATIONALE**: soundness of argument and degree of understanding of the subject area

The open-response item assignments are intended to assess subject knowledge. Your responses must be communicated clearly enough to permit valid judgment of the evaluation criteria by scorers. Your responses should be written for an audience of educators in this field. The final version of each response should conform to the conventions of edited American English. Your responses should be your original work, written in your own words, and not copied or paraphrased from some other work.

Be sure to write about the assigned topics. Please write legibly. You may not use any reference materials during the test. Remember to review your work and make any changes you think will improve your responses.

Open Response 1

1. Use the information below to complete the exercise that follows.

Mrs. Whalen, a fifth-grade teacher, is assessing Demetrius, a new student to the school, for reading fluency and comprehension. She has him read the following passage aloud.

> My name is Jake. That's my first name, obviously. I can't tell you my last name. It would be too dangerous. The controllers are everywhere. Everywhere. And if they knew my full name, they could find me and my friends, and then . . . well, let's just say I don't want them to find me. What they do to people who resist them is too horrible to think about.
>
> I won't even tell you where I live. You'll just have to trust me that it is a real place, a real town. It may even be *your* town.
>
> I'm writing this all down so that more people will learn the truth. Maybe then, somehow, the human race can survive until the Algonites return and rescue us, as they promised they would. Maybe.
>
> My life used to be normal. Normal, that is, until one Friday night at the mall. I was there with Marco, my best friend. We were playing video games and hanging out at this cool store that sells comic books and stuff. The usual.

Demetrius has trouble pronouncing nearly every word longer than two syllables: "obviously," "controllers," and "Algonites," for example. He also needs help in pronouncing the word "resist." He reads with some expression and fairly quickly, except for the words he stumbles over. When questioned about the content of the passage, he answers as follows:

Mrs. Whalen: Can you tell me something about what you were just reading?

Demetrius: There's a guy who likes video games. I think his name is Jake.

Mrs. Whalen: What can you tell me about Jake?

Demetrius: Well, he's scared. He's in trouble.

Mrs. Whalen: How do you know he's in trouble?

Demetrius: He can't give out his last name.

Mrs. Whalen: Do you have any idea what he's afraid of?

Demetrius: Not really—they're An-guh-...

Mrs. Whalen: The Algonites?

Demetrius: Yeah, them. I guess they're after the whole world.

Based on your knowledge of reading comprehension, write a response that:

- identifies two comprehension needs demonstrated by this student;

- provides evidence for the needs you identify;

- suggests two different instructional strategies to address the needs you identify; and

- explains why these strategies might be effective.

Open Response 2

2. **Read the problem below, then complete the exercise that follows.**

Mr. Del Guercio's class of 22 students had a mean score of 81.8 on the second-quarter district math assessment. Mrs. Prudhomme's class has 23 students, but 4 were absent on the day of the test (all of Mr. Del Guercio's students were present). Mrs. Prudhomme's students who were present earned a mean score of 78.7 on the test. The maximum score on the test is 100. The 4 students who were absent will be making up the test today. Can Mrs. Prudhomme's class overtake Mr. Del Guercio's, and if so, what is the lowest mean score these 4 can attain if Mrs. Prudhomme's class is to have a higher mean than Mr. Del Guercio's?

Use your knowledge of mathematics to create a response in which you analyze and solve this problem. In your response you should:

- describe two prerequisite mathematical skills necessary for solving this problem;

- identify two mathematical concepts involved in solving this problem; and

- solve the given problem, showing your work and justifying the steps you used in arriving at your solution.

General Curriculum

Answers: Practice Test 1

Answer Key

1. (C)	26. (B)	51. (B)	76. (A)
2. (A)	27. (D)	52. (A)	77. (B)
3. (C)	28. (D)	53. (B)	78. (B)
4. (A)	29. (A)	54. (D)	79. (B)
5. (D)	30. (C)	55. (A)	80. (B)
6. (B)	31. (A)	56. (A)	81. (D)
7. (A)	32. (C)	57. (C)	82. (C)
8. (B)	33. (A)	58. (C)	83. (A)
9. (C)	34. (C)	59. (C)	84. (C)
10. (C)	35. (B)	60. (D)	85. (A)
11. (D)	36. (A)	61. (C)	86. (D)
12. (B)	37. (D)	62. (C)	87. (B)
13. (D)	38. (B)	63. (D)	88. (A)
14. (C)	39. (A)	64. (B)	89. (B)
15. (C)	40. (A)	65. (A)	90. (D)
16. (C)	41. (C)	66. (C)	91. (D)
17. (B)	42. (B)	67. (D)	92. (C)
18. (A)	43. (A)	68. (A)	93. (B)
19. (B)	44. (D)	69. (D)	94. (D)
20. (B)	45. (D)	70. (A)	95. (A)
21. (D)	46. (C)	71. (B)	96. (C)
22. (C)	47. (B)	72. (B)	97. (A)
23. (A)	48. (A)	73. (A)	98. (D)
24. (D)	49. (D)	74. (B)	99. (C)
25. (B)	50. (B)	75. (B)	100. (B)

Diagnostic Grid: Questions Sorted by Subarea

Question Number	Subarea
1	Mathematics
2	Mathematics
3	Mathematics
4	Mathematics
5	Mathematics
6	Language Arts
7	Language Arts
8	Language Arts
9	Social Science
10	Language Arts/ Social Science
11	Social Science
12	Science
13	Science
14	Science
15	Science
16	Science
17	Child Development
18	Child Development
19	Child Development
20	Child Development
21	Mathematics
22	Mathematics
23	Mathematics

Question Number	Subarea
24	Social Science
25	Social Science
26	Social Science
27	Science
28	Science
29	Science
30	Language Arts
31	Language Arts
32	Language Arts
33	Language Arts
34	Mathematics
35	Mathematics
36	Social Science
37	Social Science
38	Social Science
39	Social Science
40	Social Science
41	Science
42	Science
43	Child Development
44	Child Development
45	Language Arts
46	Language Arts

(continued)

Question Number	Subarea
47	Social Science
48	Language Arts
49	Language Arts
50	Mathematics
51	Mathematics
52	Mathematics
53	Mathematics
54	Social Science
55	Social Science
56	Social Science
57	Science
58	Science
59	Science
60	Science
61	Child Development
62	Child Development
63	Child Development
64	Language Arts
65	Language Arts
66	Language Arts
67	Language Arts
68	Language Arts
69	Mathematics
70	Mathematics
71	Mathematics

Question Number	Subarea
72	Social Science
73	Social Science
74	Social Science
75	Social Science
76	Social Science
77	Science
78	Science
79	Science
80	Child Development
81	Child Development
82	Child Development
83	Child Development
84	Mathematics
85	Mathematics
86	Social Science
87	Social Science
88	Social Science
89	Child Development
90	Child Development
91	Science
92	Science
93	Science
94	Mathematics
95	Mathematics
96	Language Arts

Detailed Explanations of Answers

1. C

There are several methods available to determine the answer. Making a sketch is a classic approach to mathematical problem solving, which is helpful here. You could draw six x's, representing the six workers:

Then you could connect each x with all other x's, counting the number of connecting lines as they were added. The connecting lines represent individual meetings.

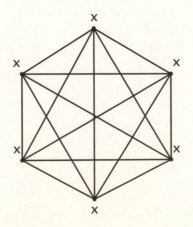

In the figure, there are 15 connecting lines, so there were 15 meetings. (You need to be sure to count the outermost lines forming the hexagon.)

*Here's another approach: Worker number 1 must have had five meetings. Once she completed her fifth meeting she was done with her meetings and could be considered out of the picture for the moment. Worker number 2 also had five meetings, but you shouldn't count the one he had with worker number 1; it's already accounted for in the first worker's tally of five meetings. So worker number 2 had only **four more** new meetings. Worker number 3 had five meetings, but you shouldn't count the first two; she had only **three more** new meetings. Continuing the pattern for all six workers, you see that you need to add together 5, 4, 3, 2, and 1 meetings. This again gives the correct answer of 15 meetings.*

2. **A**

Drawing a sketch with dots marking the possible locations of the two houses and The Soda Depot is a good idea. You can start with dots for the two houses, using inches for miles:

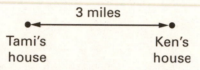

```
              3 miles
     •◄──────────────────►•

   Tami's                Ken's
   house                 house
```

If you then draw a dot representing The Soda Depot two miles (inches) to the right of Ken's house, as in the figure that follows, you see that the greatest possible distance between Tami's house and The Soda Depot is five miles.

```
        3 miles            2 miles
   •◄───────────────►••◄───────────►•

  Tami's            Ken's          Soda
  house             house          Depot
```

If you draw The Soda Depot dot to the left of Ken's house, as in the figure below, you see that The Soda Depot could be as close as one mile to Tami's house, but no closer. Only statements I and III, then, are true.

```
     1 miles      2 miles
   •◄────►••◄──────────────►•

  Tami's   Soda           Ken's
  house    Depot          house
```

3. **C**

Each combined inequality can be seen as the combination of two single inequalities. Inequality A, for instance, can be seen as the combination of the following two single inequalities:

$75 \leq x$

and

$x \leq 40.$

The meaning of a single inequality is often made clearer if you transpose the statement, placing the variable on the left. That is:

$75 \leq x$

means the same thing as

$x \geq 75.$

So, combined inequality A says that **x** (the speeds that vehicles may drive at) is greater than or equal to 75 mph **and** less than or equal to 40 mph.

You can separate combined inequalities B and D into individual inequalities in the same way:

Combined inequality B, $75 < x > 40$, means the same as

$x > 75$

and

$x > 40.$

That means that drivers have to drive **faster** than 75 mph! That doesn't match what the sign says.

Combined inequality D, $40 < x > 75$ means the same as

$x > 40$

and

$x > 75.$

That's the same as combined inequality B.

The correct answer is C, $40 \leq x \leq 75$, because that combined inequality means the same as

$x \geq 40$

and

$x \leq 75.$

That is, vehicles can travel at or faster than 40 mph, but no faster than 75 mph.

4. **A**

A bar graph works well here. The height of each of five bars would be determined by the number of votes for each lunch food.

A circle or pie chart could also be used. The 18 votes for pizza give the fraction 18/40, so pizza would be assigned 45% of the area of a circle chart, or 162°. The same approach would tell us the appropriate size of each of the other lunch food's slice of the pie chart.

A scatter plot illustrates the relationship between sets of data. A broken-line graph generally illustrates change over time. Neither is appropriate for illustrating the given data.

5. **D**

In simple notation form, the Distributive Property is as follows:

a(b + c) = (a × b) + (a × c)

*This means that when multiplying, you may have some computational options. Consider answer D. The Distributive Property allows us to break 42 down into the convenient addends 2 and 40. You can then **separately** multiply each addend by 3. Thus, 3 × 2 equals 6, and 3 × 40 equals 120. We can then (courtesy of the Distributive Property) add those products together to get 126. Only answer D above is illustrative of the Distributive Property.*

6. **B**

'Explain' is derived from the Latin explanare, so B is correct. 'Learning' is derived from Old English; 'dynamic' and 'choreograph' come from Greek roots.

7. **A**

I and III are correct. The similes make the passage more vivid by adding lifelike detail. This vivid description made the poem easier to understand for the mostly illiterate listeners. However, Homer was likely drawing on a long oral tradition of epic poetry; the epithets may not have been original to Homer, and he would not have been the first to use such figures of speech.

8. **B**

Foreshadowing is used to hint at future plot developments, not to manifest characters' or speakers' emotions. It is not used prominently in lyric poetry or in ballads.

9. **C**

Historical almanacs contain yearly data of certain events, including the time at sunrise and sunset along with weather-related data and statistics, so C is correct. Historical atlases contain a collection of historical maps. These maps may or may not include population data. Historical population data may best be found in government publications on the census. An encyclopedia article would contain a factual summary of the colonial period and the American Revolution, but may not include an analysis of the role of Fort Mackinac during the American Revolution, as encyclopedias attempt to give overviews rather than interpretations or analysis. A secondary source on Michigan during the colonial period may better address this question. Information on when the first treaty was signed and the terms of the treaty would most likely appear in a history book.

10. **C**

The Nile River's flooding was more predictable than rainfall in Greece was.

11. **D**

Productivity directly measures the prosperity and viability of farming in an area.

12. **B**

The experiment requires a control of all variables other than the one identified in the hypothesis—exposure to microwave radiation. Seeds from different suppliers may be different; for example, one brand may be treated with a fungicide. While it is likely that item III might be acceptable, without confirming that all packages are from the same year and production run, the four packages may be significantly different from each other. The best solution is to randomly divide the available seeds equally between the four test groups. Item II allows the experiment to also compare the germination rates between the different brands, but only if the seeds from each packet are isolated within each test group, and the number of seeds large enough to create a statistically significant sample.

13. **D**

The hypothesis is to evaluate seed germination as a function of microwave irradiation. Recording the overall growth or length of the seed root, while interesting, is not the stated hypothesis. Item C would be a good approach if the hypothesis were to relate seed growth to some variable, as it would more accurately reflect the growth of thicker or multiple roots in a way that root length might not measure.

14. **C**

Item I will not reflect the success of seed germination overall, one seed in a given sample may germinate early. Item III combines the number of all the sprouted seeds, losing the differentiation of the test groups. Items II and IV maintain the distinction between test groups and indicate the overall success rate of the germination.

15. **C**

The gas molecules themselves do not expand in size when heated, but the spaces between them increase as the molecules move faster. The expanding hot air leaves the balloon body through the opening at the bottom. With less air in the balloon casing, the balloon is lighter. The combustion products of propane are carbon dioxide (molar mass 44 g/mol), which is heavier than air, and water (molar mass 18 g/mol), which is lighter.

16. **C**

The upward force of air resistance partially counteracts the force of gravity when a feather falls in air. In a vacuum, or near vacuum, this force is dramatically reduced for the feather and both objects will fall at the same rate. The effect can be modeled without a vacuum pump by comparing the falling of two sheets of paper, one crumpled to reduce air resistance and the other flat.

17. **B**

Children operating at the concrete operating stage greatly benefit from direct observation. Infants operate at the sensorimotor stage; observing a demonstration of how sound waves work would be of no use to infants (A). While students operating at the formal operational level would greatly benefit from direct observation of sound waves in addition to complex theoretical descriptions, the direct observation is absolutely essential to the understanding of the concrete thinker (C). There is no Piagetian interpersonal concordance stage. Interpersonal concordance is a stage of moral development described by Lawrence Kohlberg (D).

18. **A**

The objectives given to a class should be applicable for all levels within the class to be fair and effective. It is necessary to state these objectives to the class in great detail so that they are aware of what is expected of them. Objectives should be expected to be achieved not only by certain students (B), but by the entire class. They are rarely unnecessary (D), and even though they may be found deficient during the actual learning, they should not simply be ignored when evaluating student progress (C).

19. **B**

Piaget posited four stages of cognitive development. A child develops new abilities by the end of each stage, but will not have this ability until reaching that stage. According to Piaget, children under the age of 8 will not have the understanding of language that enables them to grasp complexities (B). Therefore, teachers should use simple language with these children and not give complex directions (A). Piaget does not say that they are unable to understand any directions (C), nor does he suggest not giving any directions to children (D).

20. **B**

When designing learning activities, teachers should be aware that younger students process information more slowly than their older counterparts. Activities for younger children should thus be simple and short in duration. Because young children can answer questions, answer A is inappropriate, but they cannot answer the same questions as slightly older children (C). They can learn cooperatively, so answer D is also wrong.

21. **D**

It's true that multiplication is commutative and division isn't, but that's not relevant to their being inverse operations. Answer A doesn't address the property of being inverse.

Answer B also contains a true statement, but again, the statement is not about inverse operations.

Answer C gives a false statement. In the example shown in answer C, the order of operations tells you to compute $8 \div 2$ first, before any multiplication.

As noted in answer D, the inverseness of two operations indeed depends upon their ability to undo each other.

22. **C**

One way to arrive at the answer is to set up a proportion, with one corner labeled **x**:

$$\frac{31}{x} = \frac{5.5}{100}$$

To complete the proportion (and to find the answer), we can cross-multiply 31 and 100, giving 3100, which we then divide by 5.5, giving approximately 564.

23. **A**

The value 0.5 is equivalent to $\frac{5}{10}$ or $\frac{1}{2}$. That means that 0.5 **percent** *(which is one way to read the original numeral) is the same as one-half of one percent, so answer I is correct.*

One-half of one percent can't be the same as five percent, so answer II cannot be correct.

$\frac{1}{200}$ is equivalent to 0.5%. Here's why: One percent is equivalent to $\frac{1}{100}$. **Half** *of one percent, (0.5%, as noted above) is therefore $\frac{1}{200}$, so answer III is correct.*

24. **D**

Both state and federal government have the power to lay and collect taxes and to borrow money. Article I, Section 8 of the Constitution establishes the powers of Congress, whereas the 10th Amendment to the Constitution (the last amendment within the Bill of Rights) sets forth the principle of reserved powers to state governments. Reading state constitutions will show that states also possess the power to lay and collect taxes.

25. **B**

Multiparty systems use an electoral system based upon proportional representation. Therefore, each party gets legislative seats in proportion to the votes it receives. In the United States the candidate who receives a plurality of the votes is declared the winner.

26. **B**

The region's mountain ranges are the main reason for the high precipitation.

27. **D**

Red light is refracted less, having a longer wavelength. This is the basis for our observation of a red sunrise or red sunset as light passes through more of the atmosphere than at midday. The high number of particles in a polluted or particulate-laden atmosphere leads to intense red sunsets as the more refractive blue wavelengths are refracted away from view. Differences in refraction are also the basis of TV commercials for sunglasses with yellow lenses that improve the clarity of vision. As light from an object passes through the lens of the eye, the blue wavelengths are refracted more and may be focused before reaching the retina while the longer wavelengths are focused on the retina. Multiple images within the eye leads to the perception of a blurred image. Yellow glasses that filter out the blue wavelengths eliminate one image and give the perception of sharper, clearer vision for the wearer.

28. **D**

Early doses of pesticide were strong enough to kill most of the insects; only a few survived who, perhaps because of some genetic trait, had a slightly higher tolerance to the poison. When these pesticide-tolerant insects reproduced, they passed the tolerance to their offspring. Higher doses of pesticide are initially effective, but again a few individuals survive with tolerance to that new level. Control of pest populations generally requires access to a variety of pesticides that work through different mechanisms, and which are applied in such a way as to minimize build-up of tolerance in the insect population.

29. **A**

The physical movement and accumulation of sand is not part of the Rock Cycle, because no transformation of rock type is involved.

30. **C**

An index not only helps students find subjects and names that they want to know more about; it also helps to teach an important study skill that will be useful to them later. The other choices are often useful inclusions, but they do not always belong in a nonfiction book: for example, engaging characters (choice B) and timelines (choice A) are not going to be necessary in a nonfiction book about insects.

31. **A**

Lowry's novel is about a girl in World War II Denmark who helps a Jewish friend escape the Germans who occupy her country. It is fiction set in a fairly recent historical time, but historical fiction nonetheless. Of course, no one could answer this question without knowing something about Number the Stars. One good way to make sure that you are familiar with the best-known children's books is to look at a list of Newbery Award winners (available from the American Library Association at http://www.ala.org).

32. **C**

Picture books that feature stories about different cultures can subtly affirm cultural values through the use of pictures (choice I). In classes of younger students, students who are having difficulty with reading can often predict the course of a story simply by looking at the pictures (or can be taught to do so), and they can also better understand the main character's point of view—if the pictures accurately reflect the text (choices II and IV). Pictures do not usually help students pronounce difficult words (choice III).

33. **A**

Frost supposes his horse to have human opinions—to think that something is "queer" or unusual—when it is really just the poem's narrator who knows that the situation is unusual. There is no comparison, either stated or unstated, which would be necessary for simile or metaphor, nor is there any alliteration.

34. **C**

The **total price** of the two items in the original problem is given as $2.59, hinting that equation B or C may be correct. (In both cases, $2.59 is shown as **the sum of** two values.)

Examine the right side of equation C: Note that one value is $1.79 higher than the other. That is, in equation C, **x** could stand for the price of the pencil, and (**x** + 1.79) could stand for the price of the more expensive pen. Hence, equation C is the right one. None of the others fit the information given.

35. **B**

One way to approach the problem is to examine each scenario for reasonableness. Regardless of a runner's mile-by-mile pace in a marathon, the runner continually increases the distance covered, and the graph will always move upward, so situation I doesn't go with the graph. The number of households a census taker has left to visit **decreases** with each visit, so situation II doesn't fit either.

Both situations III and IV are examples of **steady growth**, so both match the graph. Answer B is therefore correct.

36. **A**

The western, or Pacific, coast of Canada is known as the Cordillera region. It includes some of the tallest and oldest trees in Canada, similar to northern California. The area is full of rugged mountains with high plateaus and desert-like areas. For more information on Canada's regions visit http://www.members.shaw.ca/kcic1/geographic.html.

37. **D**

Due process is the legal concept that every citizen is entitled to equal treatment under the law. The excerpt illustrates one aspect of due process, the exclusionary rule. The exclusionary rule is applied when evidence is seized in violation of due process. So the best answer is the exclusionary rule.

38. **B**

I and III are correct because part of the high-tech boom in Massachusetts of the early to mid-1980s was fueled by greater military spending under the Reagan administration, and because Massachusetts ranks 11th in terms of gross state product. II is incorrect because by the mid-19th century, farms were being abandoned in Massachusetts as the state's rocky soil could no longer produce enough food for the state's growing population. IV is incorrect because, while *the printing and publishing industry is important in Massachusetts, the service sector (including tourism) employs about one-third of the state's workers.*

39. A

The main purpose of the WTO is to open world markets to all countries to promote economic development and to regulate the economic affairs between member states.

40. A

Overgrazing, overuse, and a lack of rainfall caused the drought of the 1930s.

41. C

Black line spectra are formed when the continuous spectra of the Sun pass through the atmosphere. The elements in the atmosphere absorb wavelengths of light characteristic of their spectra (these are the same wavelengths given off when the element is excited, for example the red color of a Neon light). By examining the line spectral gaps scientists can deduce the elements that make up the distant atmosphere. Item A is true, but it explains the source of a line spectrum. Item B is true, and it explains why a blue shirt is blue when placed under a white or blue light source. Recall that a blue shirt under a red light source will appear black because there are no blue wavelengths to be reflected. Item D is a partial truth: black lights do give off ultraviolet light that the human eye cannot see.

42. B

Salt is a strong electrolyte that completely dissociates in solution. When this solution is in contact with a semi-permeable membrane, like the inflamed cells in the throat, water moves across the membrane from the side with lowest solute concentration to the side of higher solute concentration. In the case of the sore throat, water from inside the inflamed cells moves out toward the higher concentration salt water and the throat cells shrink due to the loss of water. All the items listed are colligative properties that, like osmotic pressure, are a function of the number, but not the nature, of particles in solution.

43. A

The individualized education program, or IEP, is set up to spell out the school's responsibilities. These responsibilities would usually fall upon the classroom and special education teachers (choices C and D) and the school's administration (B). During the meeting at which the IEP is discussed among school staff and parents or guardians, suggestions are normally made about how the parents or guardians can help the student, but the IEP is a document used specifically to enumerate the school's responsibilities and plans for the student.

44. **D**

Some students' disabilities (either physical or behavioral) are so severe that they cannot function in a general classroom at all. (This number is small, about 4–5% in the latest years for which figures are available.) Statement A is in fact the usual combination of settings for students with disabilities, and statement C is the result of that combination: in fact, nearly half of all students with disabilities spend over 75% of their time in the regular classroom. In addition, LREs can include conditions that are not shared by the other students, as in statement B.

45. **D**

Many of the classic stories for children exist in the realm of fancy because of the timeless quality of such tales. Fantasy allows children to explore places and events that have never taken place, and will never take place, yet somehow contain messages that we can discuss, savor, and learn from. Faith Ringgold, an author of books for children has stated, "One of the things you can do so well with children is to blend fantasy and reality. Kids are ready for it; they don't have to have everything lined up and real. It's not that they don't know it's not real, they just don't care."

46. **C**

This is the next step in the writing process.

47. **B**

A is incorrect because English dictionaries did not become available until English spelling was already being standardized. Also, people's increased purchasing power was not necessarily the reason for developing dictionaries instead of some other type of book. B identifies several developments—more written material in English, increasing literacy—that resulted from the invention of the printing press and did lead to the standardization of English spelling. English dictionaries were not the direct result of the publication of Latin and Greek classics. Also, while religious literature may have had a role in the expansion of literacy, it was not the only factor in the standardization of spelling.

48. **A**

Formal diction is characterized by more rigorous rules of grammar. "Not only . . . but also" constructions, and words such as "unexpected" and "mysterious," are often used in colloquial speech. Also, painting and other fine arts can be discussed using colloquial diction.

49. **D**

Elegies do not necessarily celebrate heroic deeds or philosophical ideas. Ballads do not necessarily commemorate the life of one who has died, and elegies are not characterized by a narrative structure. Elegies do not consider comical subjects. Ballads do have a narrative structure, though, as do epic poems that consider heroic deeds and historical events.

50. **B**

First, it is helpful to view the shaded area as the area of the square minus the area of the circle. With that in mind, you simply need to find the area of each simple figure, and then subtract one from the other.

You know that the radius of the circle is 6 units in length. That tells you that the diameter of the circle is 12 units. Because the circle is inscribed in the square (meaning that the circle fits inside of the square touching in as many places as possible), you see that the sides of the square are each 12 units in length. Knowing that, you compute that the area of the square is 144 square units (12 × 12).

Using the formula for finding the area of a circle (πr^2), and using 3.14 for π, you get approximately 113 square units. (3.14 × 6 × 6). Then, you subtract 113 (the area of the circle) from 144 (the area of the square) for the answer of 31.

51. **B**

If you can fold a two-dimensional figure so that one side exactly matches or folds onto the other side, the fold line is a line of symmetry. The figure below is a non-square rectangle with its two lines of symmetry shown.

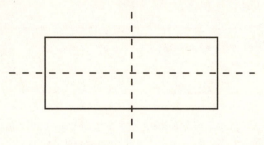

One might think that lines drawn from opposite corners are lines of symmetry, but they're not. The two halves would be the same size and shape, but wouldn't fold onto each other.

*Note that the question asked about non-square rectangles. Squares (which **are** rectangles) have **four** lines of symmetry.*

52. **A**

*To answer the question, you must recognize that triangles ADB and AEC are similar triangles, meaning that they have the same shape. That means that the corresponding angles of the two triangles are the same, or congruent, and that corresponding sides of the two triangles are proportional. Given that, you can set up the following proportion, where **x** is the distance from point A to point C:*

$$\frac{3}{7} = \frac{5}{x}$$

Solving the proportion by cross-multiplication, you see that the length of segment AC is about 11.7. Knowing that the length of segment AB is 7 feet, you subtract to find the length of BC (11.7 − 7 = 4.7).

53. **B**

*Statement I is true because the winner **could be** Mr. Greenfield and it **could be** someone else. Statement II is not true, even though Mr. Greenfield bought many more tickets than any other individual. He still has a block of only 300; there are 700 ticket stubs in the drum that aren't his. This tells us that statement III is true.*

*Finally, statement IV is false. Don't confuse the true statement "all **tickets** have an equal chance of winning" with the false statement that "all **persons** have an equal chance of winning."*

54. **D**

Both the personal correspondence of a military man stationed with the 5th RCT in Korea and an interview with Secretary of Defense George Marshall are primary sources, as they involve correspondence or testimony from individuals who were actually involved with the Korean War.

55. **A**

The peoples of the Iroquois Confederacy lived to the west, mainly in what is now New York State. The Niantic, Pequot, and Wampanoag lived in the region including what is now Massachusetts and Connecticut, before 1700.

56. **A**

The responsibility for public education belongs to the state governments. The federal government has often passed legislation to regulate and provide funds for public education, but the main responsibility for establishing and regulating education resides with the state governments.

57. **C**

Genes are the sections of the DNA molecule that determine specific traits.

58. **C**

Nuclear energy is nonrenewable. Nuclear energy has potential advantages in providing large quantities of energy from a small amount of source material, but the process of radioactive decay is nonreversible.

59. **C**

The force of friction between the book and the table is the primary force that must be overcome to move the book. An experiment to study these frictional forces could keep all other variables (size and weight of the book, speed of travel) constant while measuring the force needed to move the book using a spring scale. Different experiments could change the surface of the book by covering the book with wax paper, construction paper, or sandpaper.

60. **D**

A liquid will boil when its vapor pressure, which depends on temperature, is equal to the atmospheric pressure above the liquid. At high altitudes the atmospheric pressure is lower, thus water will boil at a lower temperature. The boiling point of water is only 100°C at 1 atmosphere pressure (760 torr). In Leadville, Colorado, elevation is 10,150 ft. When the atmospheric pressure may be as low as 430 torr, the boiling point of water may be 89°C. The lower temperature increases cooking times.

61. **C**

The description does not reflect Piaget's theory (A) and is not close to his posited stages of intellectual development. Maslow, not Kohlberg (B), is associated with the hierarchical pyramid. Although various of Vygotsky's followers have bent his theory into just about every classroom prescription possible, the Piagetian description in line 4 (D) cannot possibly be attributed to Vygotsky. The description of Bandura's modeling theory in line 3 is accurate.

62. **C**

The correct answer is to help students connect new pieces of information to what they already know. Studies of how the brain works point to the existence of an intricate web in which most pieces of information are strongly connected to others. One of the connections will probably work even if others are broken. Answer B is wrong because advocates say that the presentation should be well organized; students could possibly do a good job of learning through reading, but they would first require some training in connecting new information to what they know. Answers A and D may seem computer oriented, but they are not, and information processing advocates would reject both.

63. **D**

Vygotsky used the term "zone of proximal development" to describe the "space" in which assistance from a more intellectually developed person (e.g., an advanced peer or a teacher) will be effective in promoting learning. This term has not been used by any of the other theorists listed.

64. **B**

While the novel does contain some violent scenes, none of them are graphic enough to be considered unsuitable for young readers. The relationship between Huckleberry Finn and Jim, the escaping slave, is mostly warm and trusting rather than hostile; also, the book was written after the Civil War. It did challenge some attitudes toward race, however, because it portrayed close fellowship between two people of different races and showed a young white man's willingness to take risks on behalf of a black man's freedom. It also frankly uses vocabulary considered acceptable in the 19th century but considered offensive by many today.

65. **A**

Haiku are by definition too short to contain much elaborate description. The haiku form does not emphasize logic or direct statements. And while some haiku are humorous and/or contain lifelike details, these qualities do not characterize all haiku poems.

66. **C**

Those lines are spoken by Juliet in Romeo and Juliet, *by William Shakespeare.*

67. **D**

All of these themes have been emphasized in the works of Chinua Achebe, among other writers of world literature.

68. **A**

Walt Whitman wrote many lyrical poems, of which this is one example. Although the poem does contain instances of alliteration ("mystical moist") and assonance ("heard the learn'd"), it does not make extensive use of these techniques. Although some may see in the poem the speaker's incapacity to comprehend the astronomer's lecture, the superiority of higher education is not explicitly mentioned. Also, the poem was published in 1867, before the Modernist movement began.

69. **D**

It is helpful to compute Matt's current average. Adding up his scores, you get 522. Dividing that by 6 (the number of scores), you find that his average is 87%. Similarly, you can multiply 90 by 6 to compute the number of total points it would take to have an average of 90 (90 × 6 = 540). Matt only earned 522 points, so he was 18 shy of the A–.

70. **A**

The only way carpet from a 16-foot-wide roll will cover Ms. Williams' floor without seams is if she buys 20 feet of it. She can then trim the 16-foot width to 14 feet so that it fits her floor. Buying 20 feet of a 16-foot-wide roll means that she will have to buy 320 square feet. Her living room has an area of only 280 square feet (14 feet × 20 feet), so she'll be wasting 40 square feet (320 – 280), but no more.

71. **B**

The keystrokes indicate multiplication, and only answer B involves multiplication. Multiplication is hidden within the concept of interest. One way to compute a new savings account balance after interest has been earned is to multiply the original balance by (1 + the rate of interest). In this case, that's 1.03, then 1.04. The keystrokes match that multiplication.

72. **B**

The Silk Road was a transcontinental trade route that branched out over a vast area, including A, western China; C, northern Iran; D, northern India; and eventually the Sahara.

73. **A**

Democracy is the correct response because it is the antithesis of the authoritarianism of fascism. Indeed, the totalitarian, romantic, militaristic, and nationalistic characteristics were, in large part, a reaction against the perceived inadequacies of democracy.

74. **B**

The industrial economy of the nineteenth century was not based upon an equitable distribution of profits among all those who were involved in production. Marxists and other critics of capitalism condemned the creed of capitalists and the abhorrent conditions of the industrial proletariat. Raw materials, a constant labor supply, capital, and an expanding marketplace were critical elements in the development of the industrial economy.

75. **B**

The term "Trail of Tears" is used to describe the relocation of the Cherokee tribe from the southern Appalachians to what is now Oklahoma. The migration of Mormons from Nauvoo, Illinois, to the Great Salt Lake in Utah, the westward movements along the Oregon Trail, and, much earlier, the Wilderness Road, all took place and could at times be as unpleasant as the Cherokees' trek. They were, however, more voluntary than the Cherokee migration and therefore did not earn such sad titles as the "Trail of Tears."

76. **A**

Choice A is the best answer, since the term "casework" is used by political scientists to describe the activities of congressmen on behalf of individual constituents. These activities might include helping an elderly person secure social security benefits, or helping a veteran obtain medical services. Most casework is actually done by congressional staff and may take as much as a third of the staff's time. Answer B fails because pork barrel legislation is rarely if ever intended to help individual citizens. Pork barrel legislation authorizes federal spending for special projects, such as airports, roads, or dams, in the home state or district of a congressman. It is meant to help the entire district or state. Also, there is no legal entitlement on the part of a citizen to a pork barrel project, such as there is with social security benefits. C is not the answer because lobbying is an activity directed towards congressmen, not one done by congressmen. A lobbyist attempts to get congressmen to support legislation that will benefit the group that the lobbyist represents. Logrolling, D, is incorrect, because it does not refer to a congressional service for constituents. It refers instead to the congressional practice of trading votes on different bills. Congressman A will vote for Congressman B's pork barrel project and in return B will vote for A's pork barrel project.

77. B

Expansion occurring on the ocean floor along the Mid-Atlantic Ridge adds pressure around the edges of the Pacific Plate, creating geologic instability where the Pacific Plate collides with the continental plates on all sides.

78. B

The Moon is much closer to the Earth than to any other planet or the Sun.

79. B

Diseases caused by viruses, bacteria, or protists that invade the body are called infectious diseases. These disease-causing organisms are collectively referred to as germs. Cancers and hereditary diseases are not infectious.

80. B

Many studies have found that gifted and talented students are distributed more or less equally over the different socioeconomic levels. In fact, "gifted" classes in many school districts take on an upper-middle-class appearance because those districts identify high achievers in addition to the gifted in order to fill regular-size classes. Answers A and C are often-observed facts about the gifted and talented. Although gifted students can easily be trained to avoid statement D, they can be made to feel that simply scratching the surface of a subject is sufficient if they are not given challenging work.

81. D

Speech and hearing impairment is much more common than indicated in the table; approximately 20% of all students receiving special services in the United States have this disability. The statements in lines 1 through 3 are all true.

82. C

All children over 14 are required to be present when their IEP is being formulated; children under the age of 14 do not have to be present. Statement A is false: the IEP is a document required by law and is not to be taken as merely advisory. Statement B is also false: assessment methods can be changed during the evaluation period, but only through a meeting of all the same people who formulated the IEP. Although some resent having to deal with IEPs, and they do sometimes make a teacher's work life somewhat more difficult, students' needs might too often be ignored if the IEPs did not exist.

83. Ⓐ

Bandura—like most other educational theorists—did not approve of ranking and competitive grading practices. He believed they undermine a student's ability for appraising his or her self-efficacy by putting the means of appraisal in another's (i.e., the teacher's) hands. Statements I, II, and III are features of a Banduran classroom for modeling behavior and encouraging self-efficacy.

84. Ⓒ

The total area of the larger rectangle is

base × height = 12 × 9 = 108 sq. ft.

Therefore, the area of the shaded portion surrounding the inner rectangle is

108 sq. ft. – 80 sq. ft. = 28 sq. ft.

If the total cost of material used to cover the shaded area is $56 and we have 28 sq. ft., the cost per square foot is $\frac{\$56}{28 \text{ sq. ft.}}$ = $2.00 per square foot.

Answers A, B, and D are incorrect. Neither I nor II is necessary to determine the cost per square foot of the shaded area. D is incorrect because III is needed to determine the cost per sq. foot.

85. Ⓐ

In order to solve this problem we must first add the number of freshman girls to the number of sophomore girls (21 + 15). To find the percentage, divide this sum by the total number of students in the chorus and multiply by 100.

$$\frac{21+15}{132} \times 100 = \% \text{ of freshman and sophomore girls in chorus}$$

Answer B is incorrect; to find the percentage multiply the fraction by 100, not divide by 100. We then multiply by 100 to get the percent.

86. Ⓓ

Lincoln's immediate purpose in announcing the Emancipation Proclamation was to rally flagging Northern morale. Lincoln waited until after a major Union victory, at Antietam in 1862, so he couldn't be charged with making the announcement as an act of desperation. He recognized that the costs of the war had reached a point where preserving the Union would not be a powerful enough reason to motivate many Northerners to continue the war. Framing the war as a war against slavery would mobilize powerful abolitionist forces in the North and perhaps create an atmosphere of a "holy crusade" rather than one of using war to resolve a political conflict."

87. **B**

In the 1857 case **Dred Scott v. Sanford,** *the Supreme Court held that no black slave could be a citizen of the United States. It was in the 1954 case* **Brown v. Topeka Board of Education** *that the court held separate facilities for the races to be unconstitutional (choice A). The reverse—choice C—was the court's holding in the 1896 case* **Plessy v. Ferguson.** *Affirmative action (choice D) was limited in the 1970s and 1980s.*

88. **A**

Thomas Paine wrote several pamphlets before and during the American Revolution. **Common Sense** *was the most significant because it carefully documented abuses of the British parliamentary system of government, particularly in its treatment of the American colonies. Paine portrayed a brutish monarchy interested only in itself and pointedly argued how independence would improve the colonies' long-term situation. His argument was directed at the common man, and it struck a chord unlike anything previously written in the colonies. Its publication in 1774 was perfect in reaching the public at just the moment that their questions and concerns regarding British rule were peaking. The answers provided in Paine's essays were pivotal in the subsequent behavior of many colonists who, until that time, had been unsure of what they believed regarding independence and British rule.*

Answer B is incorrect. Paine wrote another essay called **American Crisis** *during the winter of 1776. This essay, not* **Common Sense,** *helped rally American spirits during that long, demoralizing winter. Answers C and D are also incorrect. Paine wrote to an American, not a British, audience. He also wrote* **Common Sense** *well before American independence was achieved.*

89. **B**

Giving the entire class a partially completed outline will help the learning-disabled students—who have difficulty staying on task during lectures and will have difficulty figuring out what to write down—to focus on specific information and help them learn what is important enough to write, especially if Mr. Rodriguez pauses long enough during his presentation to allow them to fill in the outline. Procedure A is not likely to be effective, because adaptations for special-needs students should be age-appropriate. Procedure C would be hard to implement without similarly rewarding the entire class, and procedure D does not give the students enough structure. Even though it would involve them in cooperative learning that might help them if their personalities mesh, it would need more teacher oversight, which would likely be hard to give. On the other hand, implementing procedure B should not add much to Mr. Rodriguez's preparation time and has the added value of improving instruction for the entire class.

90. **D**

Teachers should give students enough time to think about their answers, especially if the responses are incorrect. Answers A and C, although they might be useful in some situations, are not as good as D because they fail to provide any chance to self-correct. Answer B is always wrong (unless a particular answer is in fact close to being correct): a teacher should never give a student a false impression that an answer is close when it is not.

91. **D**

All are correctly matched.

92. **C**

The frequency of a wave is associated with pitch. Middle C has a frequency of 440 cycles per second. However, wavelength and frequency are directly related by the relationship $\nu = c / \lambda$ where ν (nu) is the frequency, c is the speed of sound, and λ (lambda) is wavelength.

93. **B**

Reptiles are not generally warm-blooded; all other statements are correct.

94. **D**

You should first count the number of spaces on the dial. There are 10 spaces. Five spaces equals 90 units, and 90 divided by 5 is 18 units. Each space is worth 18 units. The needle points to about halfway between marks 6 and 7. Thus, one half of 18, plus 6 times 18, is 117. Choice D is the correct reading.

95. **A**

You know that ten thousand contains 4 zeros, or 10^4 in place value. One million contains 10^6, or six zeros. Thus, 10^6 divided by 10^4 is 10^2 or 100. You may divide out 10,000 into one million, but that is the laborious way to solve this. Choice A is correct.

96. **C**

The "To be or not to be" speech is a soliloquy in which Hamlet utters his thoughts aloud at length. It is not an aside, since he is not speaking briefly to the audience in the midst of other action. Since Hamlet is the only one speaking, it is not a dialogue; nor is it an example of comic relief, due to the speech's serious tone.

97. **A**

The tone is serious but not necessarily urgent. 'Formal' describes a type of style, and 'didactic' describes a purpose, so these are not adequate descriptions of the passage's tone. Also, the paragraph does not focus on the UNESCO convention; this is an example of discouraging the international trade in pillaged artifacts by means of import bans.

98. **D**

Sentence 1 is important for introducing the passage's topic. Sentences 3 and 4 present and describe another way to reduce the problem of pillaging historical artifacts. Sentence 6 is relevant to the essay from which the passage was taken, but is not crucial to the development of the passage itself.

99. **C**

The paragraph is not structured around comparisons or contrasts.

100. **B**

B is not true because additional facts can be gathered and the thesis can be further refined after drafting has begun.

Answer to Open Response 1 Earning 4 Points

For Demetrius to read this text at an independent level, he needs better word identification skills and better acquaintance with the passage's genre.

If he does not know the meaning of the word "obviously," he not only misses a clue about Jake's personality, but he also goes into decoding mode, which prevents him from enjoying the text and from making connections between the text and other experiences.

Although Demetrius has two major word identification problems—decoding words phonologically and simply not having a sufficient vocabulary to read this passage—the inability I will concentrate on here is the insufficient vocabulary. Two of the words Demetrius had trouble with—"obviously" and "resist"— should be in a fifth grader's vocabulary, and they both follow somewhat unusual phonological models.

Even with better skills in this area, however, Demetrius will still have trouble with comprehension. This passage appears to be from a science fiction book, and he definitely seems unfamiliar with the genre. Thus, his first response to Mrs. Whalen's question concerning what the passage is about is Jake's affinity for video games, which may be the only thing Demetrius grasps well about the passage. When asked what else he knows about Jake, he concentrates on Jake's trouble rather than the trouble for the human race, probably because Demetrius is more accustomed to reading books in which individuals are in trouble of their own (or maybe he's just used to being "in trouble" himself).

Both strategies that Mrs. Whalen should try could be done on either an individual basis just with Demetrius or on a class-wide (or small-group) basis, depending on how many other readers in the class are at Demetrius's level. The first strategy, to increase his vocabulary, is to work with the student(s) to analyze new and unfamiliar words in all their reading. Assuming Demetrius will be worked with on an individual basis, he should read a book that is at his current instructional level (that is, one that he can read independently). He should make word lists of the words that he is unfamiliar with. He should define them and try to think of (or find) other words that have similar phonemes. For instance, his words and their phonemic analogies in this passage might be "obviously ↔ previously" and "resist ↔ insist." He may need help finding meanings or analogies, so Mrs. Whalen should have occasional short conferences with him to assess whether the word lists and their analogies are useful or even possible. This strategy will theoretically increase the number of words he knows and his ability to decipher unfamiliar words as well.

A second strategy is one that Mrs. Whalen would probably want to do with the whole class, and that would be to introduce the science fiction genre. Surely many students in the class will be acquainted with science fiction at least through movies and television shows, and they will be able to list a number of standard science fiction plots. Mrs. Whalen should diagram some of these plots on a board or overhead so that students will know what to expect as they read science fiction—for example, that big matters such as human survival are often at stake.

Demetrius already shows that he can make connections between what he reads and his own life, but his connections are flawed because he relies too much on his own life and too little on the text. By learning better word-recognition strategies and by recognizing conventions of the genre he is reading, he can raise his comprehension to a higher level.

Features of the Open Response Scoring 4

Purpose. The purpose of the assignment has been achieved. All four bullet points listed in the assignment have been addressed in an orderly way. The essay begins by stating the two comprehension needs, then gives evidence for these needs. It goes on to discuss two strategies, with reasons that the writer expects each to have a chance for success.

Subject Matter Knowledge. By indicating specific methods for implementing both strategies, this essay shows that the writer has an idea of how to improve reading, and how to assess whether the proposed methods are successful.

Support. Specific examples from the reading assessment are cited in describing the needs, and specific examples are given for the supposed strategies.

Rationale. In a sense, the "rationale" part of the scoring is covered by the other three areas: it would be hard to give a convincing argument without answering the question, demonstrating knowledge, or supporting your points. However, this area also includes the organization of the argument, and this essay methodically elucidates its points in a manner that helps the reader keep track of the overall argument.

Answer to Open Response 2 Earning 4 Points

The first step to solving this problem is to figure out how many total points each class has attained on this test. Because the mean score is calculated by adding all scores together and then dividing by the number of students, we can reverse the process to find the total points for Mr. Del Guercio's class. That is, mean = total score/(number of students), so total score = mean × (number of students).

Mr. Del Guercio has 22 students, so multiplying 22 by 81.8 gives his class's total: 1800 points. Mrs. Prudhomme's class so far has 19 students with an average of 78.7, for a total of 1496 points (rounding to the nearest point).

To attain a mean of 81.8, Mrs. Prudhomme's class of 23 will have to get a total of 23 × 81.8 = 1881 points, so her class will need 1882 total points to surpass the other class. Since the class total now stands at 1496 points, the 4 students taking the make-up test will need to score a total of 386 points (an average of 96.5) to put Mrs. Prudhomme's class ahead of Mr. Del Guercio's. Thus, her class can still overtake his, but only if the 4 students average over 96.5 on the test. (Needless to say, competitions of this sort have very little to do with effective teaching, but they are sometimes fun.)

Two mathematical skills necessary to solve this problem are (1) how to calculate a mean (addition and division) and (2) how to find an unknown quantity in an equation (by reversing the order of operations).

Two mathematical concepts involved in solving this problem are (1) understanding that knowing the total scores is necessary to compare the classes and (2) understanding the relationship between the mean score and the total number of points.

Features of the Open Response Scoring 4

Purpose. The purpose of the assignment has been achieved. All three bullet points listed in the assignment have been addressed, and most important, the problem has been solved correctly. The essay begins by stating how to solve the problem, and it goes through the problem clearly, without omitting any steps. The required mathematical skills and concepts are listed clearly at the end of the essay.

Subject Matter Knowledge. By indicating the specific method for implementing the solution, this essay shows that the writer has a clear idea of how to solve this and similar problems, and is likely capable of teaching the concepts involved.

Support. Specific calculations involved in solving the problem are detailed, and the reasons for doing those calculations are clearly explained.

Rationale. In a sense, the "rationale" part of the scoring is covered by the other three areas: it would be hard to give a convincing argument without answering the questions, providing a solution, or supporting your points. However, this area also includes the organization of the argument, and this essay presents its points in a manner that helps the reader keep track of the overall argument.

MTEL

General Curriculum

Practice Test 2

This practice test for the MTEL is also on CD-ROM in our special interactive MTEL TEST*ware*®. It is highly recommended that you first take this exam on computer. You will then have the additional study features and benefits of enforced timed conditions and instantaneous, accurate scoring. See page xi for guidance on how to get the most out of our MTEL book and software.

Practice Test Directions

Time: 4 hours

This test contains two sections: (1) a multiple-choice section and (2) an open-response item assignment section. You may complete the sections of the test in any order you choose. Directions for the open-response items appear before that section.

Each question in the first section is a multiple-choice question with four answer choices. Read each question carefully and choose the ONE best answer. Record your answer on the answer sheet in the space that corresponds to the question number. Completely fill in the space having the same letter as the answer you have chosen. *Use only a No. 2 lead pencil.*

Sample Question:

1. What is the capital of Massachusetts?

    A. Worcester

    B. New Bedford

    C. Boston

    D. Springfield

The correct answer to this question is C. You would indicate that on the answer sheet as follows:

1. Ⓐ Ⓑ ● Ⓓ

Try to answer all questions. In general, if you have some knowledge about a question, it is better to try to answer it. You will NOT be penalized for guessing.

The second section consists of two constructed-response items. You will be asked to provide a written response to the assignment. Directions for completing your written response to the open-response items appear immediately before the assignment.

Answer Sheet

1. Ⓐ Ⓑ Ⓒ Ⓓ	26. Ⓐ Ⓑ Ⓒ Ⓓ	51. Ⓐ Ⓑ Ⓒ Ⓓ	76. Ⓐ Ⓑ Ⓒ Ⓓ
2. Ⓐ Ⓑ Ⓒ Ⓓ	27. Ⓐ Ⓑ Ⓒ Ⓓ	52. Ⓐ Ⓑ Ⓒ Ⓓ	77. Ⓐ Ⓑ Ⓒ Ⓓ
3. Ⓐ Ⓑ Ⓒ Ⓓ	28. Ⓐ Ⓑ Ⓒ Ⓓ	53. Ⓐ Ⓑ Ⓒ Ⓓ	78. Ⓐ Ⓑ Ⓒ Ⓓ
4. Ⓐ Ⓑ Ⓒ Ⓓ	29. Ⓐ Ⓑ Ⓒ Ⓓ	54. Ⓐ Ⓑ Ⓒ Ⓓ	79. Ⓐ Ⓑ Ⓒ Ⓓ
5. Ⓐ Ⓑ Ⓒ Ⓓ	30. Ⓐ Ⓑ Ⓒ Ⓓ	55. Ⓐ Ⓑ Ⓒ Ⓓ	80. Ⓐ Ⓑ Ⓒ Ⓓ
6. Ⓐ Ⓑ Ⓒ Ⓓ	31. Ⓐ Ⓑ Ⓒ Ⓓ	56. Ⓐ Ⓑ Ⓒ Ⓓ	81. Ⓐ Ⓑ Ⓒ Ⓓ
7. Ⓐ Ⓑ Ⓒ Ⓓ	32. Ⓐ Ⓑ Ⓒ Ⓓ	57. Ⓐ Ⓑ Ⓒ Ⓓ	82. Ⓐ Ⓑ Ⓒ Ⓓ
8. Ⓐ Ⓑ Ⓒ Ⓓ	33. Ⓐ Ⓑ Ⓒ Ⓓ	58. Ⓐ Ⓑ Ⓒ Ⓓ	83. Ⓐ Ⓑ Ⓒ Ⓓ
9. Ⓐ Ⓑ Ⓒ Ⓓ	34. Ⓐ Ⓑ Ⓒ Ⓓ	59. Ⓐ Ⓑ Ⓒ Ⓓ	84. Ⓐ Ⓑ Ⓒ Ⓓ
10. Ⓐ Ⓑ Ⓒ Ⓓ	35. Ⓐ Ⓑ Ⓒ Ⓓ	60. Ⓐ Ⓑ Ⓒ Ⓓ	85. Ⓐ Ⓑ Ⓒ Ⓓ
11. Ⓐ Ⓑ Ⓒ Ⓓ	36. Ⓐ Ⓑ Ⓒ Ⓓ	61. Ⓐ Ⓑ Ⓒ Ⓓ	86. Ⓐ Ⓑ Ⓒ Ⓓ
12. Ⓐ Ⓑ Ⓒ Ⓓ	37. Ⓐ Ⓑ Ⓒ Ⓓ	62. Ⓐ Ⓑ Ⓒ Ⓓ	87. Ⓐ Ⓑ Ⓒ Ⓓ
13. Ⓐ Ⓑ Ⓒ Ⓓ	38. Ⓐ Ⓑ Ⓒ Ⓓ	63. Ⓐ Ⓑ Ⓒ Ⓓ	88. Ⓐ Ⓑ Ⓒ Ⓓ
14. Ⓐ Ⓑ Ⓒ Ⓓ	39. Ⓐ Ⓑ Ⓒ Ⓓ	64. Ⓐ Ⓑ Ⓒ Ⓓ	89. Ⓐ Ⓑ Ⓒ Ⓓ
15. Ⓐ Ⓑ Ⓒ Ⓓ	40. Ⓐ Ⓑ Ⓒ Ⓓ	65. Ⓐ Ⓑ Ⓒ Ⓓ	90. Ⓐ Ⓑ Ⓒ Ⓓ
16. Ⓐ Ⓑ Ⓒ Ⓓ	41. Ⓐ Ⓑ Ⓒ Ⓓ	66. Ⓐ Ⓑ Ⓒ Ⓓ	91. Ⓐ Ⓑ Ⓒ Ⓓ
17. Ⓐ Ⓑ Ⓒ Ⓓ	42. Ⓐ Ⓑ Ⓒ Ⓓ	67. Ⓐ Ⓑ Ⓒ Ⓓ	92. Ⓐ Ⓑ Ⓒ Ⓓ
18. Ⓐ Ⓑ Ⓒ Ⓓ	43. Ⓐ Ⓑ Ⓒ Ⓓ	68. Ⓐ Ⓑ Ⓒ Ⓓ	93. Ⓐ Ⓑ Ⓒ Ⓓ
19. Ⓐ Ⓑ Ⓒ Ⓓ	44. Ⓐ Ⓑ Ⓒ Ⓓ	69. Ⓐ Ⓑ Ⓒ Ⓓ	94. Ⓐ Ⓑ Ⓒ Ⓓ
20. Ⓐ Ⓑ Ⓒ Ⓓ	45. Ⓐ Ⓑ Ⓒ Ⓓ	70. Ⓐ Ⓑ Ⓒ Ⓓ	95. Ⓐ Ⓑ Ⓒ Ⓓ
21. Ⓐ Ⓑ Ⓒ Ⓓ	46. Ⓐ Ⓑ Ⓒ Ⓓ	71. Ⓐ Ⓑ Ⓒ Ⓓ	96. Ⓐ Ⓑ Ⓒ Ⓓ
22. Ⓐ Ⓑ Ⓒ Ⓓ	47. Ⓐ Ⓑ Ⓒ Ⓓ	72. Ⓐ Ⓑ Ⓒ Ⓓ	97. Ⓐ Ⓑ Ⓒ Ⓓ
23. Ⓐ Ⓑ Ⓒ Ⓓ	48. Ⓐ Ⓑ Ⓒ Ⓓ	73. Ⓐ Ⓑ Ⓒ Ⓓ	98. Ⓐ Ⓑ Ⓒ Ⓓ
24. Ⓐ Ⓑ Ⓒ Ⓓ	49. Ⓐ Ⓑ Ⓒ Ⓓ	74. Ⓐ Ⓑ Ⓒ Ⓓ	99. Ⓐ Ⓑ Ⓒ Ⓓ
25. Ⓐ Ⓑ Ⓒ Ⓓ	50. Ⓐ Ⓑ Ⓒ Ⓓ	75. Ⓐ Ⓑ Ⓒ Ⓓ	100. Ⓐ Ⓑ Ⓒ Ⓓ

Practice Test Answer Sheets

Begin Essay 1 on this page. If necessary, continue on the next page.

Continue on the next page if necessary.

Continuation of your essay from previous page, if necessary.

Begin Essay 2 on this page. If necessary, continue on the next page.

_____

_____

_____

_____

_____

_____

_____

_____

_____

_____

_____

_____

_____

_____

_____

_____

_____

_____

Continue on the next page if necessary.

Continuation of your essay from previous page, if necessary.

1. The following data represent the ages of seventeen people enrolled in an adult education class:

    32, 33, 34, 35, 36, 42, 42, 42, 43, 50, 51, 61, 61, 62, 63, 68, 79

    Adina organized the data as follows:

3	2, 3, 4, 5, 6
4	2, 2, 2, 3
5	0, 1
6	1, 1, 2, 3, 8
7	9

    The display Adina used is called which one of the following?

    A. box-and-whisker plot

    B. stem-and-leaf plot

    C. cumulative histogram

    D. pictograph

2. When infants and their mothers have strong attachments

    A. the parents are of higher economic status.

    B. the parents are usually strict disciplinarians.

    C. the children generally become socially competent.

    D. there is no correlation with social skills.

3. The Ungerville cafeteria offers a choice for lunch on their Mexican Day special. You can choose either a taco or burrito. You can choose a filling of chicken, beef, or beans and you have a choice of six different beverages. To determine the total number of possible different lunches consisting of a taco or burrito, one filling, and one beverage, which mathematical process would be most useful?

    A. factor tree

    B. conditional probability

    C. factorials

    D. counting principle

4. Research on the effectiveness of day care shows that

    A. IQ scores will always go up for children in day care.

    B. the children will have better social skills than those not in day care.

    C. intellectual performance of underprivileged children will increase.

    D. negative effects in forming relationships with others may occur.

5. Which pair of prefixes has the same meaning?

    A. *sub* and *ultra*

    B. *ante* and *pre*

    C. *intra* and *circum*

    D. *hyper* and *tele*

6. A topographical map is one which shows the

    A. population distribution of a region.

    B. climate of a region.

    C. landscape and water of a region.

    D. political boundaries of a region.

7. The spinner shown below is divided into equal sections.

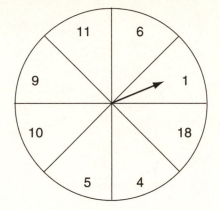

What is the probability of landing in a section with a number that is a multiple of 3?

A. ⅝

B. ⅚

C. ⅜

D. ³⁄₁₀

8. The culture of a people consists of its

I. Religion
II. Language
III. Social organization

A. I only

B. I and II

C. II and III

D. I, II, and III

9. The monotheism of the ancient Hebrews spread throughout the ancient world and also led to the formation of Christianity and Islam. This is an example of

A. cultural diffusion.

B. religious homogeneity.

C. global interdependence.

D. demographic data.

10. A nomadic lifestyle would most likely be found in the

    A. English countryside.

    B. Scandinavian fjords.

    C. Sahara desert.

    D. Canadian Rockies.

11. Studies of child abuse show that it

    A. increases during times of economic recession.

    B. is greater in single-parent households than in two-parent households.

    C. is more frequent in Western societies.

    D. occurs more often with parents who had been abused as children.

12. Which of the following is true about autism?

    A. Neurological findings are similar to those of neurologically brain-damaged children.

    B. Autism occurs in families with emotionally rejecting parents.

    C. Autism is cured in 75 percent of the reported cases.

    D. Autism is diagnosed earlier than Tourette's syndrome.

13. In the word *prediction*, *dict* means

    A. find.

    B. begin.

    C. test.

    D. say.

14. In which situation are the steps "define, analyze, and suggest solutions" most often used?

    A.   conducting an interview

    B.   writing a report

    C.   solving a problem

    D.   making an outline

15. The phrases *absent-minded professor* and *blue-collar worker* are examples of

    A.   transfer.

    B.   stereotyping.

    C.   card-stacking.

    D.   concreteness.

16. The diagram below could be used to model which one of the following?

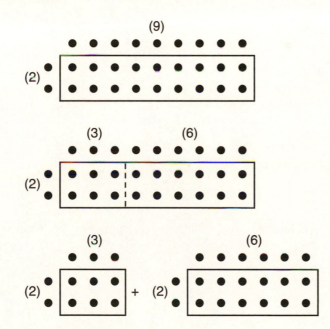

    A.   distributive property

    B.   associative property of addition

    C.   commutative property of multiplication

    D.   associative property of multiplication

17. Ms. Rosenberg writes these words on the chalkboard:

    Igneous
    Sedimentary
    Metamorphic

    She is going to teach a lesson on

    A. geography.

    B. biology.

    C. chemistry.

    D. geology.

18. Given the numbers –2, –1, -½, 0, 1, 3, which Venn diagram expresses the charateristics of the numbers correctly by type?

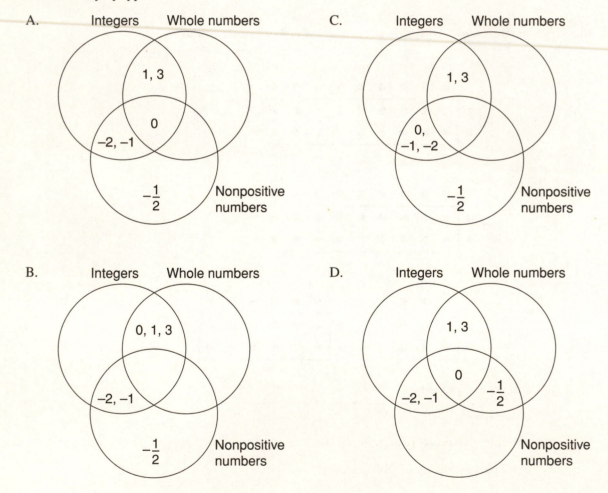

19. The diagram below displays a factor tree for the number *x*.

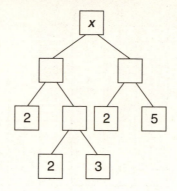

What is the value of *x*?

A. 14

B. 80

C. 100

D. 120

20. The average speed of a plane was 600 kilometers per hour. How long did it take the plane to travel 120 kilometers?

A. 0.2 hours

B. 0.5 hours

C. 0.7 hours

D. 5 hours

21. One type of allergic reaction results in constriction of the bronchial tubes, which interferes with the passage of air into and out of the lungs. This type of allergic reaction is most closely associated with

A. emphysema.

B. asthma.

C. bronchitis.

D. meningitis.

22. Given the point (1, 1), which one of the following points is the shortest distance from the point (1, 1)?

A. (5, 0)

B. (3, 4)

C. (−3, 2)

D. (0, −3)

23. In which sentence does the word *there* point to something?

A. *There* are no dragons.

B. I stopped because *there* was no room.

C. *There* is no use in stopping payment.

D. *There* is a missing page.

24. Which of the following graphs best represents your height above the ground when riding a ferris wheel?

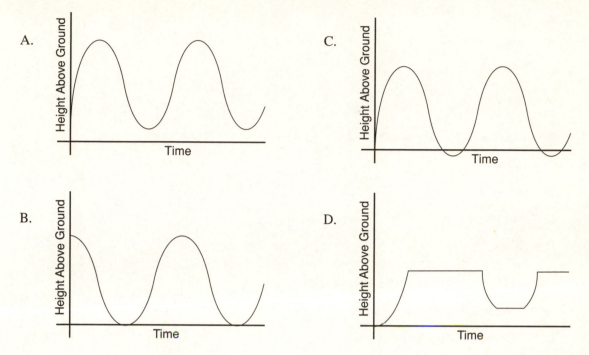

A.

C.

B.

D.

25. A teacher gave the following homework assignment to her class for the weekend. While riding in a car or walking on a street, bring paper and pencil. Look at car license plates and think of a phrase to go with the letters. For example:

   CST – Carrie Stood There

   NJL – Not Just Luck

Write down 3 plate letters and the phrase that you made up. This teacher was trying to develop her students'

A. auditory processing skills.

B. kinesthetic awareness.

C. language skills.

D. visual tracking.

26. A sweater was reduced 50% during a clearance sale. In order to sell at the original price, by what percent must the item be increased?

    A. 200%

    B. 50%

    C. 75%

    D. 100%

27. Which division of a play usually includes all the others?

    A. scene

    B. act

    C. monologue

    D. line

28. The term *colonialism* would be used to describe:

    A. Spanish conquests in the sixteenth century.

    B. The medieval system of guilds.

    C. Haitian independence from France in 1804.

    D. The Catholic Church's usage of indulgences.

29. A recipe for spinach pasta uses the following ingredients:

INGREDIENT	AMOUNT
Oranges	2
Scallions	¾ bunch
Cream	1 cup
Angel-hair pasta	12 oz.
Baby spinach	3 bags

    This recipe serves 4 people and takes 17 minutes to prepare. To serve 10 people, how many ounces of angel-hair pasta are required?

    A. 15

    B. 20

    C. 25

    D. 30

30. Mr. DeVito's class is studying immigration to the United States. Which concept would be appropriate to introduce?

    A. divestment

    B. assimilation

    C. feudalism

    D. nationalism

31. Ms. Posner wants her students to have an idea about the subject they will be studying before they begin. Which strategy should she use?

    A. outlining

    B. previewing

    C. rereading

    D. note taking

32. According to Piaget, children should be taught using manipulative materials to understand concepts particularly in which stage of development?

    A. sensorimotor stage

    B. preoperational stage

    C. concrete operations stage

    D. formal operations stage

33. Given the following numerical computation,

$$\frac{5+3(4-2)^2}{4}$$

which operation should be performed first?

    A. addition

    B. subtraction

    C. division

    D. powering

34. A teacher takes a beaker of colored water and pours it from a long, slim vessel to a short, wide vessel. The teacher is illustrating the principle of

A. natural selection.

B. deduction.

C. conservation.

D. accommodation.

35. All of the following were early influences on the Constitution of the United States:

  I.   The Magna Carta
  II. The Declaration of Independence
  III. The Articles of Confederation

A. I only

B. II only

C. I and II

D. I, II, and III

36. Given the following balanced scales,

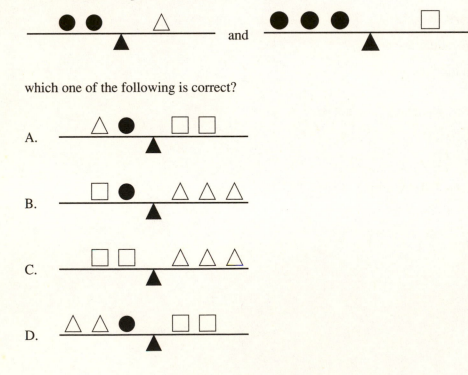

which one of the following is correct?

37. Which one of the following correctly matches the proponent with his/her theory of learning?

PERSON	THEORY OF LEARNING
A. J. Bruner	Constructivist theory
B. J.P. Guilford	Behaviorist theory
C. H. Gardner	Cultural theory
D. A. Bandura	Cognitive theory

38. The first life-forms to appear on Earth were most likely

   A.   complex single-celled organisms

   B.   complex multicellular organisms.

   C.   simple single-celled organisms.

   D.   simple multicellular organisms.

39. In developing an Individualized Educational Plan (IEP), all of the following must be stated EXCEPT:

   A.   measurable goals.

   B.   students' rights.

   C.   special education services.

   D.   specific test modifications.

40. The ancient scientist who believed that the Earth was the center of the universe was

   A.   Aristotle

   B.   Archimedes.

   C.   Ptolemy.

   D.   Plato.

41. When humans use more ground water for industry than is being replaced, the soil above the ground water may collapse and disrupt natural habitats. This human activity is an example of

   A.   species exploitation.

   B.   renewal of natural resources.

   C.   a disposal problem.

   D.   poor use of finite resources.

42. Ms. Rodriguez is teaching social studies and outlining skills. What would be the most appropriate heading for the following outline list?

    A. _____
    1. More government regulation
    2. Reform of corrupt political practices
    3. Concern for the problems of workers

A. Reconstruction

B. The Progressive Era

C. The Cold War Era

D. The New Frontier

43. The widespread use of computers has led to a national concern over

A. increased pollution of the environment.

B. guarding the right to privacy.

C. protection of the right to petition.

D. a decrease in television viewing.

44. Jose conducted a survey of 20 classmates to determine their favorite breakfast drink. The results are shown in the following table:

BEVERAGE	NUMBER OF CLASSMATES
Orange juice	6
Milk	4
Tea	2
Soda	2
Other	6

To create a pie chart for this data, how many degrees should be used for the sector representing milk?

A. 40°

B. 72°

C. 86°

D. 90°

Questions 45 and 46 refer to the following paragraph:

1. One potential hideaway that until now has been completely ignored is De Witt Isle, off the coast of Australia. 2. Its assets are 4,000 acres of jagged rocks, tangled undergrowth, and trees twisted and bent by battering winds. 3. Settlers will have avoided it like the plague, but bandicoots (rat-like marsupials native to Australia), wallabies, eagles, and penguins think De Witt is just fine. 4. Why De Witt? 5. So does Jane Cooper, 18, a pert Melbourne high school graduate, who emigrated there with three goats, several chickens, and a number of cats brought along to stand guard against the bandicoots. 6. "I was frightened at the way life is lived today in our cities," says Jane. 7. "I wanted to be alone, to have some time to think and find out about myself."

45. Which of these changes are grammatically correct?

    A. Sentence 1 — Change *has been* to *have been*.

    B. Sentence 7 — Delete *to have*

    C. Sentence 3 — Change *will have* to *have*.

    D. Sentence 4 — Change *emigrated* to *immigrated*

46. Which of these changes would make the passage flow more logically?

    A. Put Sentence 5 before Sentence 4

    B. Begin the passage with Sentence 4

    C. In Sentence 1, delete *off the coast of Australia*.

    D. Begin the passage with Sentence 2

47. In teaching higher level reading skills, Mr. Chin wants his students to recognize editorializing. Which of these best illustrates editorializing?

    A. Robert McGee was given a well-deserved round of applause.

    B. Also discussed at the Board meeting was the condition of the South Street School.

    C. The company received its charter in 1912.

    D. Just before he sat down, Mr. McPherson asked, "Has the homework been completed?"

48. The creation of wildlife refuges and the enforcement of game hunting laws are measures of

    A. conservation.

    B. exploitation.

    C. conservatism.

    D. population control.

Questions 49 and 50 are based upon the excerpt below:

" . . . But there are some occasions . . . when he considers certain laws to be so unjust as to render obedience to them a dishonor. He then openly and civilly breaks them and quietly suffers the penalty for their breach . . . "

49. This passage supports the use of

    A. military force.

    B. appeasement.

    C. civil disobedience.

    D. retaliation.

50. Which leader based his actions on the philosophy expressed in this passage?

    A. Vladimir I. Lenin

    B. Simon Bolivar

    C. Yasir Arafat

    D. Mohandas K. Gandhi

Questions 51 and 52 are based on this poem.

In a unit on ecology for a fifth-grade class, the teacher presents the following poem:

> The days be hot, the nights be cold,
> But cross we must, we rush for gold.
> The plants be short, the roots spread wide,
> Me leg she hurts, thorn's in me side.
> I fall, I crawl, I scream, I rave,
> Tiz me life that I must save.
> How can it be, I've come undone,
> Here 'neath this blazin' eternal sun?
> The days be hot, the nights be cold,
> Me lonely bones alone grow old.

51. What physical setting is the poem describing?

    A.   A forest

    B.   A tundra

    C.   A swamp

    D.   A desert

52. The type of writing in the poem can best be described as

    A.   colloquial.

    B.   narrative.

    C.   metaphoric.

    D.   factual.

53. Use the diagram below to answer the question that follows.

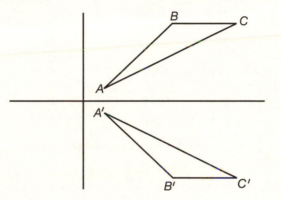

    In the figure above, triangle *ABC* is transformed to triangle *A'B'C'*.
    This type of transformation is called which one of the following?

    A.   reflection

    B.   dilation

    C.   rotation

    D.   translation

54. Mrs. Nemetski is doing a unit on literary genres. She presents the class with the following story:

    A fisherman was trying to lure fish to rise so that he could hook them. He took his bagpipes to the banks of the river and played them. No fish rose out of the water. Next he cast his net into the river and when he brought it back, the net was filled with fish. Then he took his bagpipes again and as he played, the fish leaped up in the net.

    "Ah, now you dance when I play," he said to an old fish.

    "Yes," said the old one, "when you are in a person's power you must do as he commands."

    To which genre does this story belong?

    A. narrative

    B. character analysis

    C. editorial

    D. fable

Questions 55–57 refer to the following:

A flea and a fly in a **flue**
Were caught, so what could they **do**?
Said the fly, "Let us **flee**."
"Let us fly," said the **flea**.
So they flew through a flaw in the **flue**.

—Anonymous

55. What form of poetry did the teacher present to her class?

    A. an elegy

    B. a ballad

    C. a limerick

    D. haiku

56. The repetition of the *fl* in *flea*, *fly* and *flue* is called:

    A. alliteration.

    B. onomatopoeia.

    C. imagery.

    D. symbolism.

57. A follow-up activity for this poem might include:

    I.   having students illustrate the poem
    II. asking students to write their own poem in this form
    III. having the children clap their hands to practice the rhythm of the poem

    A. I only

    B. I and II

    C. I and III

    D. I, II, and III

58. Given that the following sentence is true,

    "If turnips are not blue, then the sky is falling."

    Which one of the following sentences MUST also be true?

    A. If turnips are blue, then the sky is not falling.

    B. If the sky is falling, then turnips are not blue.

    C. If the sky is not falling, then turnips are blue.

    D. If the sky is not falling, then turnips are not blue.

59. A cycling of materials is represented in the diagram below.

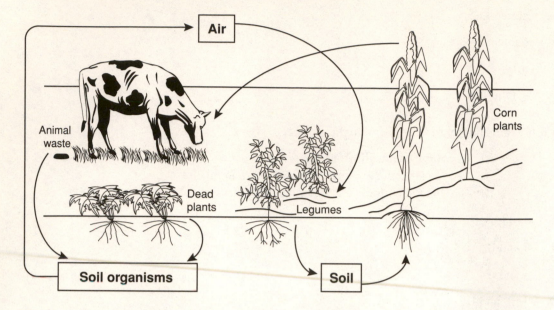

Which statement is supported by events shown in the diagram?

A. Materials are cycled between living organisms, only.

B. Materials are cycled between heterotrophic organisms, only.

C. Materials are cycled between the living and nonliving components of the environment.

D. Materials are cycled between the physical factors of the environment by the processes of condensation and evaporation.

60. The proverb "Death is a black camel, which kneels at the gates of all" is an example of

A. alliteration.

B. simile.

C. metaphor.

D. hyperbole.

61. Mr. Chan is teaching his class how to recognize propaganda. He presents his class with the slogan "Buy a brand-new Whizzer bike like the ones all your friends have." Which propaganda device is he illustrating?

A. bandwagon

B. testimonial

C. card-stacking

D. glittering generality

62. Laura *tried* to do her best.

    The judge *tried* the case harshly.

    These two sentences illustrate

    A. grammatical errors.

    B. synonyms and antonyms.

    C. rules of spelling.

    D. words with multiple meanings.

Question 63 is based on the following poem:

Richard Cory

By Edwin Arlington Robinson

Whenever Richard Cory went down town,
We people on the pavement looked at him:
He was a gentleman from sole to crown,
Clean favored, and imperially slim.

And he was always quietly arrayed,
And he was always human when he talked;
But still he fluttered pulses when he said,
"Good-morning," and he glittered when he walked.

And he was rich—yes, richer than a king—
And admirably schooled in every grace;
In fine we thought that he was everything
To make us wish that we were in his place.

So on we worked, and waited for the light,
And went without the meat, and cursed the bread;
And Richard Cory, one calm summer night,
Went home and put a bullet through his head.

63. Richard Cory represents the

    A. wisdom of age.

    B. happiness of love.

    C. deception of appearance.

    D. contentment of youth.

64. A teacher presents the following sentences to her class. Which one is correct?

A. I don't like hiking as much as I like cross-country skiing.

B. I don't like to hike as much as I like cross-country skiing.

C. I don't like hiking as much as I like to ski cross-country.

D. I don't like to hike as much as I like going cross-country skiing.

65. The flowchart below shows part of the water cycle. The question marks indicate the part of the flowchart that has been deliberately left blank.

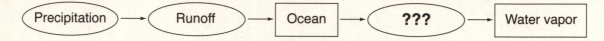

Which process should be shown in place of the question marks to best complete the flowchart?

A. condensation

B. deposition

C. evaporation

D. infiltration

66. Joshua's tie has three colors. One-half of the tie is blue, 1/5 is brown and the rest is burgundy. What fraction of the tie is burgundy?

A. $^5/_7$

B. $^2/_{10}$

C. $^3/_{10}$

D. $^7/_{10}$

67. Economic resources include all of the following EXCEPT:

A. land.

B. labor.

C. capital.

D. values.

68. Some children in Ms. Macheko's class belong to a group called The Banana Splits. What kind of group is this?

A. A group that makes different kinds of desserts.

B. A dance group.

C. A group for children of divorced parents.

D. A group to promote interracial awareness.

69. Mr. Weintraub wants to introduce a unit on consumer awareness. Which one of the following would NOT be a useful introduction?

    A. taking a class trip to a supermarket

    B. discussing the work of Ralph Nader

    C. reading a biography of Donald Trump

    D. doing a price comparison of items in different supermarkets

70. Dawn draws a picture of a parallelogram on the board. All of the following are properties of every parallelogram EXCEPT

    A. opposite sides are equal.

    B. opposite angles are equal.

    C. diagonals are equal.

    D. diagonals bisect each other.

71. Given the figure below, which one of the following equations could NOT be used to calculate the value of *x*?

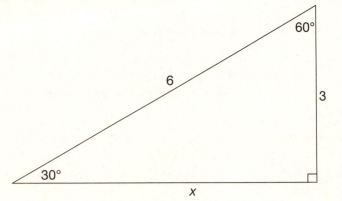

    A. $\sin 60° = \dfrac{x}{6}$

    B. $x^2 + 3^2 = 6^2$

    C. $\tan 30° = \dfrac{3}{x}$

    D. $3^2 + 6^2 = x^2$

72. In studying American history, a class is shown the film *Modern Times* starring Charlie Chaplin. The film illustrates the

    A. class struggle.

    B. evils of slavery.

    C. negatives of industrialization.

    D. horrors of war.

73. A microprocessor is used in which of these items?

    A. calculators

    B. incandescent lamps

    C. jet engines

    D. telegraphs

74. All of the following correctly pair the learning style with an appropriate teaching strategy EXCEPT

    A. Visual/Verbal Learner   Use "color coding" when reading
    Make flash cards for vocabulary

    B. Visual/Nonverbal Learner   Use charts to organize mathematics
    Stress key words

    C. Tactile/Kinesthetic Learner   Read text slowly and carefully
    Pay attention to spelling and grammar as you write

    D. Auditory/Verbal Learner   Read text aloud
    Use audio tapes

75. Which of the following was an immediate result of the early inventions in the cotton textile industry?

    A. Wages of weavers fell sharply.

    B. Cotton goods became cheaper and more available.

    C. Agricultural workers lost their work.

    D. Factories sprang up throughout London.

76. After a class has studied ancient Egyptian history, their teacher wants to show them some ancient Egyptian art and artifacts. Which would be the most appropriate place to take the children?

    A. The Museum of the Moving Image

    B. The Whitney Museum

    C. The Metropolitan Museum of Art

    D. The Guggenheim Museum

77.

> A number diminished by 5 is 3 more than 7 times the number.

If we let n represent the number referred to below, which one of the following best represents the statement shown above?

A. $n + 5 > 7n + 3$

B. $n - 5 > 7n + 3$

C. $n - 5 > 7(n + 3)$

D. $n - 5 = 7n + 3$

78.   According to research, what is true about suicide?

A.   It occurs more often in males than in females.

B.   It occurs more often during the day.

C.   It is successful every time it is attempted.

D.   It occurs more often after widowhood.

79.   Humanism was based on the value of

A.   human nature as revealed in the Greek and Roman classics.

B.   human beings ranking higher than angels in God's plan for the universe.

C.   the world as a contemptible place destructive to the human spirit.

D.   human nature as preordained.

80.   In teaching social studies, a teacher puts these two quotations on the board:

> *"By uniting we stand, by dividing we fall."*
> John Dickinson, 1768

> *"Yes, we must all hang together or most assuredly we shall hang separately."*
> Benjamin Franklin, 1776

These quotations illustrate the concept of

A.   nationalism.

B.   confederacy.

C.   equality.

D.   totalitarianism.

81. Diagrams, tables, and graphs are used by scientists mainly to

    A. design a research plan for an experiment.

    B. test a hypothesis.

    C. organize data.

    D. predict an independent variable.

82. Mrs. Korenge is teaching a unit on ecology. She tells her class,

    "A new type of fuel gives off excessive amounts of smoke. Before this type of fuel is used, an ecologist would most likely want to know . . .

    A. what effect the smoke will have on the environment."

    B. how much it will cost to produce the fuel."

    C. how long it will take to produce the fuel."

    D. if the fuel will be widely accepted by the consumer."

83. Mr. Galili is teaching the Civil War and its aftermath in social studies. He explains that the Jim Crow laws were attempts by

    A. the federal government to improve the status of African-Americans and Native Americans.

    B. the state and local governments to restrict the freedom of African-Americans.

    C. the states to ban such organizations as the Ku Klux Klan.

    D. the Radical Republicans in Congress to carry out reconstruction plans.

84. Pregnant women who drink alcohol are associated with

    A. lower weight in the fetus.

    B. higher heart rate in the fetus.

    C. more premature births and stillbirths.

    D. no differences from those women who do not drink.

85. The diagram below represents the percentage of total incoming solar radiation that is affected by clouds.

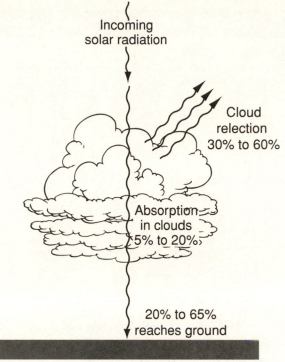

What percentage of incoming solar radiation is reflected or absorbed on cloudy days?

A. 100 percent

B. 35 percent to 80 percent

C. 5 percent to 30 percent

D. 0 percent

86. The data table below shows average daily air temperature, wind speed, and relative humidity for four days at a single location.

DAY	AIR TEMPERATURE	WIND SPEED	HUMIDITY (%)
Monday	40	15	60
Tuesday	65	10	75
Wednesday	80	20	30
Thursday	85	0	95

On which day was the air most saturated with water vapor?

A. Monday

B. Tuesday

C. Wednesday

D. Thursday

87. Ms. Posner is doing a unit on plants with her class. She took three seeds and put them in three different locations. Each seedling was grown in the same soil and each received the same amount of water. At the end of six days, the results were put on this table:

DATA TABLE		
LOCATION	HEIGHT (cm)	LEAF COLOR
Sunny windowsill	7	Green
Indirect sunlight	9	Green
Closed closet	11	Whitish yellow

What hypothesis was most likely being tested here?

A. A plant grown in the dark will not be green.

B. The type of soil a plant is grown in influences how tall it will be.

C. Plants need water to grow.

D. Plants grown in red light are taller than plants grown in green light.

88. The connotation of a word is its

     A. literal meaning.

     B. associated meaning.

     C. pronunciation.

     D. spelling.

89. The Rockefeller Foundation, Carnegie Hall, and the Morgan Library illustrate various ways that entrepreneurs and their descendants have

     A. suppressed the growth of labor unions.

     B. supported philanthropic activities to benefit society.

     C. applied scientific discoveries to industry.

     D. attempted to undermine the United States economic system.

90. The emancipation of women has had all of the following effects EXCEPT

     A. delayed marriage.

     B. falling birthrates.

     C. increased occurrence of divorce.

     D. more structured relationships between men and women.

91. The state and the federal government share the power of

     A. establishing schools.

     B. conducting foreign relations.

     C. establishing post offices.

     D. chartering banks.

92. The act of favoring incumbent legislators by arranging legislative districts is called

     A. pork barrel.

     B. apportionment.

     C. ballot stuffing.

     D. gerrymandering.

93. A school psychologist might do psychological testing to determine

    A. proper class placement of a child in regular education.

    B. the potential intellectual ability of a possible candidate for special education.

    C. the fears and phobias of a possible candidate for special education.

    D. the extent of academic achievement of a child.

94. Which substances may form in the human body due to invaders entering the blood?

    A. nutrients

    B. vaccines

    C. antibodies

    D. red blood cells

95. Water will enter the soil if the ground surface is

    A. impermeable and saturated.

    B. impermeable and unsaturated.

    C. permeable and saturated.

    D. permeable and unsaturated.

96. The greatest source of moisture entering the atmosphere is evaporation from the surface of

    A. the oceans

    B. the land.

    C. lakes and streams.

    D. ice sheets and glaciers.

97. Differences in hardness between minerals are most likely caused by the

    A. internal arrangement of atoms.

    B. external arrangement of flat surfaces.

    C. number of pointed edges.

    D. number of cleavage planes.

98. Which one of the following techniques is NOT appropriate for a kindergarten class?

    A. providing for differences in styles of learning

    B. teaching concepts by theme

    C. providing a great deal of factual material

    D. using manipulative materials

99. During a 504 meeting with the school psychologist, speech pathologist, teacher, special education coordinator, and parent, no consensus is reached about a child. What is the next step in the 504 process?

    A. The group will meet again the following month to discuss the child.

    B. The parents will move the child to another school district.

    C. The child is entitled to private school education at the district's expense.

    D. There will be a due process hearing or mediation by an impartial professional.

100. Which line correctly pairs the educational theorist with his/her theory?

    A. John Dewey   Progressive education

    B. Abraham Maslow   Effects of poverty on learning

    C. Diane Ravitch   Multicultural education

    D. A.S. Neil   Structured learning

Directions for the Open-Response Item Assignments

This section of the test consists of two open-response item assignments that appear on the following pages. You will be asked to prepare a written response of approximately 150 to 300 words (1 to 2 pages) for each assignment. **You must write responses to both of the assignments.**

For each assignment, read the topic and directions carefully before you begin to work. Think about how you will organize your response.

As a whole, your response to each assignment must demonstrate an understanding of the knowledge of the field. In your response to each assignment, you are expected to demonstrate the depth of your understanding of the subject area by applying your knowledge rather than by merely reciting factual information.

Your response to the assignment will be evaluated based on the following criteria:

- **PURPOSE**: the extent to which the response achieves the purpose of the assignment

- **SUBJECT KNOWLEDGE**: appropriateness and accuracy in the application of subject knowledge

- **SUPPORT**: quality and relevance of supporting evidence

- **RATIONALE**: soundness of argument and degree of understanding of the subject area

The open-response item assignments are intended to assess subject knowledge. Your responses must be communicated clearly enough to permit valid judgment of the evaluation criteria by scorers. Your responses should be written for an audience of educators in this field. The final version of each response should conform to the conventions of edited American English. Your responses should be your original work, written in your own words, and not copied or paraphrased from some other work.

Be sure to write about the assigned topics. Please write legibly. You may not use any reference materials during the test. Remember to review your work and make any changes you think will improve your responses.

Open Response 1

> **1. Read the information below; then complete the exercise that follows.**

> The study of different genres enables students to compare and contrast different types of literature. Although the myths within different cultures appear unique on the surface, most have common elements and themes.

- Choose one type of myth from a variety of cultures and describe its common elements and themes.

- Use this information to write a simple one page myth of the type you choose.

- Describe the prerequisite skills necessary to fulfill the tasks above.

Open Response 2

> **2. Read the information below; then complete the exercise that follows.**

> The Renaissance represents the rebirth of humanism, secularism, individualism, and classicism during the fourteenth century in Italy and later in northern Europe.

- Choose a Renaissance artist, political leader, or philosopher and show how this person contributed to the four Renaissance ideas above.

- Contrast how this person's ideas and views are different from those of the Middle Ages.

- Describe the prerequisite knowledge one must have to answer the first two bullet points.

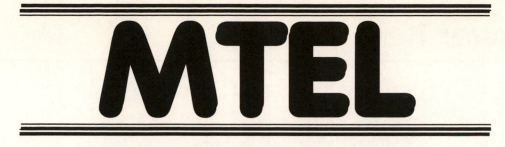

MTEL

General Curriculum

Answers: Practice Test 2

Answer Key

1.	(B)	26.	(D)	51.	(D)	76.	(C)
2.	(C)	27.	(B)	52.	(A)	77.	(D)
3.	(D)	28.	(A)	53.	(A)	78.	(A)
4.	(C)	29.	(D)	54.	(D)	79.	(A)
5.	(B)	30.	(B)	55.	(C)	80.	(A)
6.	(C)	31.	(B)	56.	(A)	81.	(C)
7.	(C)	32.	(C)	57.	(D)	82.	(A)
8.	(D)	33.	(B)	58.	(C)	83.	(B)
9.	(A)	34.	(C)	59.	(C)	84.	(C)
10.	(C)	35.	(D)	60.	(C)	85.	(B)
11.	(D)	36.	(C)	61.	(A)	86.	(D)
12.	(A)	37.	(A)	62.	(D)	87.	(A)
13.	(D)	38.	(C)	63.	(C)	88.	(B)
14.	(C)	39.	(B)	64.	(A)	89.	(B)
15.	(B)	40.	(C)	65.	(C)	90.	(D)
16.	(A)	41.	(D)	66.	(C)	91.	(D)
17.	(D)	42.	(B)	67.	(D)	92.	(D)
18.	(A)	43.	(B)	68.	(D)	93.	(B)
19.	(D)	44.	(B)	69.	(C)	94.	(C)
20.	(A)	45.	(C)	70.	(C)	95.	(D)
21.	(B)	46.	(A)	71.	(D)	96.	(A)
22.	(B)	47.	(A)	72.	(C)	97.	(A)
23.	(D)	48.	(A)	73.	(A)	98.	(C)
24.	(A)	49.	(C)	74.	(C)	99.	(D)
25.	(C)	50.	(D)	75.	(D)	100.	(D)

Diagnostic Grid: Questions Sorted by Subarea

Question Number	Subarea
1	Mathematics
2	Child Development
3	Mathematics
4	Child Development
5	Language Arts
6	Social Science
7	Mathematics
8	Social Science
9	Social Science
10	Social Science
11	Child Development
12	Child Development
13	Language Arts
14	Language Arts
15	Language Arts
16	Mathematics
17	Science
18	Mathematics
19	Mathematics
20	Mathematics
21	Science
22	Mathematics
23	Language Arts
24	Child Development

Question Number	Subarea
25	Child Development
26	Mathematics
27	Language Arts
28	Social Science
29	Mathematics
30	Social Science
31	Language Arts
32	Child Development
33	Mathematics
34	Social Science
35	Science
36	Mathematics
37	Child Development
38	Child Development
39	Child Development
40	Science
41	Science
42	Social Science
43	Social Science
44	Child Development
45	Language Arts
46	Language Arts
47	Language Arts
48	Science

(continued)

Question Number	Subarea	Question Number	Subarea
49	Social Science	75	Social Science
50	Social Science	76	Social Science
51	Science	77	Mathematics
52	Language Arts	78	Child Development
53	Mathematics	79	Social Science
54	Language Arts	80	Social Science
55	Language Arts	81	Science
56	Language Arts	82	Social Science
57	Language Arts	83	Social Science
58	Mathematics	84	Science
59	Science	85	Science
60	Language Arts	86	Science
61	Language Arts	87	Science
62	Language Arts	88	Language Arts
63	Language Arts	89	Social Science
64	Language Arts	90	Social Science
65	Science	91	Social Science
66	Mathematics	92	Social Science
67	Social Science	93	Child Development
68	Child Development	94	Science
69	Social Science	95	Science
70	Mathematics	96	Science
71	Mathematics	97	Science
72	Social Science	98	Child Development
73	Science	99	Child Development
74	Child Development	100	Child Development

Detailed Explanations of Answers

1. **B**

A stem and leaf plot shows the data in numerically increasing order. The leaf is the last digit to the right and the stem is the remaining digit or digits disregarding the leaf. For example: Given the number 27, 7 is the leaf, 2 is the stem.

stem	leaf
2	7

2. **C**

Studies have shown the importance of the infant-mother bond. It is the first socialization for the newborn and leads to social competence. It has no correlation, however, with a mother's economic situation nor does it relate to discipline.

3. **D**

The counting principle states:

If there are m different ways to choose a first event and n different ways to choose a second event, then there are m × n different ways of choosing the first event followed by the second event.

There are three stages in this example:

Stage 1	taco or burrito	2 choices
Stage 2	filling	3 choices
Stage 3	beverage	6 choices

Total possible different outcomes: $2 \times 3 \times 6 = 36$

4. C

The only correlation between day care and other factors that was borne out by testing was the increase in intellectual and academic performance in underprivileged children who attended day care as compared with those who did not attend day care. No correlation was found in the social skills of the children. We cannot say that IQ scores will always go up for those in day care.

5. B

Both ante *and* pre *mean before, so B is correct. Sub* means under, while ultra *means too or excessive, so A is wrong. Intra* is within and circum *is around, so C is incorrect. Hyper is over and tele* is across so D is wrong.

6. C

The topography of a region is specifically the nature of its landscape—mountains, deserts, plateaus, oceans, and lakes. Population distribution would be shown on a demographic map. Climate and political boundaries are separate entities.

7. C

$$\text{The probability of an event} = \frac{\text{total successful outcomes}}{\text{total possible outcomes}}$$

Successful events are multiples of 3. This includes 6, 9 and 18. There are 3 successful events. The total number of possible outcomes is 8. Probability of landing on a multiple 3 = ³⁄₈.

8. D

The culture of a people is the way in which the people live. It encompasses their religion, language, social organization, customs, traditions, and economic organization.

9. **A**

Cultural diffusion refers to the extending of an aspect of culture from one area to another and its inclusion in the culture(s) of other people. Religious homogeneity is the similitude of religion, not its spread. Global interdependence refers to the importance of one country to another, usually in terms of economics. Demographics is the study of population trends.

10. **C**

A nomadic lifestyle is one in which people do not settle in one area; instead, they roam from place to place and set up temporary living arrangements in each place. The desert is an area of nomadic lifestyle because it generally does not support agriculture and does not have sufficient water for people to settle there permanently.

11. **D**

Unfortunately, people who have themselves been abused as children, whether physically, emotionally, or sexually are more likely to repeat the pattern with their own children. Economics do not play a significant role, nor does having one parent rather than two parents, nor is it more common in Western societies.

12. **A**

The only statement that is correct is A. The neurological findings on the brain of the autistic child is very much like those of brain-damaged children. Autism is not related to the emotional state of parents and, unfortunately, is cured only in 10 percent of the reported cases.

13. **D**

The Latin root dict *means to say.*

14. **C**

To solve a problem, one must first define the problem, then analyze it, and finally, suggest possible solutions.

15. **B**

Stereotyping is applying generalizations to people, regardless of their personal characteristics. Professors are seen as people whose heads are in the clouds and are not concerned with practical matters; thus, the term absent-minded professor *is applied. Similarly, manual workers are visualized in a pejorative sense, hence the term* blue-collar worker.

16. **A**

The distributive property (of multiplication over addition) can be demonstrated algebraically as

$$a(b+c) = ab + bc$$

The diagrams in the example display as follows:

$$
\begin{aligned}
2(9) &= 18 \\
2(3+6) &= 18 \\
2(3) + 2(6) &= 18
\end{aligned}
$$

17. **D**

Igneous, sedimentary, and metamorphic are terms that describe varieties of rocks; therefore, they would be taught in a lesson on geology, which is the study of the earth's history.

18. **A**

Venn diagrams are overlapping circles which display elements of different sets. They show elements common to more than one set as well as elements unique to only one set.

$-2, -1, 0, 1, 3$ are integers

$-2, -1, -1/2, 0$ are nonpositive (<u>Note:</u> Zero is neither positive nor negative.)

$0, 1, 3$ are whole numbers

19. **D**

A factor tree decomposes an integer into its prime factors by continuously factoring a given number into two factors until there are no further factors other than one and the number. For example, the factor tree for 12 appears as follows:

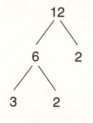

To work a factor tree backward (from the bottom up), multiply the factors to obtain the composite number they come from.

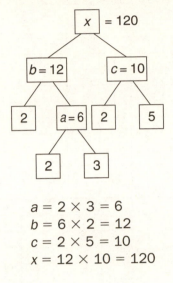

$$a = 2 \times 3 = 6$$
$$b = 6 \times 2 = 12$$
$$c = 2 \times 5 = 10$$
$$x = 12 \times 10 = 120$$

20. **A**

The plane travels 600 kilometers in 1 hour.

$$\frac{120}{600} = \frac{1}{5}$$

To travel 120 kilometers, you need 1/5 of an hour or 0.2 hours.

21. **B**

Asthma occurs when the bronchial tubes do not allow sufficient air to pass through to the lungs. Emphysema is a lung disease which is generally caused by smoking or air pollution. Bronchitis is an inflammation of the bronchial tubes, usually as part of a cold. Meningitis is an inflammation of the brain that affects the spinal cord.

22. **B**

Plot the answer choices on the x-y coordinate plane.

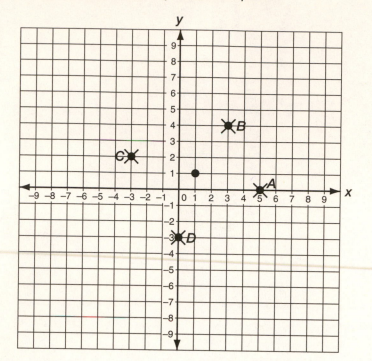

By careful examination, points A, C, and D are equidistant from the given point (1,1). Point B is closest.

23. **D**

In Sentence D, the word *there* points to the missing page. Sentence A's meaning is that no dragons exist. Sentence B says that no room was available. Sentence C states that stopping payment is futile. Therefore, the correct answer is D.

24. **A**

A person enters a ferris wheel at a height a little above ground level. He/she achieves a maximum height a while later and, after an equal amount of time, is back at the lower position. This cycle then repeats until the ride is over.

25. **C**

Making up words using given letters is a language skills and requires that students think of words and phrases. Kinesthetic awareness deals with the sense of touch, while auditory processing skills relate to the sense of hearing. Visual tracking is left-right tracking and is an important pre-reading skill.

26. **D**

The sweater's price was cut by half. Therefore, it needs to be doubled to sell at the original price. For example:

Original price: $20.00

50% sale: $10.00

To go back to the original price, you must double the sale price, which is the same as increasing it by 100%.

27. **B**

A line is the smallest unit of the choices given, so Choice D is incorrect. A monologue is a speech given by one person and is included in a scene, so Choice C is wrong. A scene is part of an act, so Choice A is wrong. Therefore, the correct answer is B.

28. **A**

Colonialism is the extension of a nation's rule beyond its borders by the establishment of settlements in which indigenous populations are directly ruled or displaced. Colonizers generally dominate the resources, labor, and markets of the colonial territory. In the sixteenth century, Spain extended its rule to parts of North America, South America, and the Caribbean. Guilds were the forerunners of modern trade unions, a system in which people who practiced similar crafts joined together. Haiti's independence from France removed the colonialism which France had imposed upon this island. Indulgences were practices of the Catholic Church in medieval times in which Catholics "bought" pardons from the church.

29. **D**

We establish a proportion relating the number of people to the ounces of angel-hair pasta.

$$\frac{4}{12} = \frac{10}{x}$$ Then cross multiply.

$$4x = 120$$ Divide by 4.

$$x = 30$$

30. **B**

Assimilation is the process in which a minority racial, cultural, religious, or national group becomes part of the dominant cultural group. Divestment occurs when a country removes itself economically, militarily, or socially from something in which it had previously invested. Feudalism was a system in which people were protected by lords in exchange for their labor. Nationalism, or patriotism, is the feeling of pride and belonging that a people has for its country.

31. **B**

Previewing is a technique that, as its name implies, allows a student to get a foretaste of what is to come. Outlining is a method of organizing material. Rereading is used to find answers to specific questions, and note taking is a method of writing down important facts.

32. **C**

The sensorimotor stage occurs in ages 0–2, when the infant is guided by senses. The preoperational stage occurs in ages 3–7, when the child uses intuitive means to grasp reality. During formal operations, ages 12–15, the child can use abstractions and reasoning skills. During the concrete operations stage, ages 8–11, the child uses tangible objects to learn about the world around him. Thus manipulative materials would best be used during the concrete operations stage.

33. **B**

The order of operations requires us to do all operations WITHIN grouping symbols first. A parenthesis is a grouping symbol. The first operation to be performed is: 4 − 2.

34. **C**

The Law of Conservation states that a material will have the same volume regardless of the shape of the container in which it is placed. Accommodation and its sister concept, assimilation is the way in which one incorporates new information in one's way of thinking. Piaget is the Swiss psychologist who did experimental work on these concepts. Natural selection is a Darwinian concept which states that a species will naturally evolve to retain useful adaptive characteristics. Deduction is a method of reasoning.

35. **D**

The Magna Carta is an English document signed by King John in 1215 that promised fair laws, equal access to courts, and a trial before imprisonment. It is the basis of our Constitution. The Declaration of Independence was the first step our country took to announce its intention to break free of English rule. The Articles of Confederation, drafted in 1777, was in effect the first constitution of the United States and led to the present constitution. Therefore, all three influenced our constitution.

36. **C**

We can analyze the four answer choices by converting each △ or □ to its ● equivalent.

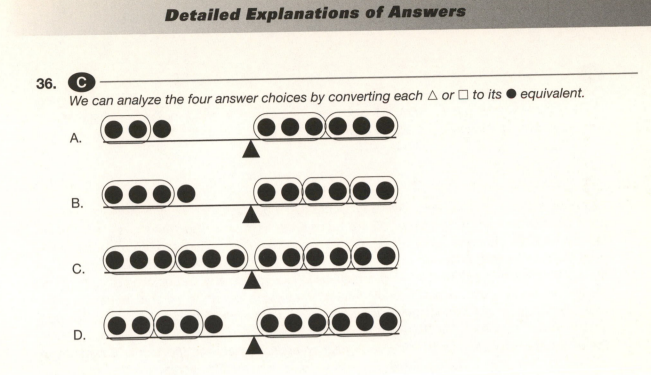

A.

B.

C.

D.

37. **A**

Jerome Bruner posited the constructivist theory, an outgrowth of the work of Piaget. He believed that the student must be an active learner, helping to shape what he learns. He believed that material should be taught in a spiral fashion. J.P. Guilford developed a theory of intelligence and intelligence testing. H. Gardner is known for his theory of multiple intelligences, and A. Bandura posited the theory of social learning.

38. **C**

The first life forms would be the simplest, so simple single-celled organisms (Choice C) is correct.

39. **B**

An IEP must contain measurable goals and objectives so that progress may be assessed. It also must state the special education services that are to be provided and the specific test modifications for state testing. Students' rights are not part of an IEP, so B is correct.

40. **C**

Ptolemy was the most important Greek astronomers of his time. He propounded the geocentric theory that prevailed for 1,400 years. Aristotle and Plato were philosophers, while Archimedes was the greatest mathematician of his age.

41. **D**

Ground water is a natural resource, not a species so Choice A is wrong. Humans are using up the water, not renewing it, so Choice B is wrong. The problem is not disposal; it is usage of limited resources, so Choice D is the best answer.

42. **B**

The Progressive Era in the early twentieth century can be described as one in which government concerned itself with reform. The progressives, as they called themselves, worked to make American society a better and safer place in which to live. They tried to make big business more responsible through regulations of various kinds. They worked to clean up corrupt city governments, to improve working conditions in factories, and to better living conditions for those who lived in slum areas, a large number of whom were recent immigrants. Reconstruction took place in the years immediately following the Civil War, which ended in 1865 and concerned itself with putting the United States back together after the war. The Cold War Era occurred in the aftermath of World War II. It involved great competition between the former Soviet Union and the United States. During the 1960 election campaign, the Democratic candidate, John F. Kennedy stated that America was "on the edge of a New Frontier"; in his inaugural speech he spoke of "a new generation of Americans"; and during his presidency he seemed to be taking government in a new direction, away from the easygoing Eisenhower style. His administration was headed by strong, dedicated personalities. The Kennedy staff was also predominantly young. Its energy and commitment revitalized the nation.

43. **B**

A great concern of educators, parents, and the general public is privacy in using computers. The Internet is a vast worldwide network and users worry that what is sent over the Internet may not be secure.

44. **B**

Four of the twenty people chose milk. That is ⁴/₂₀ or ¹/₅ of the people chose milk. Consequently, ¹/₅ of the 360° pie chart should be associated with milk.

$$\frac{1}{5}(360°) = 72°$$

45. **C**

The verb phrase will have avoided implies that an action will occur in the future. However, it is clear that the author is describing what has already happened; therefore, have avoided is the correct verb usage.

46. (A)

Paragraph 1 ends by describing all of the animals who have made De Witt Island their home. The best transition to Paragraph 2 introduces Jane Cooper and then explains why she chose this particular place.

47. (A)

Editorializing is giving an opinion about an occurrence or an issue. Choices B and C are factual statements. Choice D is a straightforward question. Choice A's use of the words well-deserved illustrates editorializing because it gives the writer's opinion about the applause.

48. (A)

Wildlife refuges are places specifically created so that animals can have a safe haven. Similarly, game hunting laws prevent hunters from killing animals indiscriminately. Exploitation is the opposite: it means using a resource for our own ends regardless of the effects upon the resource. Conservatism is a political point of view that espouses keeping status quo in society.

49. (C)

The passage discusses a person's willful breaking of a law, even though he knows that what he is doing is illegal. This is called civil disobedience. Military force is the act of using a country's military might to achieve objectives. Appeasement is a policy of giving in rather than going to war. Retaliation is revenge for a specific occurrence.

50. (D)

Gandhi is the famous leader of India who used civil disobedience to gain his country's freedom from Great Britain. Lenin was a major leader of the Soviet Union under Communist rule. Simon Bolivar, also known as the "George Washington of South America," was a general who helped many countries win their independence from Spain. Yasir Arafat was the leader of the Palestine Liberation Organization.

51. (D)

The poem describes a blazing hot environment with cold nights. Plants are small with wide roots, and no mention is made of rain; therefore, it would be a desert. The plants are not the type to be found in a forest, where there would be natural covering from the sun. A swamp would be rainy, and a tundra is a cold, icy environment.

52. **A**

Colloquial language is language used by people of a certain area. The author's use of The days be hot, the nights be cold *and* Tiz me life that I must save *is nonstandard English; thus it is considered colloquial. A narrative is a long story, while factual writing, as the name implies, gives readers facts. Metaphors are comparisons without the use of words such as like or as.*

53. **A**

A reflection is a transformation which "flips" the figure across a line to create a mirror image on the other side of the line. In our example, the triangle is "flipped" over the x-axis creating its mirror image.

54. **D**

A fable is a story that teaches a lesson; therefore, the passage can be classified as a fable. A narrative is generally a long, fictional piece. A character analysis scrutinizes one or more characters that are presented. An editorial gives an opinion on a specific subject.

55. **C**

A limerick is a humorous poem in the rhythm a a b b a. The first two lines rhyme; the second two lines rhyme, and the last line rhymes with the first two lines. An elegy is a mournful poem. A ballad is a long poem that tells a story. Haiku is a form of poetry with a 17-syllable verse, divided into three units of 5, 7, and 5 syllables.

56. **A**

Alliteration is the repetition of consonant sounds. Onomatopoeia occurs when a word actually sounds like the sound it makes. Imagery is a way to portray something by comparison. Symbolism occurs when a word or phrase represents something else.

57. **D**

Illustrating the poem would allow younger children to visualize its humor, while clapping their hands as the poem is read reinforces it rhythm. Older children could write their own poems in this style.

58. **C**

In an if-then statement, the phrase following the if *is called the hypothesis and phrase following the* then *is called the conclusion. Given an original statement, only the contrapositive is guaranteed to have the same truth value. The contrapositive is obtained by swapping the hypothesis and conclusion phrases and also negating them.*

<u>Note</u>*: The negative of "turnips are not blue" is "turnips are blue."*

59. **C**

The diagram shows cycling among air, legumes, soil organisms, dead plants, live plants, and animals. This means that the cycling occurs between the living and nonliving parts of the environment.

60. **C**

A metaphor is a comparison between two items without the use of like or as. In the proverb, death is called a black camel. A simile is a comparison that uses like or as. Alliteration is the repetition of a consonant sound, and hyperbole is an exaggeration.

61. **A**

The statement tries to influence readers by telling them that all of their friends own this particular item. This device is known as bandwagon. A testimonial is a quote by someone, whether by name or anonymous, that vouches for the product. Card-stacking is the intentional organization and arrangement of material to make one position look good and another position look bad. A glittering generality is use of an emotionally appealing word or concept to gain approval without thinking.

62. **D**

The two sentences show two meanings for the verb try. In the first sentence, the word means attempted, while the second very means judged.

63. **C**

Robinson shows the reader that although Richard Cory seems to have everything—riches, grace, and respect of others, he was inwardly very unhappy and committed suicide.

64. **A**

These sentences illustrate the grammatical rule of parallelism. The phrase before the like, as or than have to match, or be parallel to the phrase after the like, as or than. Choice B states: "to hike" and "skiing." Choice C states: "hiking" and "to ski." Choice D gives us "to hike" and "going cross-country skiing. Only Choice A shows parallelism in its use of "hiking" and "skiing." Therefore, A is correct.

65. **C**

In order to turn water, a liquid, into water vapor, a gas, the process of evaporation must occur. Condensation is the reverse—turning a gas into a liquid. Deposition occurs when something is deposited in an area, and infiltration is the process by which one item permeates another item.

66. C

The blue and the brown comprise ½ + ⅕ of the tie. Use 10 as the lowest common denominator:

$$\frac{1}{2} = \frac{5}{10} \text{ and } \frac{1}{5} = \frac{2}{10}$$

Thus the blue and brown make up ⁷/₁₀ of the tie. The balance (1 – ⁷/₁₀) or ³/₁₀ belongs to the burgundy.

67. D

Economic resources are those which provide goods and services to people. Economic resources are considered to be scarce, while wants are unlimited. Therefore, land, labor, and capital are considered resources, while values are not goods or services which are limited.

68. D

The Banana Splits is a term used for a school group of children of divorced parents that meets regularly with a mental health professional to deal with their common issues.

69. C

Taking a class trip to the supermarket would introduce students to comparative pricing of the same item in different brands, while comparing different supermarkets would show the students possible differences in pricing in the same brand. Ralph Nader was a very vocal activist in consumer affairs. Donald Trump, however, is a real estate developer and did not work in consumer affairs.

70. C

Properties of a parallelogram include

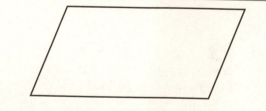

- *The sum of its angles is 360°.*
- *Opposite sides are equal.*
- *Opposite sides are parallel.*
- *Opposite angles are equal.*
- *Adjacent angles are supplementary (add to 180°).*
- *Diagonals bisect each other.*

Diagonals are only equal if the parallelogram is a rectangle or a square.

71. D

The following math facts are used in this example:

$$\sin x = \frac{\text{side opposite angle } x}{\text{hypotenuse}}, \quad \tan x = \frac{\text{side opposite angle } x}{\text{side adjacent to angle } x}$$

$$(\text{leg})^2 + (\text{leg})^2 = (\text{hypotenuse})^2$$

Choice D: $3^2 + 6^2 = x^2$ *says* $(\text{leg})^2 + (\text{hypotenuse})^2 = (\text{leg})^2$.

72. C

Modern Times is a classic film that shows the dehumanization of industrialization. Its classic scene depicts Charlie Chaplin as a cog in an ever-turning machine.

73. A

A microprocessor is a circuit that directs the other units in the computer. It is used in a micro-computer. A microprocessor contains one silicon chip, so it is small enough to be used in small pieces.

74. C

A tactile/kinesthetic learner needs tangible materials to help him/her learn. Using manipulative materials, charts, felt letters, etc. would all be useful to this type of learner.

75. D

The inventions of the cotton industry, machines such as the cotton gin and the reaper, made the work easier and quicker and led to the growth of factories in London.

76. C

The Metropolitan Museum of Art has a famous permanent exhibition of Egyptian art and arti-facts, including mummies and mummy cases. The Museum of the Moving Image, as its name implies, deals with films. The Whitney Museum deals with American art, while the Guggenheim Museum exhibits contemporary works of art.

77. D

Diminished means made smaller. This implies subtraction; therefore, a number n diminished by 5 means n − 5. Three more than 7 times the number n is 7n + 3, and finally, "is" means equals. Putting is all together: n − 5 = 7n + 3.

78. **A**

Research shows that suicide is attempted about three times more often in males than in females. None of the other statements has been shown to be true.

79. **A**

Humanism is the spirit of learning that developed at the end of the Middle Ages with a renewed confidence in the ability of human beings to determine for themselves truth and falsehood. It originated largely in ancient Greece and Rome, evolved throughout European history, and now constitutes a basic part of the Western approach to science, political theory, ethics, and law.

80. **A**

Both speakers are referring to the colonies that were later to become the United States of America. This feeling of togetherness and pride for one's country is called nationalism. Confederacy occurs when one group joins in opposition to another. Totalitarianism is the rule by a dictator—the antithesis of these quotes, while equality denotes equal rights.

81. **C**

Diagrams, tables, and graphs are different ways to display information. These would be most useful in organizing that information. They would not assist in making predictions, testing a hypothesis, or designing a research plan but could be helpful in any of these endeavors.

82. **A**

An ecologist is concerned about environmental issues; therefore, he or she would be most interested in the effect of the fuel's smoke emissions. Cost and time factors do not concern the environmentalist, so Choices B and C are irrelevant. Similarly, consumer acceptance is not the domain of the environmentalist, so Choice D is not correct.

83. **B**

The Jim Crow laws were in existence from the 1880s (post-Civil War) to the 1960s. A majority of American states enforced segregation using these laws. States and cities could impose legal punishment on people for a variety of "infractions" dealing with African-Americans. Intermarriage between the races was forbidden and in both the public and private sectors, blacks and whites were separated.

84. **C**

Studies have shown that drinking alcohol while pregnant is associated with more premature births and stillbirths among the fetuses of these women. Drinking is not associated with weight or heart rate of the fetus.

85. **B**

The diagram shows cloud reflection to be 30 percent to 60 percent and absorption to be 5 percent to 20 percent. The question asks us what percentage is reflected or absorbed, so we must add the two percentages. This gives us 35% (30% + 50%) to 80% (60% + 20%).

86. **D**

Relative humidity measures the percentage of water vapor in the air. The higher the humidity, the more water vapor exists in the air. Thursday had the highest relative humidity (95 percent), so D is the correct answer.

87. **A**

The variable in this experiment is light. The plants were grown in the same soil and given the same amount of water, so Choices B and C are wrong. The experiment does not deal with red light, so Choice D is incorrect. The three plants were given different amounts of light, so Choice A is the correct answer.

88. **B**

The connotation of a word is what the word implies, not its literal meaning. For example, the word terse means brief but connotes rudeness, while the word concise means brief but has a positive connotation. In order to understand and properly utilize words, one must know not only their denotation but also their connotation.

89. **B**

Rockefeller, Carnegie, and Morgan all made fortunes in the nineteenth century. They and their heirs set up cultural and philanthropic institutions with some of their wealth.

90. **D**

The emancipation of women gave women more opportunities to pursue their own needs and wants. Therefore, the marriage age has gone up, there are fewer children in each marriage and divorce is now a viable option to end a marriage. It has not led to more structured relationships between men and women, so D is the correct answer.

91. D

Establishing schools is a state power, so A is wrong. Foreign relations and establishing post offices are federal powers, so B and C are incorrect. Both state and federal governments can charter banks, so the correct answer is D.

92. D

Pork barrel refers to a legislator's favoring his own district with monies for projects. Apportionment refers to the way in which the number of congressmen are decided for a district. Ballot stuffing is the practice of adding bogus votes for a candidate's election. Gerrymandering is the arrangement of legislative districts to favor specific candidates, so D is the correct answer.

93. B

A school psychologist is involved with testing children for possible disabilities, so Choices A and D are wrong. The psychologist is not involved in psychological testing for the fears and phobias of children, so Choice C is wrong. He/she does test to see the potential intellectual ability of a child, so Choice B is correct.

94. C

Antibodies are substances that the body creates to fight attackers such as bacteria or viruses. Nutrients are what the body needs to maintain itself, while vaccines are given to prevent specific diseases. Red blood cells make up the blood in the human body.

95. D

Permeability refers to the earth's ability to take in a substance. For instance, a sponge is permeable to water, while raincoats are supposed to be impermeable. Saturation refers to the point at which nothing more can be added. Therefore, water can enter the soil if it is permeable and unsaturated.

96. A

Since oceans are the largest bodies of water on earth, they are the greatest source of moisture entering the atmosphere.

97. A

The denseness of internal atoms would affect the hardness or softness of a mineral. The denser the atom, the harder the mineral. Choices B, C and D would not influence the hardness of a mineral.

98. **C**

Taking learning styles into account is appropriate for every age, so Choice A is wrong. Kindergarten children learn well by theme and actually using manipulative materials, so Choices B and D are wrong. At ages 5–6, presented too much factual material is unwarranted, so Choice C is the best answer.

99. **D**

A 504 meeting has definite protocol if no agreement is reached between the parents and the school staff. The next step in the process is a due process hearing or mediation by a professional to try to come up with a viable plan for the child.

100. **D**

Each professional is correctly paired with his/her theory except for A.S. Neil, author of Summerhill, an experiment in education that allowed each child to follow his/her interests and develop as an individual regardless of age and grade.

Sample Answer to Open Response 1 Earning 4 Points

Every culture has myths. But before we describe the common elements of a particular type of myth, we first must define what a myth is. We can define a myth as a story embodying and declaring a pattern of relationships between humanity, some divine nature, other forms of life, and the environment. One type of myth common to just about all world cultures is the creation myth. Each culture's creation myth is a poetic and shared vision of how the world came into being and where humans came from.

We find creation myths among various Native American cultures, African cultures, south Asian cultures, Greco-Roman culture, as well as the cultures of the ancient Middle East in which the Sumerian, Babylonian, and Hebraic are the most popular. Just about all creation myths derive from the oral traditions of these cultures. If we compare different creation myths, we see that most use repetition for emphasis and ease of recall, the use of poetic devices such as alliteration, personification, metaphor and simile, symbolism, and a concern for numbers. It appears that creation myths share several common literary devices. The first is some divine being or beings create order out of a pre-existing nothingness or chaos. The second is that the world is created through some purposeful action by a creator or divine being. Unlike modern scientific thinking in which life occurs through random chemical processes, these ancient myths involve some creator with a plan. The third common theme is the creation of human beings who can mirror the nature of the creator. This is usually the implementation of the creator's plan. In other words, humans mirror the essence of the creator. In the Old Testament, the Hebrew god creates man in his image while in Hindu myths, when a man becomes perfect, he becomes part of the divine source. A final literary device in most creation myths is that the earth is usually created perfect, but something occurs that forces the divine being to make it a place where humans will have to toil so as to survive.

Using some of the themes and devices mentioned above, here is a simple creation myth: At the outskirts of the Milky Way Galaxy, existed a small planet, going by the name of "Perfection." It was simple, a place envisioned by the gods that portrayed picturesque qualities. It was a true work of art that boasted immense beauty, a realistic fantasy. It accommodated all the needs of the dazzling creatures that walked upon it.

However, one significant piece of the puzzle was missing. People did not inhabit this planet, and the gods felt lonely because of this lacking aspect of life. To resolve this problem, the gods set up a contest to see who could create the perfect man. This would eventually be known as the greatest competition ever to face this planet.

The God of the Skies, Flufakus, tried to shape a person from his own clouds. But with one touch, the being would drift away. The first attempt was unsuccessful.

The God of Fire, Arsenigus, made a figure out of scorching flames, but Flafakus became overwhelmed with envy. The God of the Skies rained upon the God of Fire's living inferno.

It had come down to the final contestant, the God of Soil, to present his creation. He put together a man comprised of clay, but it remained motionless. The contest took place in the middle of the night, however, the sun, in pity of the God of Soil, ascended to the middle of the sky during nighttime. Suddenly, the clay's flesh somewhat hardened, and as a result, a phenomenal creation of man transpired.

There was a mutual relationship between the gods and their creations. The gods respected man, and man respected the gods. Furthermore, men had power over every creature in the world. They were above everything that surrounded them. The only things above them were the gods, and they accepted this because without gods, they would not be in existence. Now it was true that "Perfection" was absolutely perfect.

Features of the Open Response Scoring 4

Several important prerequisite skills are needed to accomplish the above task. One has to be able to compare and contrast different types of myths within the genre. One must understand that the creation myth is just one type of myth. Other myths explain natural phenomena as well as different types of human emotions and needs. Also, one needs to understand different types of literary forms when reading myths from different cultures, i.e., the elements of different poetic forms as well as other writing styles. In addition, one must have higher level thinking skills so as to figure out the common themes among different myths and also how these myths truly represent the different cultures from which the myth derives. Finally, one must be able to apply this knowledge to create an independent piece of literature incorporating some of the common themes discussed in the creation of a myth.

Sample Answer to Open Response 2 Earning 4 Points

Although it appears that most art during the Renaissance continued the religious themes of the Middle Ages, if one looks deeper, one realizes that many art works represented the ideas of humanism, classicism, secularism, and individualism. The artist that best characterizes these views is Leonardo da Vinci. More than any other artist, he synthesized all the elements of the Renaissance.

Da Vinci's art could not have been created unless he understood secular, scientific ideas. Many of his paintings show how he used keen observation and his knowledge of science. In Florence, he was apprenticed to Andrea del Verrocchio where he learned the technical-mechanical arts. He also worked with Antonio Pollaiuolo from whom he learned the science of anatomy. He would incorporate all this knowledge in many of his paintings. He viewed art as a part of science. He felt that people need to use the sense of sight to draw scientific conclusions. Therefore, paintings and drawings were, for him, a form of secular scientific expression. Unlike artists during the Middle Ages, da Vinci was not trying to advance a religious ideal. Instead, most of his paintings reflected the use of scientific techniques that created color, perspective, and lighting that lent realism to his art. He used the study of optics to create three-dimensional images on a two-dimensional plane

Next, da Vinci's art reflects the humanistic spirit of the Renaissance, whereas the religious paints of the Middle Ages show biblical events in theological terms. Da Vinci's religious paintings depict real people acting like real people. For example, in the Last Supper, the disciples all display very human and very identifiable emotions. Their faces show different degrees of horror, anger, and shock. This is quite different from medieval paintings in which Christ's disciples all have serene, calm, and haloed looks.

Third, most of da Vinci's paintings reflect the return to classical Greco-Roman forms in painting and sculpture. His portraits and paintings remove extraneous detail and show the world as it is. Also, his paintings reflect the classical ideal of balance and harmony in nature. In addition, most of his paintings and frescos have rooms, clothes, and characters that hark back to the Greco Roman tradition, whereas, much of Gothic art lacks perspective and often appears one-dimensional and stilted.

Finally, paintings, such as the Last Supper, reflect a conflict between the Renaissance ideas of individualism and theology. During the Renaissance, the individual was considered more important than the state or church. Medieval paintings of the Last Supper usually show the disciples subservient to Jesus. On the other hand, in the da Vinci's painting, we see the disciples as individuals expressing their own feelings. In this painting, they are now unique individuals.

Features of the Open Response Scoring 4

The prerequisite knowledge needed to answer this question is as follows: One needs to understand and contrast the ideas and philosophies of the Renaissance and the Medieval period. One needs to understand various scientific concepts used in physics, such as mechanics and optics. One also needs to understand the history of science as it relates to the Renaissance. Finally, one needs to understand the history of various art forms, such as classical, Gothic, and revival.

Index

INSTALLING REA's TEST*ware*®

SYSTEM REQUIREMENTS

Pentium 75 MHz (300 MHz recommended) or a higher or compatible processor; Microsoft® Windows 98 or later; 64 MB available RAM; Internet Explorer 5.5 or higher.

INSTALLATION

1. Insert the MTEL General Curriculum TEST*ware*® CD-ROM into the CD-ROM drive.

2. If the installation doesn't begin automatically, from the Start Menu choose the RUN command. When the RUN dialog box appears, type d:\setup (where d is the letter of your CD-ROM drive) at the prompt and click OK.

3. The installation process will begin. A dialog box proposing the directory "Program Files\REA\ MTEL_Gen" will appear. If the name and location are suitable, click OK. If you wish to specify a different name or location, type it in and click OK.

4. Start the MTEL TEST*ware*® application by double-clicking on the icon.

REA's MTEL TEST*ware*® is **EASY** to **LEARN AND USE**. To achieve maximum benefits, we recommend that you take a few minutes to go through the on-screen tutorial on your computer. The "screen buttons" are also explained here to familiarize you with the program.

TECHNICAL SUPPORT

REA's TEST*ware*® is backed by customer and technical support. For questions about **installation or operation of your software**, contact us at:

> **Research & Education Association**
> **Phone: (732) 819-8880 (9 a.m. to 5 p.m. ET, Monday–Friday)**
> **Fax: (732) 819-8808**
> **Website: *http://www.rea.com***
> **E-mail: info@rea.com**

Note to Windows XP Users: In order for the TEST*ware*® to function properly, please install and run the application under the same computer administrator-level user account. Installing the TEST*ware*® as one user and running it as another could cause file-access path conflicts.

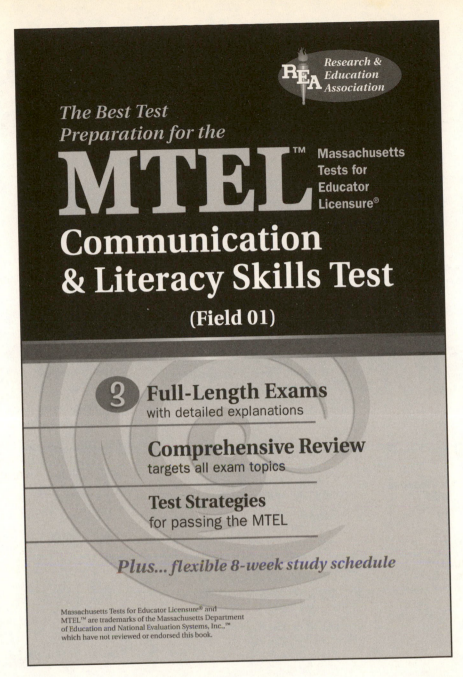

REA's Test Preps
The Best in Test Preparation

- REA "Test Preps" are **far more** comprehensive than any other test preparation series
- Each book contains up to **eight** full-length practice tests based on the most recent exams
- **Every** type of question likely to be given on the exams is included
- Answers are accompanied by **full** and **detailed** explanations

REA publishes over 70 Test Preparation volumes in several series. They include:

Advanced Placement Exams (APs)
Biology
Calculus AB & Calculus BC
Chemistry
Economics
English Language & Composition
English Literature & Composition
European History
Government & Politics
Physics B & C
Psychology
Spanish Language
Statistics
United States History

College-Level Examination Program (CLEP)
Analyzing and Interpreting Literature
College Algebra
Freshman College Composition
General Examinations
General Examinations Review
History of the United States I
History of the United States II
Human Growth and Development
Introductory Sociology
Principles of Marketing
Spanish

SAT Subject Tests
Biology E/M
Chemistry
English Language Proficiency Test
French
German

SAT Subject Tests (cont'd)
Literature
Mathematics Level 1, 2
Physics
Spanish
United States History
Writing

Graduate Record Exams (GREs)
Biology
Chemistry
Computer Science
General
Literature in English
Mathematics
Physics
Psychology

ACT - ACT Assessment

ASVAB - Armed Services Vocational Aptitude Battery

CBEST - California Basic Educational Skills Test

CDL - Commercial Driver License Exam

CLAST - College Level Academic Skills Test

COOP & HSPT - Catholic High School Admission Tests

ELM - California State University Entry Level Mathematics Exam

FE (EIT) - Fundamentals of Engineering Exams - For both AM & PM Exams

FTCE - Florida Teacher Certification Exam

GED - High School Equivalency Diploma Exam (U.S. & Canadian editions)

GMAT - Graduate Management Admission Test

LSAT - Law School Admission Test

MAT - Miller Analogies Test

MCAT - Medical College Admission Test

MTEL - Massachusetts Tests for Educator Licensure

NJ HSPA - New Jersey High School Proficiency Assessment

NYSTCE: LAST & ATS-W - New York State Teacher Certification

PLT - Principles of Learning & Teaching Tests

PPST - Pre-Professional Skills Tests

PSAT / NMSQT

SAT

TExES - Texas Examinations of Educator Standards

THEA - Texas Higher Education Assessment

TOEFL - Test of English as a Foreign Language

TOEIC - Test of English for International Communication

USMLE Steps 1,2,3 - U.S. Medical Licensing Exams

U.S. Postal Exams 460 & 470

REA's Test Prep Books Are The Best!
(a sample of the <u>hundreds of letters</u> REA receives each year)

" The gem of the book is the tests. They were indicative of the actual exam.
The explanations of the answers are practically another review session. "
Student, Fresno, CA

" I just wanted to thank you for helping me get a great score
on the AP U.S. History... Thank you for making great test preps! "
Student, Los Angeles, CA

" Your Fundamentals of Engineering Exam book was the absolute best
preparation I could have had for the exam, and it is one of the major
reasons I did so well and passed the FE on my first try. "
Student, Sweetwater, TN

" I used your book to prepare for the test and found that the advice and the
sample tests were highly relevant... Without using any other material, I earned
very high scores and will be going to the graduate school of my choice. "
Student, New Orleans, LA

" What I found in your book was a wealth of information sufficient to shore up my basic
skills in math and verbal.... The practice tests were challenging and the
answer explanations most helpful. It certainly is the Best Test Prep for the GRE! "
Student, Pullman, WA

" I really appreciate the help from your excellent book. Please keep
up with your great work. "
Student, Albuquerque, NM

" I used your *CLEP Introductory Sociology* book and rank it 99%– thank you! "
Student, Jerusalem, Israel

(more on next page)

REA's Test Prep Books Are The Best!
(a sample of the <u>hundreds of letters</u> REA receives each year)

" The last formal English grammar class I had was more than 25 years ago, and I did not know how I was going to prepare for this [MTEL] test. Then I found [REA's MTEL] book! It was a very accurate representation of the test material. I would not take the test without using this review—whether you graduated from college one year ago or 25 years ago "

MTEL Test Taker, Chelmsford, MA

" I did well because of your wonderful prep books... I just wanted to thank you for helping me prepare for these tests. "

Student, San Diego, CA

" My students report your chapters of review as the most valuable single resource they used for review and preparation. "

Teacher, American Fork, UT

" Your book was such a better value and was so much more complete than anything your competition has produced—and I have them all! "

Teacher, Virginia Beach, VA

" Compared to the other books that my fellow students had, your book was the most helpful in helping me get a great score. "

Student, North Hollywood, CA

" Your book was responsible for my success on the exam, which helped me get into the college of my choice... I will look for REA the next time I need help. "

Student, Chesterfield, MO

" Just a short note to say thanks for the great support your book gave me in helping me pass the test... I'm on my way to a B.S. degree because of you! "

Student, Orlando, FL

(more on previous page)